1066

A New History of the Norman Conquest

Within a year and a day Devils shall stalk through all this land and harry it from one end to the other with fire and sword and havoc of war.

St Edward the Confessor

About the Author

Peter Rex is a retired history teacher. He was Head of History at Princethorpe College for twenty years. His other books include *William the Conqueror: The Bastard of Normandy*, *The English Resistance: The Underground War Against the Normans*, *The Last English King: The Life of Harold II*, *Edgar: King of the English*, *King & Saint: The Life of Edward the Confessor* and *Hereward: The Last Englishman*. He lives in Ely.

1066

A New History of the Norman Conquest

PETER REX

AMBERLEY

This book is dedicated to the memory of all those English men and women who perished during the Norman Conquest of England.

This edition first published 2011

Amberley Publishing Plc
Cirencester Road, Chalford,
Stroud, Gloucestershire, GL6 8PE

www.amberleybooks.com

Copyright © Peter Rex, 2009, 2011

British Library Cataloguing in Publication Data.
A catalogue record for this book is available from the British Library.

ISBN 978 1 4456 0384 1

Typesetting and Origination by Amberley Publishing.
Printed in Great Britain.

Contents

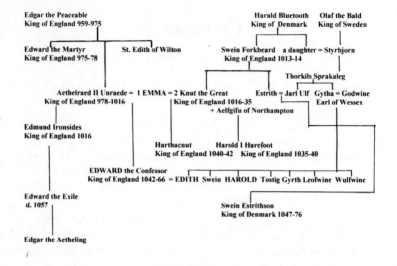

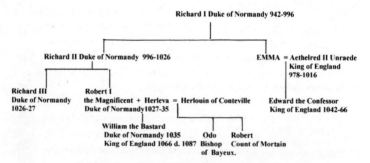

Duke William was the great nephew of Queen Emma and so in no way descended from her. There was therefore, strictly speaking, no hereditary claim at all and he was not a member of King Edward's kin, therefore he was not 'aetheling' born.

Top: Anglo-Danish dynasties of the eleventh century.

Bottom: William of Normandy and the English throne.

Introduction

Even after well over a thousand years since it was accomplished, the Norman Conquest of England still holds a peculiar fascination for many people. There had been other invasions and successful conquests of this country from the Roman invasion in the reign of the Emperor Claudius and the advent of the Angles, Saxons and Jutes in the fifth century to the Viking invasions of the ninth and, early in the eleventh century, the conquest by Cnut the Great and his Danes. But the invasion by Duke William, the bastard of Normandy, was, in many respects, qualitatively different.

Cnut the Great had imposed his rule on the country and inserted many of his higher ranking supporters into positions of power and influence, allowing the rank and file of his armies to acquire lands left vacant after the battles between the English and the Danes. But he had not, for the most part, supplanted the native English nobility or carried out a massive transfer of land and power. Indeed, two of his highest ranking nobles were Englishmen raised to the rank of Earl and given the status and power of provincial governors; Earl Leofric in Mercia, the son of an English Ealdorman and Godwine, the thegn of Sussex, in Wessex.

But Duke William did not only make himself King, as others had done before him, nor did he merely add yet another cohort of nobles to the ranks of those already in power, instead he virtually eliminated the whole of the existing governing class and transferred the ownership of their estates to his own somewhat mixed collection of followers, Bretons, Flemings, Poitevins and, above all, Normans.

This book is an attempt to convey the manner in which this invasion and conquest was devised, planned and executed. It describes the steps taken to establish, in the eyes of other European princes and of the Papacy, Duke William's 'right' to the English throne, by asserting an 'hereditary' claim to the throne, as a relative of the saintly, recently deceased, King Edward, who was alleged to have actually designated the Duke as his heir, and by manoeuvring the King's successor, Harold II, the former Earl of Wessex, recognized even by the Normans themselves as the 'Dux Anglorum' (Duke of the English), just as William himself was Dux Normannorum (Duke of the Normans), into a false position wherein he could be convincingly portrayed to the other Princes as a faithless and perjured vassal and, therefore, a usurper.

A tremendous propaganda campaign preceded the Conquest which was written up afterwards (when all those who might have been able to refute it were dead, dispossessed or in exile) and a wonderfully executed pictorial version was made, the Bayeux Tapestry, to ensure that the message was conveyed even to those who could neither read nor write. So well-crafted was the campaign that much of it still impresses the minds of modern historians who are unable to free themselves from its insidious influence.

Most of this account is devoted to a stage by stage description of the Conquest itself and its effects on the nobility and clergy of England and upon the ordinary people. Duke William's military preparations are described and his launching of the invasion. Much space is devoted to the Battle of Hastings and the Bastard's terror campaign which intimidated the survivors into surrender. This is followed by an account of the reaction which set in when the true nature of Norman rule was revealed and the struggle, in vain, to remove the Norman Yoke. Then the story moves on to explain how the Norman settlement was carried out; the dispossession of the English, the Harrying of the North, the 'cleansing' of the English Church and so on. It ends with the mysterious revolt by two Norman earls and the execution for involvement in it of Earl Waltheof, son of Cnut's great earl, Siward of Northumbria.

In writing this book I acknowledge my debt to the work of all those scholars whose works have been consulted and without which it would not have been possible. They are, of course, in no way responsible for the views and interpretations contained in it and any errors are my own.

I am grateful, as always, to the Librarian of St John's College, Cambridge, for his permission to use the College Library.

Prologue

The Death of King Edward

In early January, 1066, Edward, King of the English, son of Aethelred II, lay dying in his Palace of Westminster. He had fallen ill some time towards the end of the previous November or early in December and, by the Feast of the Holy Innocents, 28 December, had been unable to attend the consecration of his beloved Westminster Abbey.

The nature of his illness was not understood by contemporaries and was complicated by suspicions of 'sickness of mind', that is a 'deep sorrow' or melancholy, brought on by the way in which his wishes concerning the response to the threat of civil war in Northumbria had been frustrated. In modern times he would have been treated for depression. But that winter of 1065 was a harsh one with intense cold and the King's illness became a physical one intensified by his age. By Christmas Eve his condition grew worse. On Christmas Day he could no longer disguise his weariness and arrangements were made for the consecration to be carried out in his absence.

As his condition became more serious he lost appetite and refused to eat, taking to his bed in distress as his condition worsened. By 28 December he had developed a fever 'being consumed by the fire of his illness' and the aged king began to accept that his end was approaching. 'Becoming drowsy because of his body's heaviness' he lapsed into deep but troubled sleep and his attendants sought to rouse him. Much of what he said proved unintelligible to his hearers. Archbishop Stigand, who was present, remarked *sotto voce* to Earl Harold, 'He is broken with age and disease and knows not what he says'. But then, after two or three days, he rallied enough to describe what was troubling him.

During his sleep, he is reported to have said, he had dreamed of two monks whom he had known as a young man in Normandy. They told him that they had a message for him from God. All the nobles and higher clergy of the kingdom, they said, were 'servants of the Devil' and in consequence 'one year and one day after the day of your death, God has delivered all this kingdom, cursed by Him, into the hands of the enemy and devils shall come to roam at large through all this land with fire and sword and havoc of war.' They had then related the parable of the Green Tree which was the description of something impossible and therefore meant that the day when the 'woes of England' would cease was never. Ailred of Rievaulx adds that the King said 'The Lord has bent His Bow, the Lord has prepared His Sword. He brandishes it like a warrior. His anger is manifested in steel and flame'.

The Norman D Day:
Dawn, Thursday 28 September 1066

William, Bastard Duke of Normandy and Count of Rouen awoke aboard his flagship, the 'Mora', gift of his wife, the Duchess Matilda. It was a magnificent gift, probably the largest vessel in the fleet. Its sails were scarlet and the figurehead was a sculpture of a young child holding a drawn bow as if ready to fire upon an enemy. This is not shown in the Bayeux Tapestry[1] which instead has a figure at the stern holding a banner and blowing a trumpet. William found that his vast invasion fleet, packed to the gunwales with men, horses, arms and supplies, was nowhere to be seen. From his vantage point aboard ship he could see the horizon, about six miles in all directions, but not a ship was there.

Unperturbed, the Duke ordered a nearby sailor, one of the oarsmen, to shin up the masthead and report. But the oarsman also could see only the open sea and the sky, though from there the horizon was some twelve miles in any direction. It was not yet sunrise though dawn was breaking.

Duke William ordered a full meal to be brought to him and proceeded to eat breakfast 'as though in his hall at Rouen', and drank a large glass of spiced wine. By the time he had finished the sun had risen, burning away any traces of mist. It would now have been about 6.45 a.m. when a rising tide, as William's shipmaster, Stephen son of Airaud would have known, would enable the Duke's fleet, if it arrived, to beach in England by 9.00 a.m. that day.

As no ships had yet appeared, the Duke ordered another man to be sent up the mast and this time the sailor reported that he could see four ships then many more, like a forest of masts, emerging perhaps from mist on the horizon. Once the fleet had caught up with the Mora, the Duke weighed anchor and led the way towards England, hoping to catch the morning tide, fully intending to lead his men to victory. William of Poitiers describes the voyage in language derived from Livy's account of Scipio's voyage.[2]

So this burly warrior with the deep guttural voice led his men against England. Great in stature but not ungainly, he was capable of enduring great hardship, a characteristic he shared with his opponent, King Harold. So, a big man with long arms and legs, he might well have looked not unlike Henry VIII. (A portrait was made of William when his coffin was opened in 1522. It has not survived but there is a possible copy of it, which shows a large and dominating monarch, massive in bulk, with a full-fleshed face and russet hair).

It is possible, even likely, that Duke William was by now aware of the invasion in the north of England by King Harald Sigurdson, known as Hardrada, King of Norway. He had landed about a fortnight earlier, perhaps even at the same time as the Duke had moved from Dives to St Valery-sur-Somme. But Duke William could not have known of the result of any battles that might have been fought. He was ignorant therefore of the defeat of the brother Earls, Edwin, of Mercia, and Morcar, of Northumbria, at Gate Fulford, near York, on the 20 September and of King Harold Godwinson's stunning victory over the Norwegians at Stamford Bridge on Monday 25 September, five days later. But, perhaps through the monks of Fécamp based at Steyning, Rye and a place, now lost, called 'Rameslie' in Sussex, or Norman sympathisers at the court of King Harold, the Duke would have known that the English King had left the South Coast unguarded since at least 8 September. Duke William was, in any case, accompanied on the crossing by monks from Fécamp who could provide him with information about suitable landing areas. Remigius of Fécamp (later made a bishop) had provided a ship for the fleet and paid for twenty knights to accompany the Duke.

But Duke William could not have known, when he launched his invasion fleet on Tuesday 27 September, intending to cross as much of the Channel as possible during the hours of darkness and to make landfall early in the morning the following day, which king he would have to fight, Harald of Norway or the 'faithless vassal', Harold Godwinson. He had launched the invasion largely out of sheer pride; once he had challenged Harold's right to the throne he could not afford to back down lest he become the laughing stock of Western Europe.

The Mora had ended up some twelve miles ahead of the Norman fleet. It was a well found ship, large and commodious, carrying only the Duke himself, his entourage and their horses. It was less heavily laden and had made better time. Ships like this were capable of carrying up to sixty men plus beasts, horses and baggage.

So the Norman fleet entered Pevensey Bay which formed a shallow lagoon (where Pevensey Levels now lie), some four miles wide, and penetrated inland as much as six miles. Since 1066 the sea level there has receded and the present day coastline is very different. In 1066 the coastline ran from Beachy Head to Rye with inlets and penetrations leading to Pevensey harbour near the Roman Fort of Anderida where the sea reached its walls. One arm extended inland to Ashburnham. Local legend claims that Standard Hill in Ninfield was the actual landing point and certainly the ancient inlets of the bay did reach as far in as Ninfield. At Bulverhythe the coast penetrated inland as far as Crowhurst. It is likely that the fleet spread out all along the bay, from where Eastbourne and Bexhill now lie. Further along lay Hastings and its harbour and then the coast turned northwards to the Brede Estuary, going inland as far as Sedlescombe. Beachy Head itself would have been an identifiable landmark known to Duke William's pilot who could have laid a course north west by west from St Valery in the hope of sighting the cliffs.[3]

All now went according to plan. The landing was accomplished, at about the third hour, or 9.00 a.m., and, in practice, allowing for the tide and time for the leading vessels to be beached, that meant mid-morning. The landing was unopposed and the Norman army began to disembark. The Duke, having disembarked himself, then 'glorified God's mercy from the very depths of his heart', missing no opportunity to paint himself as God's champion. There was no interference from the English fleet which had moved to London shortly after 8 September, during which move it had been badly damaged in the storm in the Channel which had also struck the Duke's fleet when it emerged from its harbours around the Dives estuary. So the English had not been able, nor thought it necessary, to resume their watch for the coming of the Duke. King Harold could well have concluded that, as the weather was so adverse with winter approaching, William was not going to come that year.

The Duke's fleet, of some 700 vessels of varying sizes, came in on a rising tide, having the advantage of noon High Water. The larger vessels dropped anchor offshore and those aboard had to drop over the side and wade ashore. Even horses would have been led down gangplanks and through the surf to the beach. Many other craft were not much more than barges, of shallow draft, propelled by a single sail, and intended for a one way trip. These were simply beached.

The invasion force, composed of squadrons of knights with their horses, companies of archers and crossbowmen, and many contingents of men-at-arms, (heavily armed and armoured footsoldiers), is reported by an Aquitanian source, to have been 14,000 strong, of whom at least 10,000 would have been actual fighting men, perhaps more.[4] Given 700 ships, that suggests an average of twenty soldiers per vessel with plenty of space for horses, supplies and the numerous support staff required; smiths (who acted as armourers) ostlers and grooms, carpenters, cooks and large numbers of miscellaneous servants. They are all pictured in various plates of the Bayeux Tapestry making preparations for the invasion and landing at Pevensey. The Ship List of William the Conqueror, a document based on an original written at Battle Abbey, lists 776 ships, names fourteen magnates as contributing them together with 280 knights.[5]

The Duke had ordered vessels carrying infantry and archers to beach first and send in armed men as an advance guard. These men fanned out across the bay, meeting no overt opposition, so set pickets and a watch in case of a surprise attack. The barons and knights supervised the unloading of their precious horses and the grooms and ostlers led their charges ashore to be exercised, fed and watered. Other servants unloaded baggage and supplies of all kinds, including tents for the Duke and his magnates. Cooks and their staffs set about preparing food. When all was ready and the encampment secure, the Duke and his nobles came ashore.

As he came up the beach, the Duke tripped and fell, his fall causing great consternation among his men, but as he rose it was seen that he had grasped handfuls of earth. William fitzOsbern, who was nearby cried 'You have England in your grasp, Duke, you shall be king!' Duke William, also seeking to turn aside a bad omen, replied, 'By the Splendour of God! I have taken seisin of my Kingdom, the earth of England is in my hands.' A soldier on guard seized a piece of thatch from a nearby cottage and offered it to the Duke who said, 'I accept it, and may God be with us!'[6]

Pevensey Bay, at that period, was a large and relatively shallow lagoon with much marshy ground to the east and north. Since then the area has silted up as sea levels fell and the shoreline has advanced some miles further south. It is not certain that the Duke had deliberately selected Pevensey but the area was well known to the monks of Fécamp, who could have provided vital information about suitable landing sites. Pevensey could have been chosen in order to avoid the Channel ports and their defences, especially Dover, Sandwich and Romney.

Under King Edward these ports, and possibly some others, had provided small fighting ships with a crew of twenty-one men, used for coastal defence. Each port was also fortified with its own burh. There were forty or fifty of these vessels.

Pevensey was not really the best location for a bridgehead, as the marshes restricted passage further inland, so the Duke was content merely to occupy the old Roman fortifications at Anderida where a motte and bailey castle was quickly erected, using prefabricated parts brought from Normandy to provide the palisades and the watch tower. It was located in the south east corner of the old borough at Anderida and protected by a bank and ditch. The Duke had in fact brought the essential wooden parts of several castles in easily assembled sections ready for speedy assembly once a motte or mound (usually at least ten or twenty feet high or more) had been built and the bank and ditch dug.

Evidence from Domesday Book, of reductions in the annual profit produced by estates (and so a reduction in their produce) immediately after the Conquest, reveals that the area to the west of Pevensey (south of the present A27) and extending as far as the borough of Lewes, had been ravaged by the Normans. This suggests that the invaders had set about replenishing their supplies with fresh meat and produce as soon as they had secured the area. That was to have the fitting consequence of causing dysentery among the Normans. This ravaging also served as a warning to the local inhabitants and was meant to intimidate them. Having taken what they wanted, the Normans then destroyed the farms. This had been planned in advance since Duke William knew he could not, even with so large a fleet, feed such a large force. He also knew that, as an invader, he could, as he did, feed his men by ruthlessly ravaging the area around his beachhead. King Harold, however, could not have done that, the people of Sussex were his own people.

On either the 29 or 30 of September the Duke decided to move his fleet along the coast to Hastings, while the knights and foot soldiers moved along the coast, ravaging as they went to intimidate the inhabitants. One part of the army went around the northern shore of the harbour, as the trail of 'wasted' vills listed in Domesday Book shows, (they lost up to three quarters of their values), and the other part passed along the coast where the trail of destruction is even more marked. The Normans would have moved from one location to another by line of sight as they had no maps to guide them, taking their bearings from the sun and the shoreline. It is reported by Norman chroniclers that young men and girls and even widows were taken captive, no doubt to be used as servants, as well as all the cattle being stolen. The rest of the English in the landing area had fled, taking their goods and cattle with them. That was to make it essential for the ravaging to be extended in order to seize supplies. The fleet moved on the morning tide and took about two hours to reach its destination. There was still no sign of organised resistance. The local levies of the Fyrd had been stood down on 8 September and then many of them had gone north with King Harold to Stamford Bridge. The Norman move was made necessary by the exposed nature of Pevensey Bay, the restricted amount of space available, because of the marshes, and the need to secure a port with a harbour. The relocation of the whole fleet must have occupied several days.

The Norman fleet now anchored or beached in the Bulverhythe Estuary and Coombe Haven, and the army billeted itself on Hastings. Duke William knew he had to protect his fleet. The town lay on the coast at the southern edge of a sort of peninsula, about ten miles by six, protected on three sides by the sea and two rivers, the Brede and the Cuckmere. The only way inland lay to the north over the ridgeway across Andredeswald (the Weald of Kent). The road led inland between Sedlescombe and Catsfield and was the Roman road to Maidstone. The Duke ordered the construction of a second castle to control the town and its surrounding area. He had now established a defensible bridgehead and occupied a harbour to which reinforcements and further supplies could be brought and by way of which he and his men could escape if the need arose. So William, who was waiting for the English reaction, remained close to his castles and his ships. Further evidence of the reduced value of estates reveals ravaging around Hastings also.

The Duke's major strategic aim was now to escape from the bottleneck and choose a suitable location at which to offer battle to whichever opponent presented himself. Hastings had been chosen because the road to London lay to the north of the town and would allow William's scouts to watch for the arrival of any opponents. The peninsula between Hastings and Rye belonged to Fécamp Abbey. This decision dictated the location of the battle which ensued.

Either at Pevensey, but more probably at Hastings, the Duke reviewed his fleet and found that two of his ships were missing. He learnt also of the fate of a Norman cleric who had prophesied that William would be victorious without a blow being struck. The unfortunate fellow had fallen overboard and been drowned during the crossing. The Duke remarked, sardonically, 'A poor diviner he must have been who could not foresee the manner and time of his own death. Foolish would be he who put his faith in the words of such a soothsayer'.

A few days later it was discovered that the missing vessels had become separated from the rest of the fleet and had landed at Romney where both ships were destroyed and the crews slain by the inhabitants. In due course the men of Romney were to pay a heavy price for their temerity.[7]

The Norman landings had, of course, not gone unnoticed. Various local thegns had been keeping watch on Norman movements at both Pevensey and at Hastings (Hastings itself was connected by an ancient route which ran up over the Weald from the isthmus, formed by the Brede and the Bulverhythe and lead on via Lewes to London). At least one man had watched the disembarkation of infantrymen and archers and had seen the knights and their horses. He would have been struck by the military appearance of these men with their short razor cut hairstyle, short back and sides, thin on top with a thicker quiff at the front, not unlike a U.S. Marine's hair cut. The Bretons among them were probably distinguished by having beards, whereas the Normans were clean shaven.

The thegn who had observed the landing had ridden off to London to warn King Harold. In all likelihood more than one man had had the same idea. It would have taken in the region of five days for news of the landing to reach York, a distance of close on 250 miles from Hastings. The very earliest that Harold could have been told of William's arrival would have been on the 3 or 4 of October. Some writers thought he had heard of the Norman invasion while still at York celebrating his victory at Stamford Bridge, but it is more probable that he heard while already on his way back to London. Time has to be allowed for his having organised affairs at York, leaving Maerleswein, Sheriff of Lincolnshire, to govern the province in the absence of Earl Morcar. Only after that, and after leaving the treasure won in the battle in the safe keeping of Ealdred, Archbishop of York, did he set out on his return, reaching the city of London by 5 October.

Meanwhile, the Duke began what became his trademark in dealing with the English, a methodical march along the south coast, ravaging as he moved, that is, destroying and burning everything in his path and eliminating the unfortunate inhabitants. Without waiting for any hostile action to materialise, he ordered the Norman army to begin a systematic scorched earth policy around and to the north of Hastings. The Duke himself, escorted by a party of twenty-five knights, went on a foraging expedition, to obtain supplies and reconnoitre the area between Hastings and the Weald. He could easily have penetrated as far as Telham Hill or even Starr's Green in the valley below where the battle was to be fought. He had to return on foot, walking at least part of the way back, because the ground was so rough and uneven. At one stage he carried not only his own hauberk (removed because of the heat) but also that of his companion, William fitzOsbern.

According to one Norman writer, William of Poitiers, there were alleged to have been a series of negotiations between the Duke and King Harold in the days before the battle. The Duke is reported as sending a monk of Fécamp with his messages for King Harold. What was said in these exchanges, as presented in this account, allows the writer to rehearse the Norman justification for the invasion which, stripped of all embellishments, boils down to a claim that King Edward had made the Duke his heir, that Harold had been sent to Normandy to repeat the bequest, swearing to assist the Duke in claiming his inheritance, and that Harold had broken his oath, seized the throne and in doing so, had betrayed his lawful lord, Duke William. King Harold is presented as scornfully rejecting all this and claiming that he, not William, had been designated as his successor by the dying King.[8]

But the short time scale of events, days rather than weeks, before Hastings does not permit of any lengthy exchanges between the Duke and the King, only for a final challenge on the part of the Bastard and its rejection by King Harold. Instead, the content of the speeches put into the mouths of the rivals by the Norman writer represents the arguments presented by the Duke early in 1066, shortly after Harold's elevation to the throne by a unanimous decision of the Witan (the Council of magnates and bishops).

However, while the Duke was at Hastings he did receive a message from another source. The Staller, (that is, an office holder with 'seat and special duty' at Court), Robert fitzWymarc (of Breton origin) sent a strongly worded warning to the Duke. He told him of Harold's crushing defeat of the Norwegians at Stamford Bridge and the deaths of Harald Sigurdson and Earl Tostig.

He told the Duke that King Harold was advancing against him 'with all speed... and... with innumerable soldiers all well-equipped for war' in comparison with whom William and his Normans were 'a pack of curs'. Duke William would be well advised to retire behind his entrenchments and should not 'dare to offer battle'.

The Duke, possibly believing that the message came from or was inspired by Harold himself, told the Staller that it would have been better for him 'not to mingle insults' with his message and that for his part, he intended to offer battle 'as soon as possible'. He boasted that he would offer battle even if he had only ten thousand men and not the sixty thousand (sic!) he actually had. That last number is, of course, an impossible exaggeration and signifies only that he claimed to have many more than ten thousand.[9]

The Duke, still with his fleet at this time, is then described as dealing with a message from Harold, delivered by an unnamed English monk. If such a last minute message did arrive, then the Norman historian has probably reversed the order of events. What the monk is reported to have said reads more like a rebuttal, by Harold, of arguments already presented by the Duke.

William of Poitiers, by his own admission, was not present with the Duke before the battle and could not have known what, if anything, passed between Duke William and King Harold. But he would have known the content of the Duke's original challenge to Harold in the early part of the year. According to the account he gives, Duke William is supposed to have sent a monk of Fécamp to deliver his reply.

So, having first admitted that no one had told him what the Duke said before the battle, William of Poitiers then proceeds to tell his readers what was said! This was a convention of historical writing at that time, dating back to the writings of Roman historians. The writer simply invented suitable speeches for the protagonists as a means of conveying the sort of things they would have been expected to say. The Norman scribe simply repeats what he knew William had already said, earlier in the year, in justification of his invasion, and what Harold's known response had been.

The only new element in the exchanges was Duke William's issue of a formal challenge to King Harold that they settle the issue by single combat. That, 'Ordeal by Battle', was a Norman custom unknown in England, unacceptable therefore to King Harold, and the Bastard would have known that quite well. Such challenges were frequently made before battle in Normandy, in an effort to wrong foot an opponent to the challenger's advantage.

No doubt brief messages were exchanged in which King Harold sent a herald to tell William, 'Return with your followers to your own country!' and the Duke replied, 'The Kingdom is mine! Let Harold surrender it. I am ready to risk my life in battle!' Harold is reported to have cried, on hearing this, 'Tell the Duke that I say, Let God decide between me and thee!' and to his companions he said, 'We march at once; we march to battle!'[10]

The scenes presented in the Bayeux Tapestry of events before the battle permit of such an interpretation. The Knights are shown going out from Hastings on foraging expeditions. A Norman called Vitalis is asked whether he has seen Harold's army and an armoured man is shown reporting to King Harold the presence of the Duke's army. So, by about Monday the ninth or Tuesday the tenth of October, Duke William was aware that he was going to have to fight for the crown. What, then, were the events which had brought matters to this critical point?[11]

A Disputed Coronation:
Saturday 6 January to 1 May 1066

King Edward, the Confessor, had died of his illness, probably pneumonia, on the night of 4/5 January, possibly around midnight on the fourth. The Chroniclers report him dead on 5 January and buried on the 6th, but the 'Life of King Edward who lies at Westminster', written under the patronage of his widow, Queen Edith, says he died on the 4 January. He was then buried on the 6 January, the Feast of the Epiphany, in accordance with his last wishes, in his newly consecrated Abbey Church at Westminster.[1]

Shortly before his death, the King had rallied sufficiently to make an oral declaration of his last will and testament, known in the eleventh century as a man's 'verba novissima' or last words and regarded as especially binding. Such a will, made in the presence of clerical and other witnesses, by long-standing custom took precedence over and cancelled any previous bequests. King Edward's last words were witnessed, as his Life and the Bayeux Tapestry confirm, by his wife, the Queen, by his under-king (subregulus), Earl Harold, by Archbishop Stigand of Canterbury, and by Robert fitzWymarc, Steward of the Royal Palace. It is likely that other favourites and servants of the King were present, such as his household priests and chaplains and other French servants (who were singled out for mention by the King). It is remarkable, given the Norman claims, that Duke William of Normandy was not present. Yet, if he had been Edward's designated heir, it would have been natural for him to have been summoned to attend so that he could be recommended to the Witan.

According to the account given in the King's Life, and rather surprisingly, the dying man first asked that his wife, the Queen, be taken under the protection of Earl Harold, her brother. He is reported as saying, 'I commend this woman and all the kingdom to your (i.e. Harold's) protection; serve and honour her with faithful obedience as your lady and sister, which she is, and do not despoil her, as long as she lives, of any due honour got from me'. The King then also asked that the Earl accept 'fealty' from the French favourites, protecting and retaining them in his service or, if they preferred, permitting them to return home across the Channel with safe conduct. Lastly, he asked to be buried as he had arranged, in the new Abbey and that his death be immediately made known to the people so that they might pray for his soul. He was then given the Last Rites of the Church and received Holy Communion. Shortly after that he died peacefully.[2]

All other sources, even Duke William's panegyrist, William of Poitiers, accept that the King directly bequeathed the crown to Earl Harold, subject to the approval of the Witan, (the Council of Magnates and Higher Clergy) so it looks as though the author of the Vita, seeking to protect his patron, the Queen, deliberately sought to reduce the significance of the King's last words, by implying that Earl Harold was in some way to be subordinate to Edith, or that he was to be a regent for the real heir. This latter point can be ruled out since no such heir is named. The author of the Vita Edwardi appears to have altered the order in which the King gave his instructions, running them together by inserting the bequest of the Kingdom after the demand that Edith be given special protection. King Edward would surely have dealt primarily and first of all with the disposal of his kingdom, saying something like, 'I commend this realm to my noble Earl, Harold, who has always faithfully obeyed me as his lord and neglected nothing needful to me' (see the poem on the King's death in the Worcester and Abingdon versions of the Chronicle) and then went on to commend Queen Edith to Earl Harold's protection and to ask that Edward's French servants be permitted to swear fealty to the Earl as they would to a king. The verb 'commendare' is full of legal significance, the King was placing the Kingdom, and Queen Edith, under the protection of Earl Harold, so that the Kingdom and everyone in it became his vassals and were subject to him. The verb can also mean 'grant', and the Anglo-Saxon Chronicle is clear that King Edward granted the Kingdom to Earl Harold, subject to the approval of the Witan.

The requests the King makes, that Earl Harold should give his protection to Queen Edith and accept the service of those of his French favourites who wished to remain in England, are made as though the Kingdom has already passed into Harold's hands. The Bayeux Tapestry, by placing the scene in which the king lies dying, and is addressing Earl Harold and others, immediately above that in which he is shown dead, and both after the funeral procession, allows for the direct juxtaposition of the death bed speech to the scene in which courtiers give the crown to Earl Harold, so linking the speech to the transfer of the crown. The text then reads; 'Here King Edward in his bed addresses his faithful men; here they gave the king's crown to Harold' and immediately afterwards 'Here sits Harold King of the English.' The cause and its effect is very plain. The Anglo-Saxon Chronicle records a tribute to the King and adds that he 'committed the kingdom to a distinguished man, a princely Earl, Harold himself, who at all times loyally obeyed his lord in words and deeds, neglecting nothing of which the nation's king was in need.'[3]

That the King nominated Harold as his successor was never denied, even by the Duke. The Normans simply chose to ignore the binding nature of 'verba novissima', claiming that Edward's alleged promise to the Duke took precedence because of his kinship (as Edward's great-nephew) and that the Earl, as allegedly the Duke's vassal, ought to have refused the nomination. There is no evidence that King Edward ever made any public declaration in favour of the Duke, other than Norman assertions, and, had he done so, it would surely have been recorded in the Chronicle. Nor was there a written will, since, had it existed, William would surely have produced it.

As soon as the King had been buried, on the Saturday, the Witan met to ratify the bequest and the Coronation followed immediately. It was not a matter of undue haste and there was nothing improper about it. It was a matter of simple convenience and a response to the need for a King to be chosen as soon as possible. The sixth of January was a major feast day, the Epiphany, and the magnates and higher clergy were still present, having remained at court because of the king's imminent death and to witness his burial. They had assembled in December for the usual Christmas Witan, had remained for the consecration of Westminster, and then hung on because of the situation. The evidence of witness lists to charters issued at around this time reveal that everyone of importance was present. It was not a Witan liable to be overawed by the prestige of Earl Harold. Given the constant threat presented by the Scandinavian kings, aware that the exiled Earl Tostig could well attempt a come back, and possibly aware also (as Harold was) of the ambitions of William the Bastard, it was essential that a king be chosen and it made complete sense to take advantage of the fact that the Witan was already assembled

All sources confirm that the crown was offered to, and accepted by, Earl Harold, as King Edward's nominated heir. He was then consecrated, anointed and crowned, using the established coronation ritual, by Archbishop Ealdred of York, who was in possession of a valid Pallium bestowed on him by Pope Nicholas II (so avoiding any doubts as to the coronation's validity arising from the anomalous position of Archbishop Stigand). Thus 'the funeral baked meats did coldly furnish forth' the coronation banquet.[4] Thereafter, as the Chronicler comments sadly, Harold had 'little quiet the while that he possessed the kingdom'.

Harold made a solid beginning as king. He proceeded to cement an alliance with the Earls of Mercia and Northumbria, Edwin and Morcar, by marrying their sister Ealdgyth. It has been suggested that the marriage was intended as a signal to Duke William, that he could not expect King Harold to fulfil any promise to marry the Duke's daughter. Harold went north to York, accompanied by Bishop Wulfstan of Worcester (who was well known at York as he had been Archbishop Ealdred's suffragan bishop there since 1062). The new King's objective was to assure the northern magnates, many of whom had not been present at Westminster, of the legitimacy of his succession and to convince them that the Law of Cnut, which he had confirmed for them in King Edward's name in October 1065, still stood. In doing this he showed himself, as Florence of Worcester comments, 'pious, humble and affable to all good men'.

On his return to London he proceeded to take in hand the government of the kingdom, issuing a new coinage bearing his own image. It showed him crowned and bearded and facing left (whereas King Edward's last issue showed him facing right). He is described as paying due reverence to all 'bishops, abbots, monks and clerks' and to have been 'pious, humble and affable to all good men'. King Harold began with the smack of firm government, giving orders to 'his earls, ealdormen, sheriffs and thegns' for the imprisonment of all 'thieves and robbers and disturbers of the peace of the kingdom'. Such 'malefactors' were to be treated with great severity. Harold began well, abolishing laws he regarded as unjust and replacing them by better ones.[5]

He then began to prepare for the worst and make preparations for defence, 'labouring in his own person by sea and land for the protection of the realm', not necessarily in expectation of a Norman invasion but certainly in expectation of trouble from his exiled brother, Earl Tostig, from Viking raiders and from the possibility of a Danish or other Scandinavian attack. Much of this action would have been taken at an Easter Witan on the 16 April.

As for William the Bastard, he heard the news of Harold's accession while out hunting at Quevilly, near Rouen. It cannot have taken long for the news of the Confessor's death to have reached Normandy. Merchants made frequent crossings of the Channel for trade between England and Normandy; some of the former servants of King Edward, not all of whom took service with King Harold, probably returned home almost immediately; the monks of Fécamp often communicated with their estates in England. Any one of these might have been the first with the news. Indeed, 'at the end of the reign' of King Edward, Harold had repossessed the estate at Steyning, granted, probably on lease, to Fécamp by King Edward and evicted the monks. He could have done it as soon as Edward died. In response to it, Duke William confirmed the Abbot in possession of Steyning in the following June, a grant which would take effect only 'if God should give him victory in England.'

Duke William, having heard the news, returned to Rouen in fury and no one dared to speak to him. Once in his ducal apartments he sat for some hours contemplating his options until roused from his brown study by William fitzOsbern. The Duke then waited for a Council of his magnates to assemble. The immediate response of the Duke, supported by his counsellors, was to send messengers to England to register his protests at what he chose to label as English perfidy. The Norman Duke demanded that Harold surrender the crown of England to him and to 'fulfil the faith which he had pledged with his oath', or so William of Jumièges claims in his account of the Duke's reaction. So the Norman claim was carefully crafted to present the Duke as the champion of feudal ethics, such as they were, against Harold who was depicted as a perjurer.[6]

King Harold naturally refused to acknowledge the Norman claims and was subsequently accused by Duke William of having 'seduced all the English people away from obedience to the Duke'. The Bastard is described, after Hastings, as having 'laid low the people opposed to him, which, rebelling against him, its King, deserved death'. Of any obligation to obey the Duke of Normandy, the English were, of course, quite oblivious, the Duke's claims were mere rhetoric. What Harold would have done was to follow English precedent and require all men to attend the courts of Shire and Hundred where the oath of fealty to the King of the English was administered.

In his account of the Duke's career, William of Poitiers, writing some years after the Conquest was an established fact, used what was known of the exchanges between the King and the Duke early in 1066 in constructing his version of events before the battle of Hastings. He had to do this because, as he himself admitted, he was not present in England before the battle and he relies on his informants for his account.

The argument William of Poitiers, and similarly William of Jumièges, used to justify the invasion, was that King Edward had bequeathed the Kingdom of England to Duke William so that the Duke was Edward's heir and had been promised the throne by him. This line of argument and the talk of Harold having contracted a marriage alliance, had been tried out on similar lines when Duke William had laid claim to the County of Maine in 1063, despite the fact that it had been controlled by Anjou since 1025. William claimed that it had previously been granted to the Dukes of Normandy and that it had been bequeathed to Duke William by Count Herbert II who had died in 1062. The Count had been an exile (like King Edward) and William had agreed to promote his claims. The Duke also claimed that he had married one of his daughters to Herbert and arranged a marriage between his son, Robert Curthose, and Herbert's sister, Margaret! There is no evidence that the marriage to Herbert ever took place and the Duke's daughter is never named. Only William of Poitiers reports all this. The parallel between these claims and those made concerning England seems more than coincidental. Not only that, but Walter III of the Vexin and Mantes, elder brother of Earl Ralph of Mantes and, like him, a nephew of King Edward, had married Biota, a daughter of Count Herbert's aunt, so that Walter also had a claim to the County of Maine. He and his wife Biota conveniently, for William, died while they were his prisoners. Orderic Vitalis accused William of having poisoned them! (Food poisoning is more likely). Geoffrey of Mayenne had vigorously opposed the Duke's designs, supporting the claim of Count Walter. In consequence of this claim William had invaded and devastated Maine in 1063, 'setting fire to it to destroy the whole town and massacre the guilty' (that is, those who had opposed him). Margaret had died before the marriage to Robert could take place (another parallel) but Duke William nonetheless made himself Count of Maine. William of Poitiers comments that William took possession 'of the principality of Maine, as he did of the Kingdom of England, not simply by force but also by the law of justice'.[7]

He attributes to King Harold an admission of the truth of Duke William's claim that King Edward had made the Duke his heir and that the king had sent Harold to Normandy to confirm that this had been done. He says that when in Normandy Harold had 'sworn homage and… pledged… the security of the kingdom' to the Duke. King Harold is unlikely to have made any such admission. These words are put into his mouth by the Archdeacon simply to allow the presentation of the Duke's case. However, Harold's rejoinder, also given by the writer, rings true. King Harold insists that King Edward, whom he calls his lord (so implicitly denying that William could have been his lord), had, as he lay dying and acting within his rights, bestowed the Kingdom on the Earl. Harold then asserts that in England it was the 'unbroken custom, since the coming of Saint Augustine, to treat deathbed bequests as inviolable'. He, Harold, therefore, will 'break the friendship and the pacts' which he had made with Duke William in Normandy. The nature of this friendship and of the pacts in question is not explained. These exchanges, allegedly made in the days before the Battle of Hastings, reflect the content of the diplomatic exchanges which were made in the Spring of 1066. Remarkably none of these reported exchanges mentions the question of the hostages allegedly sent by King Edward to Duke William.[8]

The Duke's challenge probably reached King Harold around 17 January, possibly after his return from York (a late and otherwise unreliable source claims that William's challenge was ten days after the death of King Edward, which is not inherently improbable). Harold took various decisions in the days following 17 January. He had ecclesiastical vacancies to fill. The abbacy of Ely was vacant, and then Abbot Ordric of Abingdon died seventeen days after King Edward, on 22 January. Harold then appointed his supporter, Thurstan, as Abbot of Ely, and Ealdred, also called Brichtwin, Abbot of Abingdon. The Abingdon Chronicle links both appointments to the period after the Coronation rather than to the Easter Witan. The Chronicle of Evesham claims that Abbot Manni had become paralysed and had asked King Edward to appoint a coadjutor as abbot as he could no longer carry out his duties. The King accordingly appointed Aethelwig to govern the monastery, in Manni's name, and he was consecrated by Bishop Ealdred, which points to 1058 as the date. Manni does not seem to have died until 1066, as Aethelwig is said to have ruled as his substitute for about seven years and some months, but when he did, King Harold confirmed Aethelwig's appointment as abbot, and in a sense, his abbacy commences from that year.

William of Poitiers, determined as usual to justify the Duke's actions, alleges that the Duke at least twice tried to persuade Harold to listen to reason over the claim, offering to guarantee to him his position as Earl of Wessex and repeating the offer of one of his daughters in marriage (ignorant of Harold's marriage to Ealdgyth) and using the offer as a gambit in the ensuing diplomacy. William of Poitiers says that Duke William 'did not desire his (Harold's) death but wished to increase for him the power of his father Godwine and give him in marriage to his own daughter.' These repeated references to an offer of marriage should be taken seriously. William had used the same ploy in staking his claim to Maine. William of Jumièges confirms the idea that the Duke challenged Harold as soon as he heard the news and asserts that William offered Harold 'half the Kingdom' and the hand of his daughter in marriage! Some identify the daughter as Agatha. Other versions say that the offer was that he could have his earldom of Wessex. This is romance not history.

The Heimskringla, reporting what was known about the matter in Scandinavia, claims that a marriage had been arranged, between Harold and a daughter of the Duke, by his wife, Duchess Matilda, during a private conversation when Harold was in Normandy, and that the Duke's aim in invading was to punish Harold for not proceeding with the marriage. The Annals of the Abbey of St Bertin at St Omer in Flanders (a neutral source) say that Harold was slain because he was the man 'who had refused to accept the daughter of William himself in marriage'. The Chronicle of St

Andrew's at Cambrai is similar, arguing that the war was due to Harold's having broken his promise to marry William's daughter. These are Flemish sources, independent of Normandy. Some other accounts make the marriage the principal cause of the invasion, others accept it as a subsidiary cause. It does look as though Earl Harold had been made to swear that he would marry the Duke's daughter as Henry of Huntingdon insisted was the cause of the dispute. Betrothals in the eleventh century were sworn to and thus required the taking of oaths. Richard the Fearless of Normandy, when he promised to marry Hugh's daughter, had done homage to Hugh Capet. Harold also appears to have sworn homage to William and possibly to have accepted knighthood from him. Neither of these two actions necessarily involved any promise about the throne of England. But homage could easily be transformed into a pledge to assist the Duke in all that he desired, which included becoming King of England. When Harold failed to do as William claimed to have a right to expect he could be represented, in the eyes of the feudal lords of Western Europe, as a faithless vassal and so a traitor to his lord, who had perjured himself. The Bayeux Tapestry goes to great lengths to maintain its theme that a traitor causes both himself and others to perish. The stress placed on Harold's alleged perjury was used to cover up the weakness of the Norman claim.[9]

All sources agree that there were repeated exchanges between the rivals and imply that the Duke was endeavouring to put Harold in the wrong in the eyes of the Norman barons and of the rulers of the rest of Europe. So, as David Bates remarks, William, by obtaining Papal approval, 'achieved a remarkable coup which immediately transformed a buccaneering enterprise into a legitimate assault on a usurping king'. Harold is presented, no matter what the details, as a sworn vassal who has turned against his lord. The Duke's final offer was apparently an almost desperate plea that Harold at least marry his daughter! William's intermediary in all these diplomatic overtures was Hugh Margot, a monk of Fécamp.

These various offers and their rejection could not have been concealed and William fitzOsbern, the Duke's Seneschal and right hand man, urged his master to act. William then told Harold that if he was not prepared to comply with his demands, then he, William, would come in arms against him, 'Quicker than he thinks will he know our designs, and he shall have more certain knowledge of them than he wants, for he shall see me in person. Take him back this message; tell him that if he does not see me within one year in the place which he now strives to make safe against my coming, he may rest quiet for the rest of his days and need fear no harm from me'. This was said to one of Harold's spies captured in Normandy who was told that

Harold had no need to 'throw away gold and silver in buying the fidelity and fraud of men like you to come clandestinely among us to ferret out our plans'.[10]

Harold on one occasion apparently remarked sardonically that the daughter he had been expected to marry was dead, and that in any case, as King, he could not marry a foreigner without the consent of his Witan. He added that any alleged oaths regarding the handing over of the kingdom were invalid in any case. As for the other part of the agreement, that his sister should marry a noble Norman, well, his sister was dead, 'If you, Duke, still wish to have the body as it is now, I will send it to you, lest I be judged to have broken the oath which I swore.' In Harold's eyes only a marriage alliance had been agreed to. All this is much in the style of the Sagas which present the relations between rival sovereigns in such personal terms.

By the time all these diplomatic manoeuvres were completed, Easter had come and gone, on 16 April, and the Chronicle reports succinctly that Harold had been told 'that William the Bastard would come hither and win this land'. No English source makes any attempt to explain why the Duke intended to invade. All these events are then linked to the appearance of Halley's Comet. It was seen first on 24 April, a Monday, and shone for at least seven nights. Its appearance was noted all over Europe and associated variously with King Edward's death or, later, to that of Harold and the Norman invasion. Some might have reported, as a result of that dreaded sight, seeing phantom ships out at sea threatening invasion. The Bayeux Tapestry hints as much, showing such ships in the lower border, below the scene in which King Harold is informed of the coming of the Comet. Two birds, possibly intended as birds of ill-omen, perch on the roof of the King's palace. Even William of Poitiers was to make use of the comet's appearance. He addresses King Harold, saying 'The Comet, Terror of Kings, in shining at the commencement of your reign, announces your approaching ruin.' As Shakespeare was to write, 'When beggars die there are no comets seen, the heavens themselves show forth the death of Princes'.

The longest period of the Comet's visibility being claimed in some sources was thirty days (possibly an exaggeration) while others reported fourteen days. Variations could be due to whether the 'seeing' was good and not affected by cloud, and the eyesight of the observers. Aethelmaer, the 'flying monk' of Malmesbury was said to have remarked, on seeing the Comet, crouching in terror, 'You've come have you? You've come you source of tears to many mothers. It is long since I saw you; but as I see you now you are much more terrible. For I see you brandishing the downfall of my mother country.' In 1066 he was of advanced age and might have seen the

Comet when he was a child, seventy-six years earlier.[11]

King Harold then began to assemble 'a larger land army and fleet than any king in this land had ever done'. But the Duke also was far from idle. William had not waited until the negotiations were at an end. He took urgent steps to launch a great diplomatic offensive against Harold, seeking to form a grand coalition against the English or at least to secure the Norman frontiers against attack during his own absence. He secured a rather vague agreement with the German Emperor, Henry IV, who agreed, through his counsellors, to come to the aid of Normandy if it should be attacked. William's father-in-law, Baldwin V, was Regent of France where Philip I was still a minor, and ensured French neutrality, giving permission for French knights to join William's army. William already controlled Maine and his southern frontier and the campaign against Brittany in 1064 had ensured there would be no interference from that quarter, despite the bluster of Duke Conan.

Agents were sent out to recruit stipendiary knights (mercenaries) throughout Europe and men came in from France, Brittany, Aquitaine and Poitou, Flanders and Burgundy and possibly from Sicily, Apulia and Calabria.

With the aid of the guileful Lanfranc of Pavia, Abbot of Le Bec-Hellouin, a case was put together for presentation before the Curia at Rome and an embassy was sent, headed by Gilbert Maminot, Archdeacon of Lisieux, to present the case to Pope Alexander II. In it, King Harold was branded a perjurer and a usurper who had been crowned and anointed, as the Normans maintained, by the schismatic Archbishop of Canterbury, Stigand (who was himself accused of simony and pluralism). William's agents, in his name, promised the 'reform' of the English Church, which was described as corrupt and staffed by ill-educated clergy. The Pope must have been gratified to have William approach the Roman tribunal for a decision. He would also have been influenced by Lanfranc's advocacy as he had been a friend of his and studied under him.

King Harold was not informed that a case was being laid against him at Rome and Duke William, who controlled all the Channel ports from the Breton border in the West to Flanders in the East, saw to it that no English deputation would be allowed to travel to Rome.

The Duke's party also won the support of the prime mover at Rome, Archdeacon Hildebrand (who succeeded Alexander under the name of Gregory VII). He, despite the horrified murmurings of those cardinals who were opposed to his policies and who were worried by the prospect of Christians shedding Christian blood, which an invasion would involve, won over the Pope. In a pained protest, Hildebrand, then Pope Gregory, in a letter dated 24 April 1080, reminded William that 'even before I ascended the papal throne... how diligently I laboured for your advancement to royal rank. In consequence of which I suffered dire calumny through certain brethren insinuating that by such partisanship I gave sanction for the perpetration of great slaughter'. As Archdeacon of Rome, Hildebrand was widely regarded as the power behind the Papal Throne. Cardinal Peter Damian was reported to have said that if anyone wished to thrive at Rome, they should say at the top of their voice, 'More than the Pope, I obey the lord of the Pope.'

Duke William received the Pope's mandate to depose the usurper and reform the Church. As William of Poitiers (in what has been described as 'a monstrous exercise in hypocrisy') put it, Duke William's purpose was 'not so much to increase his own power as to reform Christian observance in those regions'. The Normans claimed the grant of a Papal Bull to this effect (which, if issued, has not survived), but no quotations were made from it and evidence to this effect is late and uncorroborated. More importantly, the Duke was given a Papal banner, with the arms of St Peter (possibly the crossed keys), to be carried before him into battle, ensuring the Saint's protection, and a ring said to contain a few hairs from St Peter himself. Although the concept of a 'crusade' had not yet been formulated, this Papal endorsement of the attack on England was a step in that direction. Several other such banners had been granted to supporters of the Papacy in the wars in Italy in the decade before 1066. Alexander had organised what amounted to a crusade in Spain after the King of Aragon was murdered by a Moslem. The Pope had also blessed an invasion of Sicily and, in 1063, had sent a Papal banner to Roger de Hauteville, granting absolution to all those who joined him to fight the heathen.[12]

At some unspecified date, (the Norman writers are notoriously casual about chronology), but probably after the return of the delegation to Rome, the Duke summoned a council at Lillebonne at which he put before his barons his intention to enforce his claim against England and demanded their participation. The most likely date would have been Easter since he is said to have taken six months to prepare for the invasion. It was the most important Feast day of the year and an opportunity for William to put his case to the barons. His hardest task was in fact to persuade his own men to support the projected invasion.[13]

He could not expect his men to accompany him overseas as a matter of feudal obligation, so he proceeded to put before them the basis of his claim to the English throne and his desire to punish Harold, presented as a faithless vassal and a perjurer. But many of the barons were unhappy at the prospect of invading England. They argued that the English had formidable naval power and that England was a rich and powerful country and had a large army. England, they said, was many times richer than Normandy. In any case, they said, 'who could hope that our ships will be ready in time or that enough oarsmen can be found within a year?'

But the Duke responded vigorously to this, arguing that Harold sought to dismay the Normans and alarm them but that their power could only grow, whereas Harold was spending money uselessly, squandering gold and silver without increasing his power. 'Without doubt,' he said, 'victory will go to he who can bestow not only what is his own but also what is held by his enemy. Nor will lack of ships hinder us, for very soon we will rejoice in the sight of a fleet.' He went on to assert that 'Wars are won not by numbers but by courage. Harold will fight to retain what he has wrongfully seized whereas we shall fight to regain what we have received as a gift and lawfully acquired. Strong in this knowledge, we shall overcome all dangers and win a happy victory, great honour and high renown'.

Nonetheless, many exaggerated the resources of Harold and minimized their own. It proved, as Orderic Vitalis recorded, to be a more difficult task than William had anticipated to persuade the barons to support the enterprise of England. William was saved by the cunning of William fitzOsbern. He discussed the matter with his fellow magnates in the Duke's absence, allowing them to give free rein to their doubts and concerns and promising to convey them to the Duke as their spokesman. When the Council reconvened, fitzOsbern spoke up, as he had promised, but to the consternation of the assembled barons, spoke only of their loyalty and love for the Duke and promised in their name to provide the ships and men required, personally promising sixty ships himself. Other supporters of the Duke, notably his half-brothers Odo, Bishop of Bayeux, and Robert, Count of Mortain, offered one hundred and one hundred and twenty ships respectively. Other leading men chimed in, offering ships and men. The great Norman houses supported William; Eu, Montgomery, Beaumont and Avranches offered sixty ships each; Evreux, not to be outdone, offered eighty, de Montfort forty, and so on and the Duchess Matilda presented her husband with the largest ship in the fleet, the Mora. In all 812 ships were promised and several contingents of knights, totalling about 280 men.

Later, in the twelfth century, Robert Wace reported that his father told him there were exactly 696 ships at St Valery, although elsewhere in his work, the 'Roman de Rou', he writes of 776 ships. The discrepancy is easily accounted for. Some ships were probably not ready in time and others were lost in the storm during the move from Dives to St Valery. The monk Hugh of Fleury claimed there were 700 ships and that William had 150,000 troops, an obvious exaggeration. Other writers threw numbers about with abandon, probably confusing the number of vessels which actually formed the fleet with the various vessels used to load supplies.[14] The objectors had been outmanoeuvred and found themselves committed to the enterprise.

Duke William did not rely solely on the resources of Normandy for knights and foot soldiers, and the greater part of his army consisted not of the feudal contingents of his barons but of stipendiary soldiers hired from all over Europe. The building of the ships and the gathering of the host took William almost six months. A prime factor was the construction of transports capable of carrying horses as well as men and supplies. Many of the vessels, as the Bayeux Tapestry shows, were of quite shallow draft, often with low sides, more like barges than sea-going vessels. The heads of the horses are shown clearly visible above the level of the ships' sides and this might not be merely an artistic convention. The ships have a single, square sail and there is no sign of oarsmen. Such vessels would depend entirely on a favourable wind from the west and south to carry them directly across the Channel to England.

Some have speculated that the original intention had been to make for the Isle of Wight, but this had been frustrated by Harold's naval dispositions. In addition the winds in August blew either from the south west or, more often, from the north east. A north easterly wind had destroyed Duke Robert the Magnificent's fleet off Jersey and a south westerly wind had blown Earl Harold to Ponthieu in 1064.[15]

But, if the barometer fell and pressure over the British Isles was reduced the south westerlies became southern winds and that was what the Duke no doubt hoped would happen. The winds remained unfavourable throughout August and morale was damaged. North easterly winds brought Harald of Norway and left the Duke stranded. So Duke William decided to move along the coast to Saint Valery, with disastrous results.

Feints & Diversions:
Monday 1 May to Wednesday 27 September 1066

Shortly before 1 May 1066, King Harold called out the whole strength of the kingdom for its defence, stationing men principally along the south coast of England in the expectation of a direct Norman assault. The area to be defended extended around the East coast into the Thames Estuary where Harold's brother, Earl Leofwine, held his earldom with lands on both sides of the estuary and the river Thames, and around into East Anglia where the other brother, Earl Gyrth, held Norfolk and Suffolk as his earldom. The Northern shores of England, from the Wash to the Humber and up along the Northumbrian coast, were left in the charge of the brother Earls, Edwin and Morcar. Unlike earlier Kings, Harold had chosen London as the centre of his government, from whence he could best conduct the defence of his kingdom. He celebrated both Easter and Pentecost in London, leaving Winchester to his sister, Queen Edith.

King Harold kept these forces on the alert throughout the summer months, through May and June into August and September, no mean achievement in itself. Detachments of Housecarls and King's Thegns, the professional household retainers of the King and his brother earls, were stationed wherever a landing was most expected, with members of the shire fyrd at ports and burhs (fortified towns) along the South Coast.

An entry in Domesday Book, referring to the customary obligations of Berkshire, suggests that in many, but not necessarily in all, shires, it was expected that one man should join the King's army on campaign for every five hides of land in the shire. Other evidence suggests that the system was that one man served for every six carucates in Danelaw areas. (These measures, hides and carucates, originally referring to areas of cultivated land sufficient to support one man and his family, were, by the eleventh century notional assessments of the taxable value of an estate, [rather like rateable values once used to raise taxes for the upkeep of local government]).[1]

The men raised for fighting in this way, if the Berkshire Customs can be accepted, had to be provided with one pound each (in silver pennies) to cover their living expenses for two months (that is, four shillings from each hide). King Harold, therefore, called out a first levy of the fyrd, as the English army was known, to cover the months of May and June, and then a second to cover July and August, but his attempt to retain the fyrd on active service during September failed in the face of the need to release men to bring in the harvest, and, as supplies were running low, the fyrd was disbanded on Wednesday, 12 September. The Chronicle remarks, 'then were the provisions of the men exhausted and no man could any longer hold them there'. King Harold was unable to keep the fleet at sea and that too went out of service shortly after the 12 September, hoping to avoid the equinoctial gales, returning to its base at London. It was caught in the same storms that almost wrecked Duke William's invasion fleet.[2]

The exiled Earl, Tostig, had spent much of the winter at the Court of his uncle by marriage, Count Baldwin V of Flanders (as Tostig's wife, Judith, was Baldwin's niece). There he had nursed his grievances against his brother Harold, now King of England, and pondered how he might seek his revenge. The Count had done little to encourage the aims of the Earl but he did allow him to recruit men and ships from Flanders. When news of King Edward's death and his brother's elevation to the kingship reached the Earl, Tostig was undoubtedly enraged and determined to do what he could to win his way back to power in England and depose his brother. He hoped to imitate his father, Earl Godwine, who had won his way back to power in 1052. Another exiled Earl, Aelfgar of Mercia had also won restoration to power, twice, with the help of Welsh and Viking forces.

Having gathered ships and men, Earl Tostig at first tried to win the support of Duke William. Arriving at William's Court, he sought an audience with the Duke and, audaciously, reproached William for allowing a perjurer to occupy the throne that rightfully belonged to him. The Earl promised to gain the crown for the Duke should he decide to enter England with a Norman army. Orderic Vitalis even suggested, in his account of this meeting, that Duke William and Earl Tostig were friends of long-standing because they were, as he put it, married to two sisters, that is Judith and William's wife, Matilda. (In fact the ladies were cousins.)

Duke William, however, had no intention of assisting the Earl in the recovery of his earldom, only in using him to cause trouble for his brother, King Harold. He encouraged the Earl to make an attack on the English coast, allowing him to leave Normandy from the Cotentin Peninsula. However, Earl Tostig was unable to do much, he could not even reach the English coast, because King Harold had 'covered the sea with ships and soldiers'. His way would have been barred by the coastal guard ships put out by such ports as Sandwich, Dover and Romney. Nor could he, because of adverse winds, return to Normandy. Concluding that he did not have sufficient resources to keep his promises to Duke William, the Earl instead decided to seek the assistance of other kings.

Leaving the Channel, he first visited King Swein of Denmark. The King made fair promises of assistance to the Earl, which he did not carry out, contenting himself with allowing Earl Tostig to recruit ships to his service. The Earl then turned, as a last resort, to King Harald of Norway.[3]

Having reached the court of the Norwegian King, he made more or less the same offer to him that he had made to Duke William. He is reported to have said to King Harald, 'I offer your Majesty my person and my service' adding that he hoped to recover 'the possessions and honours inherited from my father which are due to me'. Orderic Vitalis then claims that the Earl accused his brother, King Harold, of having robbed him of his earldom and of being both a usurper and a perjurer. Orderic is putting words into Tostig's mouth intended to bolster the Norman claims. Tostig is made to demand of King Harald, 'Humble the pride of my perfidious brother by waging war; keep for yourself half of England and grant the other half to me so that I may serve you faithfully as long as I live'. Orderic is assuming that Earl Tostig used the same arguments in talking to King Harald as he had no doubt used in seeking the aid of Duke William. The suggestion that Harold of England was 'perfidious' certainly fits Tostig's known attitude; back in October 1065 he had accused Harold of plotting his downfall, charging him with having persuaded the Northumbrians to revolt against him.

The Earl's arguments did not, in themselves, persuade King Harald to act, but they certainly fired his ambition and he was gratified by the Earl's attempt to enlist his aid. It is unlikely that King Harald had entertained ideas of an invasion of England while King Edward still lived, as the Norwegian king had displayed no interest in English affairs before 1066. Earl Tostig is said to have done homage to King Harald and so became his vassal. He had argued before the King, as he had before the Duke, that the majority of English nobles would support him if he effected a return.

Some of King Harald's men were unwilling to chance an attempt on England. His leading adviser, Ulf Ospaksson, is said to have argued strongly against it, warning the king that it would be by no means easy because of the 'army, called in England the King's Housecarls'. He said that they 'are formed of men so valiant that any one of them is worth more than two of your best men'. He added that it was a force 'without equal anywhere and equally at home with the battle axe or the sword'.

But King Harald now decided to imitate the example of Swein Forkbeard and of Cnut the Great, and make himself master of England. In that way he would both avenge the death of his half brother, St Olaf, King of Norway, who had been slain at Stiklestad (1030) and 'realise at the same time his own great desire to win this kingdom'. Before setting out on his campaign against England, in August, King Harald visited St Olaf's shrine at Nidaros, where he prayed for his aid and trimmed the saint's hair and beard as he lay in his coffin.[4]

Earl Tostig then, returned south, leaving King Harald to prepare his fleet, having arranged to rendezvous with him off the north coast of England in the following summer. King Harald immediately set in train orders for the assembly of his forces for an invasion of England and the building of an invasion fleet. These preparations took him, just as they did Duke William, six months to accomplish. The Norwegians, like the Normans, were ready early in August. The conversations between Tostig and the two princes had to have taken place in February 1066. Having concluded his business in the north, Earl Tostig returned south, probably visiting both Flanders and Denmark and recruiting mercenary ships, planning further raids on England.

Some have cast doubt on such an early meeting between the Earl and King Harald on the grounds that there had not been enough time, early in 1066, for Tostig to reach Norway and return before Easter, but that underestimates the rapidity with which Earl Tostig moved between January and May in what might be seen as an example of 'shuttle diplomacy'. The need to guard the South Coast was then vindicated in mid May when the exiled Earl, 'with as many Housecarls as he could muster', appeared with an armed fleet off the Isle of Wight, where he had held a respectable amount of land. He effected a landing and seized both supplies and men. From there he made raids all along the South Coast, though obviously repelled everywhere he went, until he reached Sandwich. As these attacks followed the appearance of Halley's Comet, it must have seemed to many that the woes it foretold were upon them.

By now, King Harold, who was in London, had heard of his brother's activities and set out with the Fleet to intercept the Earl. Tostig, no doubt informed by sympathizers that King Harold was on his way, press-ganged some of the Sandwich butsecarls (trained fighting seamen), though some also volunteered to join him, and made good his escape, sailing around the coast of East Anglia and eventually on into the Humber estuary. Geoffrey Gaimar, writing in the twelfth century, reported that as Tostig sailed from Sandwich to the Humber, he raided a place called 'Wardstane' (now lost) and the Isle of Thanet. There he met his former lieutenant, from when he was Earl of Northumbria, a thegn called Copsige who had arrived from Orkney with a few ships. The two then raided another unidentifiable location, 'Brunemue', somewhere on the East Anglian Coast, perhaps Burnham Staithe (Bruneham), and then went on into the Humber. There he raided Lindsey in northern Lincolnshire, setting fire, in time honoured fashion, to several villages and killing many men.

But the Earls, Edwin and Morcar, came against him with their levies and drove him out. The Earl had arrived with sixty ships but after he was expelled from Lindsey he was deserted by the greater part of his fleet and left with only twelve ships, those in his personal service and those Copsige had brought from Orkney. The ships manned by mercenary sailors, provided for him by King Swein Estrithson of Denmark, and those manned by sailors press-ganged in Sandwich simply refused to stay with him and returned home. They had no intention of following Earl Tostig further north towards Scotland.

King Malcolm III, called Canmore, received Earl Tostig and made him welcome. He allowed him to stay at his Court, probably at Dunfermline, all that summer. King Harold, who had spent considerable time and resources in building up his fleet and waiting for more ships to join him, had moved to repel Tostig's raids and now took his fleet down into the Channel where he spent much of the summer cruising, mainly between Sandwich and the Isle of Wight. As the Chronicle put it, he had 'gone out with a naval force against Duke William'.

Duke William, meanwhile, remained active, basing himself at Fécamp on the north coast of Normandy, not only supervising the construction of his fleet, but continuing to recruit more and more men. Supplies of all kinds were gathered from the surrounding countryside. This was easy to accomplish as the area around Caen was rich in cereal production and provided plenty of hay for the horses. The plateau of the Auge and the fields and valleys of the rivers Dives and Touques produced cattle. The Duke then set a blockade on all the ports along the Channel coast from Flanders to Brittany in order to prevent King Harold from sending agents to present his side of the case at Rome, and to arrest any Englishmen seeking to spy on his preparations. Robert of Montgomery was the principal lord in the area within which the army encamped and from which embarkation was intended. He took an active part in this preliminary phase of the expedition.

The Duke next held a Council with his barons at Bonneville-sur-Touques in June, shortly after Pentecost, and another at Caen when he attended the dedication of Matilda's Holy Trinity Abbey on 18 June. In a gesture of overweening confidence, the Duke confirmed Fécamp in possession of Steyning in England in the event that God gave him victory. Most of the major figures in Normandy were present. Extant charters show that the Duke was meeting regularly with his chief men throughout the months leading up to the invasion of England. He was in fact holding a series of rallies to keep up morale. Full cooperation from his men had to be maintained if the venture was to have any chance of success. His main assistants in these preparations were William fitzOsbern and Roger of Montgomery. He also met Eustace, Count of Boulogne and Aimeri, Vicomte of Thouars, from Poitou.

Duchess Matilda was, at some point, named officially as Regent in the Duke's absence, supported by Roger Beaumont and Roger of Montgomery. The Duke's eldest son, Robert, was associated with the Regency Council. He was less than twelve years old but had already, in 1063, been designated as William's heir. This was a crucial point in 1066 when his father was about to set out on a hazardous enterprise from which he might not return. Robert was again proclaimed heir in 1066 and the magnates were required to swear an oath of fealty to him. He confirmed his father's gifts to the Abbey of Marmoutier 'at the request of his father, who was then preparing to cross the sea and to make war against the English'. Other Norman barons made grants to various churches, especially to Holy Trinity, dated 'when the duke of the Normans set out across the sea with his fleet'.

The Norman fleet began to assemble around the mouth of the river Dives towards the end of July and was fully ready by 12 August. More ships were still being built throughout the summer, in the harbours around Dives. The fleet was delayed at Dives for a full month before moving to St Valery, where it remained allegedly awaiting a favourable wind 'for thrice five days' before setting out for England on 27 September. The move to St Valery must therefore have been made before the 12 September, the very time when King Harold was moving his fleet to London. (It is reported that there was no delay or need to wait for a wind in 1067 when William, now King, returned from Normandy, and that casts doubt on such a reason as necessary to explain a month's delay.) There was another more potent reason why the Duke delayed his departure, and that was the presence in the Channel of King Harold's fleet, as 'he went to Wight and lay there all the summer and the autumn'. Duke William needed more than just a favourable wind, he had need of an unopposed passage, good seamanship, and knowledge of Channel crossings. That knowledge was available to him from the sailors in the little ports controlled by Fécamp Abbey for the sake of cross-Channel trade. But fear of King Harold's fleet must have been uppermost in his mind.

During the time of preparation the Duke is described by William of Poitiers, in a fulsome and odiously flattering manner, as demonstrating both wisdom and foresight in the manner of his preparations. He is lauded for his generosity towards those recruited to his service, although he was promising them wealth which could only be theirs if the invasion succeeded. The Duke is reported to have absolutely forbidden his men from resorting to pillage in order to support themselves while waiting for the crossing to begin, and to have taken particular steps to prevent foreign mercenaries from taking any of their subsistence by force. He is credited with having made generous provision for his men out of his own pocket for a whole month while the invasion fleet was delayed at Dives by contrary winds. He must also have taken the opportunity to see to it that his men were trained in the manoeuvres subsequently used at Hastings.

William of Poitiers boasts that 'the crops waited undisturbed for the sickle without being trampled by the pride of the knights or ravaged by the greed of the plunderer. A wealthy and unarmed man, watching a swarm of soldiers without fear, might follow his horse, singing, wherever he would'. But anyone reading this might be forgiven for wondering whether 'he doth protest too much'. It is stretching credibility too far to suggest that all was as disciplined and peaceful as the aforesaid Archdeacon of Poitiers maintains. Reading between the lines, one might suspect that Duke William had been forced to make an example of those caught trampling crops and plundering the homes of the peasantry and that he was driven by great necessity to buy in provisions when he was delayed much longer than he had expected by the adverse winds.[5]

The fleet had been assembled at the mouth of the Dives and, given the alleged size, must have occupied all the neighbouring inlets and estuaries around Dives. It could be that the target date had been 15 August, the great Feast of the Assumption of the Virgin Mary. But no south wind materialized and the fleet was becalmed at Dives. Most of the ships were mere barges propelled by a single forward facing sail and wholly at the mercy of the prevailing wind. The English fleet was still waiting menacingly along the coast. The Bayeux Tapestry permits an estimate of the size of some of William's ships. The type shown in the Tapestry resembles the Scandinavian 'Drakkar' but it is thought that use was actually made also of the type known as 'Kaupship' which were of deeper draft and high sided. Some of the ships shown have holes marking the location of 'tholes', the pins securing oars when in use. The largest has sixteen holes, (suggesting a similar size to that of the Gokstad ship which was about seventy-five feet long). The majority of the rest show ten or twelve holes, suggesting a length of forty-five to fifty-five feet. The larger vessels could carry sixty men or some horses and thirty men, the smaller ones ten men and a few horses. A ship of Abbot Baldwin of Bury's time could carry sixty men, thirty beasts and sixteen horses plus baggage.[6] All this suggests an average complement of twenty men per ship. If there were, as Wace suggests, about 700 vessels, then the total force would be 14,000 men, the figure provided by the Chronicle of St Maixent. Not all of these would have been effective fighting men, allowance has to be made for servants, baggage handlers, ostlers, cooks etc. Duke William could therefore have had between ten and twelve thousand fighting men.

At last, and early in September, possibly by Tuesday 12 September, and shortly after King Harold had been forced to disband his forces, and dismiss his fleet, (partly by the need to release men to bring in the harvest and partly by the ending of the two monthly period of active campaigning before the onset of the equinoctial gales), Duke William took advantage of a brief change in the direction of the wind either to make a first attempt at a crossing or to move along the Norman coast. No doubt the disbandment was also reported to the Duke by his friends in England, and he wanted to seize the window of opportunity so presented to him. It is likely that the Duke and his men had exhausted all local supplies of food and fodder for men and horses and he could not afford to plunder supplies reserved for the journey to England.[7]

The fleet at this point probably amounted to between 800 and 1000 ships (depending on how small a vessel an observer condescended to include in the total), some of which would have been lighters intended only for ferrying men and supplies out to the ships. It is not certain, therefore, that the Duke intended a crossing on this occasion, he might only have intended to move to a new embarkation site. Whichever it was, he had miscalculated and his fleet was caught by one of the sudden changes in the weather for which the Channel is notorious. A tempest descended on the Channel and the fleet was caught up in it. The fleet set out and 'was blown from the mouth of the Dives and the neighbouring ports… driven by the breath of the west wind to moorings at St Valery'. The Carmen de Hastinge Proelio also states that the winds were unfavourable and the sea rough, it claims that winds buffeted the fleet, became very violent and many ships were wrecked.

The Norman account of the matter, while stressing that the Duke was 'neither daunted by the delay, nor by the contrary wind, nor by the loss of ships, nor even by the craven flight of many who broke faith with him', in effect admits, by listing these perils, that the venture came close to a disaster. The eventual total for the fleet which actually set sail for England is put, by one source, at a little less than 700 ships, so that the number lost or damaged, together with the ships of those who now deserted him, could have totalled in the region of a hundred vessels. The armada had also lost vital quantities of supplies the loss of which the Duke sought to conceal by increasing the daily rations as far as he could.

He also lost far more men, drowned or otherwise killed by the storm than the sources admit, so that he had to resort to having the bodies collected and buried secretly in order to lessen the effect knowledge of the losses would have had on his men. Strenuous efforts had to be made to restore morale, putting 'courage into the fearful and confidence into those who were downcast'. The effects of this setback can be illustrated from a Charter for Holy Trinity, Rouen, in which Osmund of Bodes is described as a man worn out and wounded in the Duke's campaign against England during a storm involving the Duke's fleet. The storm had driven the fleet eastwards until it was able to find refuge at St Valery. There it took shelter and sat out the storm as the weather remained adverse with much rain.

The removal to St Valery coincided with the decision of King Harold, following the disbanding of the fyrd, to move his fleet to London. The English fleet also was caught by the storm, 'and many perished before they came' to London. The interesting possibility is that the two fleets might well have, even if only briefly and in a confused manner, come into contact during the storm. The English sources are quite definite in saying that King Harold 'went out against' the Duke with a naval force and Domesday Book states categorically of the thegn Aethelric of Kelvedon, Essex, that 'the above named Aethelric died in a naval battle (proelium navale) against King William'. He had returned sick, and presumably injured, and left his lands to Westminster Abbey. Eadric, who is described as the 'Rector Navis Regis Edwardi' (Commander of King Edward's Ship), was exiled after the Conquest as one of those who had fought against the Duke. He fled to Denmark. Even the Gesta Herewardi or Deeds of Hereward, refers to a certain 'Bruman' who went to sea against the Normans, and encountered a Norman ship full of priests which he sank with all hands. The English were known to believe (as King Harold's spies reported to him) that the Norman soldiers were all priests because they cut their hair so short!

One Norman knight is known to have died at sea. Roger fitzTurold made a will bequeathing his lands to the Church of the Holy Family at Rouen. In it he announces his intention to join Duke William 'and was going to sail across the sea with him', but he died on the voyage. The deed of bequest was never completed. Finally, it is recorded in the Chronicle of Nieder-Alteich on the Rhine, *c.*1075, that the men of Aquitaine fought a naval battle against the English in 1066, that is in the summer of the year of the Comet. It does look as though some sort of minor naval skirmish occurred when the two fleets encountered each other during the storm. It was, however, the storm which did the most damage. The reasons for the storm are plain. In 1066 the Autumn Equinox was on 16 September under the Julian Calendar then in operation (six days behind the Gregorian date of 22 September.) It was the season of equinoctial gales. Harold had moved his ships a few days before the Equinox, knowing it was due, and William had moved from Dives to St Valery at about the same time.[8]

The sojourn at St Valery was a miserable one for the Norman army, drenched by torrential rain and exposed to violent winds. Men began to despair and to grumble in their tents. Some were reported to have said 'The man is mad who seeks to seize the land rightfully belonging to others! God is against us, for He denies us a wind; his father (Duke Robert) had the same idea and was prevented in the same way; there is a curse on this family It always conceives more than it can perform and finds God in opposition to it.' These sentiments began to spread and to weaken the resolve of the men. The Duke prayed often in the church of St Valery and anxiously watched the weathercock on the church steeple for a sign that the wind had changed. Throughout August, into September, there had been a series of Atlantic lows bringing storms and much rain until, on the 27 September a ridge of high pressure brought warmer weather and clear skies. Eventually, in an effort to sustain morale and in a last ditch appeal to God and His saints, the Duke had ordered that the body of St Valery be brought out of the Church in solemn procession so that all might invoke his intercession with God as they prayed for a favourable wind, and, no doubt for better weather. Lo and behold! The longed for southerly wind began to blow, and was doubtless seen as a response to the earnest prayers, as all men raised hands and voices in thanksgiving. A mad rush ensued.

Eagerly the knights and foot soldiers, scarcely waiting for word from the Duke, hastened to board their ships, eager to commence their long awaited voyage. The launch was so rapid that it was made while some men were still calling for their companions and others forgot to wait for their followers or their provisions, so eager were they not to be left behind. Duke William himself urged his men to make haste, determined not to miss the evening tide. That is estimated to have been at its peak at about 3.20 p.m., and the fleet had to catch the ebb tide or be delayed another day. The sailing was to be overnight so that the English coast would be reached soon after dawn the next day when the tide there was high. They also needed daylight for the landing in order to avoid making landfall on an unknown or hostile shore.

Duke William sent round a herald with orders that the ships should wait at anchor once they had reached the open sea until the whole fleet was assembled and in order. They were to wait until they saw a light displayed at the masthead of the Mora, the Duke's flagship, and until a trumpet call signalled that they should all weigh anchor. In a fanciful image, William of

Poitiers compares the Duke to Xerxes when he crossed the Hellespont to invade Greece. As Xerxes crossed on a single bridge of boats, he says, so Duke William crossed the Channel with a single fleet.[9] The Carmen, with poetic exaggeration, describes how William's fleet covered the sea with the red glow of torches.

So, shortly after high tide the fleet set sail, each ship carrying a light at the masthead so that others could locate it. The Duke's ship led the way out into the Channel, guided by his pilot, Stephen, who was skilled in the study of the winds and the stars. (A 'Stephen the Steersman' is recorded in Domesday Book as owning two houses in Southampton which was probably one of the King's favourite ports of embarkation, very convenient for Winchester and the New Forest.) The fleet had some fifty-five nautical miles to cross, mostly in dusk or darkness, except perhaps for the light of a crescent moon. When the moon finally set there would only be starlight and the lanterns on the ships.[10]

Navigation was by dead reckoning and the open sea was divided into eight equal portions directed towards the horizon. There were the four cardinal points, north, south, east and west, and mid points between them were named in relation to the mainland. The positions of the sun and major stars were noted and the steersman would be guided at night by the Pole Star, or on long summer evenings by the Sun.

The Duke's pilot took the Mora as far across the Channel as he dared, by dead reckoning, before eventually dropping anchor. The heavily laden vessels followed the Mora, some wallowing in the Channel currents. The bad weather had now abated. It had been having a serious effect on the lee shores from Cap de la Hève to Cap d'Antifer. The transports used by the fleet were of shallow draft (easy to beach) and broad in the beam, not unlike barges or gondolas. They were capable, at best, of only four or five knots. Similar vessels have been found in Roskilde Fjord in Denmark. The Mora was much the largest, perhaps like other vessels found in Scandinavia and, if so, about fifty-four feet in length and some eight feet wide. The Bayeux Tapestry[11] shows vessels with differing numbers of men and horses, suggesting vessels of differing sizes.

The fleet sailed on into the September twilight and into the Channel as darkness fell and made further progress too hazardous. They dropped anchor after perhaps eight or nine hours at sea, so that it was now after midnight. Dawn would be at about 5.00 a.m. and the Duke, when he awoke, finding the Mora isolated, ate breakfast and waited for his ships to arrive. He then weighed anchor and the fleet sailed on until it could sweep into Pevensey Bay. It was not long after dawn on Thursday 28 September, that it arrived.[12]

The Thunderbolt From the North:
Saturday 12 August to Friday 13 October 1066

All through the summer months King Harold had expected the coming of the Normans rather than of the Norwegians. He cannot have known of the link up between Earl Tostig and King Harald Sigurdson of Norway until early September. The Heimskringla (of Snorri Sturluson) relates that Earl Tostig had originally visited the Count of Flanders and the King of Denmark, voyaging by way of Friesland, and that he came at last to Viken, in Norway, before returning to Flanders in the Spring.

Some have speculated that Duke William did have some idea of Earl Tostig's plans and movements and so timed his own attack accordingly, but the vagaries of the wind upon which both invaders depended would almost certainly rule that out. Duke William is unlikely to have known much of Earl Tostig's movements once he had been driven out of the Channel. King Harold, on the other hand, probably thought Tostig was still tucked up safely at the Court of King Malcolm.

Duke William had been confined to Dives during August, held there by contrary winds, and possibly fear of the English fleet, until early September. The wind which confined him there blew from the north-east and was therefore favourable to King Harald Sigurdson. The Sagas maintain that King Harald, having persuaded his men to support a bid for the English throne (which was made a little easier by the death of Ulf Ospaksson, a leading adviser of the King, who had opposed an invasion of England), gathered the nucleus of his fleet in the Solund Isles in August, probably also around the 12th to 15th, and then moved in clearly defined stages across the North Sea. The Sagas claim that Earl Tostig had already been in contact with the Norwegian King earlier in the year and say that Harald had taken six months to prepare his campaign.

King Harald then moved to the Sogn Fjord near Bergen, taking with him the treasure he had amassed in Byzantium when he was a leading member of the Varangian Guard. He made a pious visit to the shrine of his half-brother, St Olaf, at Nidaros. The autumn was providing a northerly wind and warm weather. On the journey southwards King Harald landed first in the Shetland Isles, at the Sumburgh Roost and Fair Isle, recruiting more ships and men, and then arrived in the Orkneys, possibly putting in at Scapa Flow. From there the journey took the Norwegians to the Pentland Firth and Duncansby Head and on to the Firth of Forth.

He left behind his wife, the Russian Princess Elisef (Elizabeth) and his daughters but was joined by the two brother Earls of Orkney, Paul and Erlend, and their men. He had acquired another ally in Orkney, Godred Haraldsson, known as 'Crovan' (of the White Hand), with men from the Western Isles and the Isle of Man.

Modern replica longships can travel at twenty knots in calm waters but that falls to five knots in the open sea. The 300 miles from Norway to Orkney could have been achieved under sail in a few days, but oars would have been needed to avoid being drawn onto the rocks after the Norwegians reached the Scottish coast. The square-rigged vessels of the eleventh century could not sail close to the wind, needing a following wind to make progress. It is thought that a day's sailing could be 90 to 155 miles depending on the conditions. It would therefore have taken some ten days to reach the Firth of Forth.

Sources disagree about where the King and the Earl met to join forces. Some insist on Scotland but a meeting on the river Tyne is reckoned to have been more probable. King Harald must have been somewhat dismayed to find that Earl Tostig only had twelve ships. From Tyneside the fleet sailed on and made a landing at 'Klifland' (that is, Cleveland); the Norwegians now only making about three to five knots in the rough seas off the Northumbrian coast. However, daylight lasted for about sixteen hours that far north at that time of year, allowing steady progress. Other landings were made along the coast, for the customary ravaging by an invading Scandinavian army. One was probably at Teesmouth and, according to the Sagas, certainly at Skardaburg (Scarborough) and then in Holderness.[1]

There is no clear indication of the timing of the landings on the Tyne and elsewhere, but some time early in September seems about right. The Chronicle claims definitely that King Harald and Earl Tostig met on the Tyne 'as previously arranged', another indication that they had met earlier in the year.

At Scarborough, named for its founder, Thorgils Skarthi (the Hare-lipped), the invaders positioned themselves on the high ground overlooking the town, built a bonfire and proceeded to burn down the town by throwing burning logs down onto the houses; 'in this manner, King Harald subdued the countryside wherever he went'.

From Holderness, where there had been some resistance which was easily overcome, the fleet rounded Ravenspur (Spurn Head) into the Ouse where it joins the Humber, and made its way up the river to Riccall. One good reason for deciding on Riccall was that it bottled up the fleet of the Earls Edwin and Morcar on the River Wharfe, to which they had retreated and from which they had hoped to launch an attack. Once in the Ouse, the Norwegian fleet had used only oars. King Harald had, possibly on the advice of Earl Tostig, timed his arrival for a season when the English rivers would be swollen by September rains. King Harald could have intended to take advantage of the rising tide on the Ouse which creates a 'bore', so that his fleet could travel with the tide while it flowed upstream, without using oars, and then when the tide slackened, the oarsmen could take over. It would have taken some ten hours to reach Riccall.[2]

The river turns right at Riccall, creating a sort of ox-bow lake where the ships could easily have been beached. To settle any nearer to York meant moving onto flat ground and risking an opposed landing.

From this account of King Harald's movements and the known date of his first battle in England, at Fulford near York, Wednesday 20 September, it can be estimated that landfall on the coast of Northumbria had been around Thursday 14 September. Messengers could therefore have reached York, alerting the citizens there and the Earls Edwin and Morcar of the coming of the invaders, by the evening of 15 September. That allowed the Earls to move their fleet into the Wharfe, blocking an approach by water to the City of York. They then were able to mobilize their levies and household troops from Mercia and Yorkshire.

How large a force they had is unknown but, as the ensuing battle in which they confronted the army led by King Harald and his ally Earl Tostig lasted for most of the day, it must have been considerable. The King had a fleet reckoned at 300 ships and such a fleet could have brought a force of some 12,000 fighting men. A substantial number were left to protect the ships at Riccall leaving King Harald with some 10,000 men. The Earls probably had somewhat fewer, perhaps eight or nine thousand. But such figures are only estimates.

King Harald determined to seize the city and advanced on York from the south. The Earls had decided not to risk a siege and the subsequent destruction of York, so they moved out of the city to confront the Norwegians at a place called Fulford, 'the foul ford' (now a suburb of York). There, according to Florence of Worcester, Earl Morcar's men (in particular) 'fought so bravely after the onset of battle that many of the enemy were laid low. But after a long contest the English were unable to withstand the attacks of the Norwegians and fled with great loss, and more were drowned in the river than slain in the field'.

The Scandinavian Saga writers were convinced that Earl Waltheof, son of the mighty Earl Siward Digera of Northumbria, was present at the battle. As the great Earl had died in 1055, his son Earl Waltheof must surely have been old enough to fight by 1066. His elder half-brother, Osbeorn had died in battle against the Scots in 1054, so Waltheof could easily have been about eighteen years old in 1066, having recently reached the age at which noble youths could be granted an earldom (he had his earldom in the East Midlands). The Sagas boast that 'Waltheof's warriors by weapons slain were lying fallen thickly in the fen' after the battle. The young Earl was to play a prominent part in the later risings against the Norman King and to distinguish himself during the capture of York from the Normans in 1069.

So, early on the morning of Wednesday 20 September, the Vigil of St Matthew's Day, the Earls moved their army down along the causeways (or causeys) to the Foul Ford where a beck or stream (now called Germany Beck) entered the Ouse from the east. They intended to forbid entry to York to the Norwegian King and prevent him from ravaging the countryside. King Harald marched his men up from his ships at Riccall, some ten miles south, and found his line of march blocked at the ford. To avoid giving battle meant a long detour round to the east which would open the Norwegian army to the favourite tactic of warfare by ambush, which suited the Northumbrian mode of fighting. King Harald therefore accepted the offer of battle, though on this occasion the sources are silent about any preliminary exchange of words before battle commenced.

As the King approached the ford, leading the stronger left wing and centre of his force and leaving Earl Tostig to lead the weaker and less experienced troops who formed the right wing, he found that the beck had cut a deep and wide ditch across his front, leading down to the Ouse. His side of the ditch was lower than the opposing side occupied by Earls Edwin and Morcar. To attack meant going down into the ditch, crossing the ford and fighting back up the opposite side against ferocious opposition. Yet Earl Tostig chose to do exactly that.

Earl Edwin and his Mercians confronted King Harald, positioning themselves on the river bank built up by the flooding of the Ouse, their right flank protected by the river. Earl Morcar, commanding the left wing, had his flank protected by a wide area of marsh, impossible for fighting. Both sides opened the battle with an exchange of volleys of arrows and then as the archers exhausted their ammunition, the opposing shield walls, phalanxes of heavy infantry, launched a barrage of javelins, the throwing spears known to the English as ategars.

The front lines were about 400 yards long, permitting a deployment of some 2000 men in each shield wall, and were now about thirty feet apart. King Harald signalled by trumpet for his right wing to advance against the English left in what could have been a deliberate gambit to tempt Earl Morcar forward. As Tostig's men moved forward, down into the ditch, Morcar made what he probably thought was a decisive move. His men in their shield wall formed into wedges protected on three sides, and overhead, by shields, and, from their superior tactical position, charged down upon the enemy, punching holes in the opposing shield wall and sending Earl Tostig's men into retreat. Each time Morcar pushed forward, the same thing happened as Tostig gave way. This meant that the English left wing became more and more extended as Tostig's men backed away.

All this fighting, from the first showers of arrows onwards must have taken several hours. Heavily armed men, hacking and jabbing away at their foe, tire rapidly and cannot advance very quickly against determined opposition. Such fighting is exhausting and necessitates periods of rest while both sides labour for breath while maintaining their position.

Meanwhile, King Harald had deployed to the left, pushing up against Earl Edwin's position on the riverbank and both armies fought obstinately and bloodily, giving little ground. Seeing how fully extended Earl Morcar now was and realising that the Earl's right flank was now exposed, King Harald launched his counter stroke. Ordering his banner, Landwaster, to the fore and sounding a trumpet call for a rapid advance, he swung the whole weight of his centre against Earl Morcar's flank, leaving enough men to hold back Edwin as he did so. He was thus able to punch a gaping hole in the English line, swing round to the right, and roll up Morcar's flank. The Earl had to give ground to avoid being encircled and swing round to face the new threat. He then found his force pushed sideways into the marsh, on his left.

King Harald then dispatched his left wing to push Earl Edwin back along the river bank, dividing the English army in two, and the Earl had to retreat to fend off an attack on his left flank. He was left desperately fighting a losing battle as he was pushed back along the bank, or into the river, able only to confront the enemy on a very narrow front. As Harald himself claimed in a stanza of poetry of his own making, he had 'ordered a war-blast to be blown and urged his men on'. Once the King had crossed the ford, Earl Edwin played little further part in the battle other than to make a fighting retreat. King Harald now moved to destroy Morcar's men utterly and there were appalling casualties on both sides as Morcar found himself enveloped both front and rear. Those of his men who were not cut down were crushed and trodden underfoot. The sagas say that the beck was running with blood and that the Norwegians were able to walk 'dry shod over the marsh the bodies of the slain'. The rising tide then engulfed the bodies of the dead, giving an impression that they were drowned rather than slain.[3]

Eventually the English fled, some up river to York and others back along the beck towards Heslington. The Norwegians believed that Morcar himself was slain and possibly it had looked that way as his Standard fell and his Housecarls died to a man around it. A rather free translation of the saga reads:

> The gallant Harald drove along,
> Flying and fighting the whole throng.
> At last confused, they could not fight,
> And the whole body took to flight.
> Up from the river's silent stream
> At once arose dread splash and scream.
> But those who stood like men this day
> Round Morukari's body lay.

About Earl Waltheof, the skald wrote:

> Earl Waltheof's men lay in the fen
> By sword down hewed, so thickly strewed
> That Northmen say they paved the way
> Across the Fen for the brave Northmen.[4]

After the battle, all the people in the area despaired of raising any further opposition. York submitted and opened its gates and on Sunday 24 September, King Harald held a 'Thing' (in English a gemot or moot) at which he accepted the homage of the citizens. It was arranged that hostages would be selected from among those of wealth and position all over the district. Earl Tostig would have known from whom to seek hostages as he had previously been Earl in Northumbria. King Harald then returned in the late afternoon to his ships at Riccall, having arranged for another meeting to take place the next day at Stamford Bridge when the hostages would be handed over and he would decide who would rule York in his name. He would then distribute estates to be held under his rule and lay down a code of laws.

There is little direct evidence of all this fighting but investigation of burials in York, in Fishergate, reveals a group of some twenty-nine skeletons of men, many of whom had been killed in a single incident, with injuries consistent with having been slashed and cut with swords, or stabbed with sharp pointed weapons such as arrows or spears. Many have skull injuries and some have been decapitated. They are of mid-eleventh century date, consistent with the Battle of Fulford.

While all this was happening, King Harold Godwinson, Harold II of England, who had been in London following the dispersal of his army and the return of his fleet to the Thames, heard of the coming of King Harald and his Norwegians. He learned of this certainly shortly after the attack on Scarborough. He immediately began sending out writs of summons, calling on men within two days riding of London, to join him on campaign in the North. Other messengers were sent out to ensure a supply of fresh horses along the route as the King rode north. He had some 200 miles to travel at possibly forty miles a day, so it could be done in about five days. As he arrived at Tadcaster on Sunday 24 September, he probably left London at the latest by Tuesday 19 September. That allows for messengers to report the decision of Edwin and Morcar to offer battle but not the result of that battle.

So King Harold rode north, collecting men as he went, forming an army of mounted foot soldiers. It was not the custom for the English to fight on horseback in Continental style. They rode to battle and then dismounted to form the shield wall. Horseflesh was too valuable to waste in battle unnecessarily.

The Roman de Rou of Robert Wace, a twelfth century source, lists the shires he believed contributed men to Harold's army. If the report is correct, then Harold called in men from Kent, Surrey and Sussex, who could have reached London quite quickly, and then from East Anglia and from the shires along the Great North Road as he travelled through them. So he arrived late on Sunday at Tadcaster and rode on immediately to York. Had he been able to arrive earlier, he might have caught King Harald just as he set out for Riccall. His arrival was a great relief to the citizens of York and he and his men rested overnight around York, setting guards to prevent news of the English King's arrival reaching the ears of Harald Sigurdson.

Early next day, Monday 25 September, the rival kings set out towards Stamford Bridge, King Harold having been told of the arrangements for a meeting there by the men of York. The English rode due east and the Norwegians marched north east from Riccall, with a force much reduced by the losses at Fulford, possibly up to a quarter of the army. The weather in the North of England was warm, an early 'St Martin's Summer', and it was a hot day. King Harald made the disastrous decision to allow his men to take only helmets, shields and weapons but no heavy mail coats.

At Stamford Bridge several routes converged, probably explaining King Harald's choice, including a Roman road and the Minster Way from York to Beverley. Roads converge there from Bridlington, Malton and Thornton-le-Street. He intended to send out parties of men to collect taxes and obtain supplies of fresh food. The Sagas suggest that his men spent part of the morning at Stamford Bridge rounding up sheep and cattle. He had left a considerable force of men at Riccall, again to guard the ships, under the command of his prospective son-in-law, Eystein Orri. The Saga claims that they drew lots for the duty so that for every two men who were to go to Stamford Bridge a third was to remain at Riccall.

Because his men were out, as it were, cattle rustling and sheep stealing, a sizeable portion of the Norwegian army was on the north bank of the River Derwent when King Harold and the English army was first noticed. It is also worth noting that Benoît de St Maur claimed that William fitzOsbern had said that Harold defeated 'vint milliers' Norwegians (20,000). That is a totally unlikely number but 'vint' might be a scribal error for 'cinq', or 5,000 men, with two to three thousand down by the ships.

Saga accounts of the battle suggest that there was a pause before battle commenced and that King Harold offered the Norwegians stiff terms for avoiding a battle. But English sources maintain that King Harold took the Norwegians by surprise and swept down upon them before they were ready for battle.

'Then', according to the Chronicle, 'came Harold, King of the English against them unawares beyond the bridge; and they met till far on in the day and they fought very sternly'. Furthermore, in a late tradition, added to one version of the Chronicle, the English were held at bay, unable to cross over the bridge and attack the rest of the Norwegians, because a giant Norwegian held the bridge against them single-handed, until an Englishman went under the bridge in a small boat and stabbed him from below with a spear.

The contradiction is best explained if it is assumed that a large section of the Norwegian army was caught in the open on the north bank and fiercely attacked by the English and that King Harald brought more men to their aid across the bridge but was driven back across it and there formed a shield wall in the open fields. The English, having killed the man who held the bridge possibly then offered to accept the surrender of the rest of the Norwegians, and especially Earl Tostig. King Harold is said to have ridden up close to the Norwegian lines, as one of a small party of men, and then offered Earl Tostig peace terms.

The skalds who composed the sagas embroidered these exchanges to illustrate the character of the leaders. King Harold is magnanimous, as befits the eventual winner, Earl Tostig is loyal to his ally, and King Harald is grudgingly respectful towards his rival.

The Sagas relate that the first the Norwegians knew of King Harold's approach was when the dust raised by a large body of men was seen approaching from the direction of York. It was taken to be the approach of the escort for the hostages. Then it was reported that this was a large body of armed men with spears and shields which glittered like ice in the sun, and King Harald realised that an enemy was approaching.[5]

King Harold and his English army then swept down without further warning on the Norwegians on the North bank. Having arrived on horseback and catching a large body of men in the open, with weapons but without armour, the English simply rode them down, slashing and spearing them as they tried to defend themselves. That would explain reports by the Sagas that the English used cavalry tactics. The men so caught would have caught up their shields and formed a shield wall in a mass facing outwards and the English are said to have ridden around them in a circle. King Harald came over the bridge with a shield wall formation formed into a wedge or phalanx and was able to get most of his men back across the bridge as the English recoiled from his ferocious attack. King Harald is reported to have said that 'The Englishmen shall have a hard fray of it before we give ourselves up for lost'. He sent three men to run all the way to Riccall to summon reinforcements and ordered his banner, the famous Landwaster to be set up, borne by a man called Frirek, and charged into the battle.

The fighting at this stage was loose and light and the Norwegians managed to hold their line of battle despite heavy losses. They now formed a semi-circular shield wall and fought their way back to the bridge. There would have been a pause while both sides regrouped and rested and the English tried, at first in vain, to cross the bridge. At this point, in all likelihood, the English King made his offer, riding forward on a black horse with a silver blaze on its forehead. King Harald also rode up to the river bank, accompanied by Earl Tostig, but, they say, due to the rough ground, his horse stumbled and the weary King fell off. Undismayed, he jumped to his feet, saying 'A fall forebodes a good journey'. But King Harold, seeing this, said, 'I think his luck has left him'. He then offered the enemy his terms.

Earl Tostig could have a full pardon and be restored to his earldom, even up to one third of the kingdom would be his. But the Earl scornfully rejected this, referring only to the enmity he had received from Harold in 1065. Instead, he asked what would be offered to King Harald Sigurdson. The answer came that King Harald would 'give him seven feet of English earth, or as much more as he may be taller than other men'. Earl Tostig simply told the English to prepare for battle as he, Tostig, would never desert King Harald.

The English returned to their lines and King Harald asked the name of the English spokesman. Earl Tostig told him, 'That was my brother, King Harold'. The Norwegian commented sourly, 'For too long was that concealed from me or this Harold should never have been able to tell of our men's slaughter'. Then he added, grudgingly, 'That was a little man but he sat well in his stirrups'. As King Harald was much taller than other men, all men looked small to him. Reputedly he was five ells in height which would mean seven feet six inches, but that could be an exaggeration. Before resuming the battle he is said to have composed two poems. The first says:

Without hauberks do we go to array to receive blows from the blue blades.
Helmets shine! I have not my hauberk. Our gear is down by the ships!

Dissatisfied, he then made another invoking the Norse goddess:

Hilde of combat, who bade me hold my head high,
in bloody battle where blades and skulls are clashing!

The skald, Thiodulf, answered him:

Should our king in battle fall, a fate God may give,
His son shall vengeance take.
Never shone the sun on two nobler eaglets,
And them we'll ne'er forsake![6]

But the English forced their way across the bridge and combat was resumed. King Harald again formed the outward facing circular shield wall and the English found it no easy matter to attack it, some still perhaps attempting attacks on horseback. This was in no sense a cavalry action but an attempt by mounted men to strike with sword or spear downwards against men on foot in the open. King Harald again brought forward Landwaster and led a charge in such a rage that he ran out in front of his men, hewing men down with his huge sword held in both hands so that the English were unable to withstand him and almost took flight. But 'Norway's King had nothing to shield his breast in the battle and yet his war-hardened heart never wavered whilst Norway's warriors were watching the blood sword of their leader slicing down their foemen'. Then an arrow took Harald in the throat and he 'received his death wound'.

All those with the king when he fell died with him, leaving Earl Tostig to lead the resistance and retrieve the banner Landwaster. In an exhausted pause, King Harold again offered quarter to his brother and was refused. Then, as the Norwegians raised a last war shout, help arrived as Eystein Orri and the remaining Norwegians from the ships arrived for a final charge, called 'Orri's Storm'. They fell on the English in full armour, having run in it all the way from Ricall, and many Englishmen died before the impetus of the attack ran out. Orri's men were unable to fight on, exhausted by their race. So towards evening the remaining Norwegians fell, Earl Tostig was slain in the final moments, and the slaughter ended as darkness fell.

Much of this account comes from the Heimskringla of Snorri Sturluson, who rested his work on 'songs which were sung about the Kings who have ruled in Norway... in the presence of the chiefs themselves and their sons... no one would dare to relate to a chief what he and all those who heard it knew to be false and imaginary, not a true account of his deeds because that would be mockery not praise'.

Nonetheless, there was some confusion in the accounts rendered by the sagas, caused by the fact that two Kings named Harold died in battle within three weeks of each other. But although some have said that the account of Stamford Bridge reads, in places, like an account of Hastings transferred north, with the English playing the part of the Normans and attacking the Norwegians playing the part of Englishmen, there are still distinct differences. The Norwegians fight in the open, on flat ground, unarmoured, whereas at Hastings the English shield wall was drawn up on the crest of a ridge. Although the English at Stamford Bridge attacked, apparently, on horseback, there was no question of a massed cavalry attack by armoured knights.

The confusion lies in the minds of historians who forget that King Harold's men had hunted down Welshmen in 1063, like huntsmen chasing foxes, and might well, coming upon an enemy caught without hauberks and in the open, have ridden straight in against them. Even the story of King Harold having been killed by an arrow (in his case allegedly in the eye) looks like an echo of the death of Harald Sigurdson, called Hardrada, hit in the throat by an arrow.

After the battle proper, the mopping up began. Some Norwegians were pursued back to their ships and there could have been a last stand there which resulted in some of the ships being burned. But once the Norwegians surrendered, King Harold was merciful. The survivors, the two Orkney Earls and King Harald's son Olaf were allowed to return home to Orkney and Norway in twenty-four ships, out of the 300 in which they had come. That indicates just how complete and devastating the defeat had been.[7] Skeletons were found at Riccall in the 1950s, which show slashed arm bones and evidence of spearthrusts. Earl Tostig was recognizable only by the wart that lay between his shoulder blades. He was buried at York. King Harald's body was taken to Norway and buried at Nidaros alongside the saint, King Olaf his half-brother. Prince Olaf sailed with his men from 'Hrafnseyt' to the

Orkneys. That could mean from Hull, the port 'on the seyt', where Sayer's Creek is a tributary of the Humber. Others sailed from Ravenspur. Godred Crovan also survived 'a very great slaughter of the Norwegians' in England, and returned to the Isle of Man. Orderic Vitalis was to report that even in his own day, early in the twelfth century, 'travellers cannot fail to recognize the field, for a great mountain of dead men's bones still lies there and bears witness to the terrible slaughter on both sides'.

Having rested at York on Tuesday 26 September, King Harold contemplated his return to London, as yet unaware of the imminent arrival of Duke William and his Normans, but knowing he had left his southern flank unprotected. The King left behind the plunder gained from the Norwegian host, including the remains of King Harald's treasure, in the safe keeping of Archbishop Ealdred at York, despite the complaints of some of his men who had no doubt hoped for a share of it. The Normans were to allege that some men deserted the King because of this, but it is more likely that he lost men because of the wounds they had suffered and because their period of service had run out. The Lincolnshire sheriff, Maerlesswein, was appointed to govern Northumbria, because Earl Morcar, possibly recovering from wounds and the fact of defeat, was probably with his brother, Earl Edwin, at Chester in Mercia.

On Wednesday 27 September and the same day that William set sail from St Valery, Harold lost no time in returning south, concerned at what might have developed during his absence. At some point during his return he met messengers coming up from the south to alert him to the Norman landing. By then he could have been as far south as Nottingham and he began sending out fresh orders for more troops to be levied. He could also have met contingents summoned earlier on his way north which had not had time to join him, as Wace reports that he was joined by men from as far away as Salisbury and Bath.

Down in Winchester, Queen Edith's writer, author of the Life of King Edward, penned these words:

> Who will write that Humber vast and swollen with raging seas, where
> namesake kings had fought, has dyed the ocean wave for miles around with
> Viking gore?[8]

King Harold can hardly have reached London much before Sunday 1 October, gathering men from his former earldom of Wessex and from the earldoms of his brothers Gyrth and Leofwine. Some of the constituent parts of this new army can be identified. The men of Kent, who claimed an ancient right to form the vanguard of the English army certainly raised new levies and were present at Hastings, eager to confront an enemy daring to invade their shire. The Londoners, led by Aesgar the Staller, claimed the right to carry the King's Standard, which for Harold was the Dragon or Wyvern of Wessex (while his personal Standard was that of the Fighting Man, an armed figure worked in gold and jewels). The names of thegns slain at Hastings are recorded in Domesday Book, though not frequently. They indicate the widespread nature of the shires from which Harold had been able to call up men. Domesday names men from the South East and East Anglia, from Huntingdonshire, Hampshire and Berkshire, and from towns like Peterborough, Winchester and Bury St Edmunds.

The King remained in London for some five days; it was now ten or eleven days after Stamford Bridge, and a week after the landing at Pevensey. Messages were received from the Norman Duke, demanding that King Harold surrender his crown and insisting on the Duke's 'rights'. Norman sources do their best to paint a picture of dissension in the English ranks, claiming that many men deserted Harold and that he quarrelled with his brother Gyrth. The Earl is said to have suggested that he lead the attack on Duke William on the grounds that he owed nothing to him and, as he had taken no oath of any kind, would not be foresworn if he fought him. He also, it was claimed, argued that it was a prudent course to take. Harold was fatigued, having fought a strenuous battle and undertaken two taxing rides and so needed time to recover. Furthermore, should Gyrth be defeated, Harold could still call up yet another army and attack a much weakened Duke.

Harold is described as angrily rejecting all this, striking his brother and kicking his mother who clung to him in an effort to hold him back. This is mere slander, Norman disinformation. Gyrth could well have made some of these suggestions, especially as it would have been a prudent course of action. But Harold knew full well that his presence on the battlefield was crucial, a fit king just had to defend his title to his crown. Furthermore, Duke William was ravaging the lands of the Earldom of Wessex, sowing terror across the land as he had done in Maine, and Harold owed a duty to his people to defend them and he had seen for himself the aggressive methods used by the Duke. England had no fortifications like the castles of Normandy, and was not organized for ceaseless warfare, Norman style. The manors of southern England had only wooden halls defended by little more than an earthen wall and a ditch surmounted by a palisade, of little use against Norman methods of warfare.

King Harold paid a visit to his Church of Waltham Holy Cross to pray for its protection. Later accounts, written in the knowledge of his defeat, claim that the Figure on the Cross bowed its Head, and that this was taken as an evil omen. The story was almost certainly intended to explain why the Figure on the Cross at Waltham showed Christ with His Head bowed, as at the moment of His death. Earlier figures representing the Crucifixion show Christ with head erect, and crowned, and Waltham's Figure was therefore unusual.[9]

Then Harold ordered the mobilization of his forces, ordered that they meet him in Sussex and left London with his Household Troop of Housecarls and King's Thegns, and those of his brother Earls. He was to meet all those who rallied to him at the 'hoary apple tree', and so moved to the crest of Caldbec Hill on the evening of Friday, the Thirteenth of October.[10]

The War Between Duke William & Harold, King of the English:
Friday 13 October to Sunday 15 October 1066

After the arrival of the Normans at Pevensey and during the days afterwards as they moved from Pevensey to occupy Hastings, local English thegns kept watch on the enemy. These were not fighting men (who had all gone north with the King) but those too old or infirm to fight. They watched the knights and men-at-arms disembark and, no doubt, kept well out of the reach of marauding troops of Normans who ravaged the area, plundering it for fresh supplies. The Duke was applying the accepted principles of medieval warfare, based on the book 'De Re Militari' by the Roman general Vegetius; 'the main or principal point in war is to secure plenty of provisions for oneself, and to destroy the enemy by famine is more terrible than the sword'.

At least one man (but in fact probably several) set off at once for York or London to warn the King that the Duke of the Normans was in Sussex with a huge army. Even a local ceorl is reported to have carried news to London of the ravaging. It is likely that Harold was already on his way back to London when he received the news. He had left Maerleswein, Sheriff of Lincolnshire, to govern the north (the Earls Edwin and Morcar were still too shocked and exhausted by their defeat at Fulford to be of much use) and Archbishop Ealdred had been given charge of the plunder acquired from the defeated Norwegian army.

As the King hurried south in another whirlwind ride, accompanied by his mounted household troops and housecarls, he sent messengers out in all directions summoning a second levy of men to rendezvous with him in London. They came to him from as far afield as Wessex, and from East Anglia and Eastern Mercia. Most would have come from the earldoms of Harold himself and of his brothers Gyrth and Leofwine. The handful of references in Domesday Book to men who fell at Hastings lists men from Hampshire, Winchester and Berkshire as well as from all over East Anglia. The Normans reported the English army as a vast host gathered together from all the provinces of England.

Having arrived in London ten days after Stamford Bridge was fought (and about a week after William's landing at Pevensey), the King spent several days awaiting the arrival of fresh warriors. It was now 5 October, and Harold set out to confront the Norman Duke on 12 October. It is likely that it was in this brief period, while Harold was gathering his forces in London, that the final challenge was made by the Duke. Although William of Poitiers, for his own dramatic purposes, has Duke William send an ambassador, Hugh Margot, a monk of Fécamp, to demand that Harold surrender the throne, it is likely that it was King Harold who sent a monk as his herald, to command William to leave the country, since William of Poitiers has the Duke ask for safe conduct for his envoy so that he can respond to Harold's demands.

Harold's emissary said, as he had been bidden to do, 'Thus King Harold commands you; The Kingdom is mine by right, granted by my Lord, the King, by a deathbed grant. Withdraw from this land with your forces, otherwise I shall break friendship and all agreements made with you in Normandy and place all responsibility for that on you!'[1]

The Norman account gives a full statement of the Norman case, probably derived in fact from the exchanges between William and Harold earlier in the year and from the legal brief presented to the Pope by the Norman legation. It is unlikely that such a long drawn out argument was made at this point. William of Malmesbury reports that the Duke offered three options; that Harold should abdicate in his favour or agree to rule as his vassal or to settle the question by single combat. William insisted, as he always did, that he was King Edward's legitimate heir and therefore 'Let King Harold yield up the kingdom that is mine by right. I am ready to risk my life in combat to decide whether the kingdom should be his or mine!' King Harold grew pale, his face distorted with rage, he threw back his head and made his final response to Hugh Margot saying that he was to tell the Duke that he would let God decide between the two of them.

'Return, thou fool! Tomorrow, with the Lord as arbiter of the Kingdom, the rightful claimant shall appear! The Holy Hand of the Lord will deal justly!'

To his surrounding magnates the King then said:

'We march at once, we march to battle!'

and Hugh Margot was dismissed.

A Norman anecdote is recorded which claims that King Harold quarrelled with his brother Earl Gyrth because he argued that he, unlike the king, was free of any oath or obligation to Duke William and could safely lead the English army without incurring any accusation of perjury. Equally unlikely, simply because there could not have been any witnesses, is the suggestion that King Harold said to Earl Gyrth that Saturday, 14 October, was the day of his birth and his lucky day, but that the Earl replied that it might prove to be the day of his death. The tales are meant to demonstrate King Harold's arrogance and hubris in daring to fight Duke William.

Harold, King of the English, who did not hesitate to advance with all speed into Sussex, therefore brought the English army to Caldbec Hill near Hastings on the nineteenth day after the defeat and fall of Harald Sigurdson in the most significant feat of English military strength since Brunanburh in 937. His army emerged from the wooded slopes of the Andredesweald at the place arranged in advance, known locally as the 'Hoar Apple Tree', possibly a boundary marker between Hundreds or the meeting place of the Hundred Court. Local tradition at Battle claims that the windmill on Caldbec Hill marks the site of that hoary apple tree.

All Norman accounts stress the huge size of the English army, despite their assertions that Harold fought after having been deserted by many of his men and coming to battle only with those prepared to stand by him, and Norman fears of a sudden attack by night. It was not unusual for those whose nerve failed to leave the ranks of an army before battle commenced, but the majority of the English warriors stood by King Harold. However, on the contrary, the English Chroniclers, stress the King's lack of numbers and the state of unreadiness of the English army. Such a contrast in reporting is only to be expected.

Harold was brought to battle, they say, 'aere his folc gefylcad waes', before his army was in battle array, or 'before all his army was come up' and even that he 'well knew that some of the bravest Englishmen had fallen in his two (former) battles and that one half of his army had not yet arrived' and so 'joined battle before a third of his army was in order for fighting'.

The English sources were seeking to explain away the defeat while the Normans were trying to magnify the degree of their success. It is usual to interpret the reference to battle commencing before one third of his army was in fighting order as evidence that the rest were not ready, but it could really mean that two thirds were in array and that one third was still moving into position. How could an army in such disarray as has been suggested have repelled the Norman attack so vehemently? Because the chosen position was in fact so relatively constricted, with men still moving along the road from Caldbec Hill to join the array, observers might well have thought that the English were not yet in battle array when what they were seeing was the arrival of further reinforcements. King Harold cannot have both fought with too small a force which was not in battle order and with one so large that he had to send men away because there was no room for them.

The real evidence for the size of the English army lies in the warning delivered to Duke William by Robert fitzWymarc, who told him that King Harold was on his way with 'innumerable soldiers all well equipped for war', in comparison with which the Duke's men were merely 'a pack of curs', and in the fact that the Normans were unable to overcome English resistance for almost nine hours of intense fighting, which suggests that the two armies were almost evenly balanced. Norman sources repeatedly stress the size of the English army and how long it took for Norman attacks to make any impression on it.

King Harold in fact, in the end, elected to fight on ground of his own choosing. He knew the area around Hastings well and had estates of his own both north and south of the battlefield. He had six hides at Crowhurst near Hastings itself and land at Whatlington just north of the battlefield while both his mother, Gytha, and his father, Earl Godwine, held estates all over Sussex. Steyning, previously the property of Fécamp Abbey was in Harold's possession when he became King.

Duke William just had to accept the offer of battle. He would have been running short of supplies as his men exhausted what they could find locally. A retreat was equally perilous. The sea was becoming increasingly dangerous as winter approached and it was rumoured that King Harold had sent his fleet to blockade any retreat. The Carmen de Hastinge Proelio talks of 500 ships, that is 'quingenta', an absurd number, but this might be a scribal error for quinquagenta, which means fifty, a much more likely figure. But if the Duke could defeat Harold he would have the resources of the whole kingdom from which to provide for his men. Failure by the English would still have allowed King Harold, if he still lived, time in which to summon even more warriors.

Duke William, early on the morning of Saturday 14 October, had moved up to the crest of Telham Hill, some 200 feet above sea level, from which he was able to observe English movements on Calbec, looming higher at 260 feet. He saw that the hill was the last spur of the Andredesweald, covered at that time by trees, jutting out towards the south and blocking the road to London which ran up over it. The rising and possibly boggy ground would cause problems for his cavalry. He could not have imagined a site more unfavourable to the attacker than the hill at Senlac. He watched as the English army emerged from the forest and the woods all around 'glittered full of their spears'. The vanguard was brilliant with the gilded banners of the Fyrd, with its solid wall of shields and the bejewelled Battle Standard of the King, the 'Fighting Man', marking his position. Norman hearts must have quailed at the prospect of attacking such an enemy.

The battlefield has a curious resemblance to that of Waterloo, though on a much smaller scale. Both battles featured a ridge with a long lane at the top, and a forest behind it, facing down towards a muddy valley with a main road cutting across it.[2]

Later accounts report that the Normans had spent the previous night in prayer while the English had spent it carousing, drinking and singing. This is mere fantasy. The Duke simply ordered his men, after evening devotions, to settle down and rest, before his alarm at reports of the coming of the English caused him to order the army to be kept under arms all night. That had been back at Hastings. There had been fears of a night attack by the English and the Duke at first had ordered those men available in the camp, since some had been sent off foraging, to stand to and arm themselves while the foragers were hastily recalled. On the morning of the battle he roused his men early and they had attended Mass and taken Communion. Wace says that Bishop Odo made his men swear to give up eating meat on Saturdays if they survived the battle.

The English, having ridden, and in many cases marched, for some days, and come some sixty miles in two days from London, were tired and no doubt those who could slept soundly. It is likely that they ate and drank cheerfully and noisily before going to sleep. Robert Wace reports the common drinking toasts of the English, 'drinkail and wassail, let it come, drink to me, drink my health' and so on. They too were roused before dawn and began moving down onto the plateau chosen by King Harold as the most defensible position available. Knowing that the Normans used cavalry, he had chosen to take the high ground so that they would have to ride up hill against him. Both sides had posted sentries to guard against an attack by night.[3]

Duke William had conceded the high ground to King Harold who had chosen to fight a defensive battle. The Duke moved his men down the slopes of Telham Hill to the neighbourhood of Starr's Green and Black Horse Hill. There he set them in order in a prearranged array. All this would have taken both sides several hours to accomplish. The Normans could see the Englishmen emerging from the forest above them, down along a quite narrow neck of land out onto a plateau, shaped like the head of a hammer, at the base of the upper part of Caldbec Hill. It runs along the 250 foot contour line. The present Battle High Street runs where the neck of land once lay.

The chosen position safeguarded the English flanks. The land on each side of the approach to the plateau fell away sharply on each side of a watershed and could not be attacked by cavalry. In front of the plateau the ground fell away quite steeply, as it also did to the right. The left approach was less steep but the ground petered out there into marshy and sandy areas not easily negotiable by horses. This was perhaps the area called 'sandlacu', rendered by Orderic Vitalis as 'Senlac', and in modern terms 'Sandlake'. Estimates of the gradients around the English position cannot be accepted as applying to the location as it was in 1066, there have been far too many alterations made, starting with the building of Battle Abbey. It is probable that the whole approach to the English position was far steeper than it is now.

The English army crowded out onto the plateau in a dense mass of closely packed fighting men. So restricted was the available space that many men retired from the ranks and, no doubt, were held in reserve. So densely packed were English soldiers that it was claimed that during the battle the dead, and wounded, were unable to fall to the ground, held in place by the press of men around them. This is, naturally, poetic licence. They presented a very different appearance from that of the Normans. Englishmen, as befits the men of a nation accustomed to over twenty years of relative peace, wore their blond hair long and flowing and favoured large elaborate moustaches, shaving the rest of the face. King Harold himself was a tall, robust man, and, as his campaign in Wales demonstrates, capable of great feats of endurance. In Wales he had campaigned up and down the country with such energy that he 'left not one that pisseth against a wall'. It was said that in many places stones had been set up to record his victories saying 'Hic fuit Victor Haroldus', one might almost render that as 'Harold was here!'[4]

All attempts to estimate the size of the rival armies are dependent upon so many variables, that a definite conclusion has not yet been accepted. The consensus used to be that the two sides numbered about 7,000 men each but that is now regarded as possibly too low and figures of 10-12,000 or even more are now thought more likely. Viscount Aimeri de Thouars is probably the source of the suggestion, in the Chronicle of St Maixent, that Duke William had 14,000 men. That has been described as a 'startlingly reasonable number'. The English probably had even more. The numbers were certainly large enough to sustain a battle which lasted from full daylight, 'at the third hour' or 9.00 a.m., until sunset, some nine hours in all. It was a fiercely fought struggle, which could have gone either way, in which certainly hundreds and possibly thousands of men died on both sides and many more were wounded.[5]

English chroniclers, concluding from defeat that God was not on the English side, tended to attribute defeat to lack of numbers, but the Normans nonetheless found English resistance difficult to overcome until very late in the day. King Harold's tactic was to confront Duke William with a solid shield wall and wear down his attacks, intending that, if he could not drive the Normans from the field, he could at least reduce their numbers and make another battle impossible for them. If he still held his position at night fall, he could make a tactical withdrawal into the Weald, summon reinforcements, and resume his assault on the Normans, possibly with a larger army and fresh troops. Duke William, on the other hand, had to win, a draw would not be enough. He had never fought a set piece battle such as this. Varaville, Mortemer and Val-ès-Dunes had all been far more mobile affairs. Hastings was 'a new kind of battle' to the Normans, with one side doing all the attacking while the other stood firm.

The sun had risen above the horizon by 6.30 a.m and the Normans had set out from their camp and marched to Telham Hill. At that time of year full daylight comes late, shrouded in October mists. The Duke now ordered his men, who had ridden and marched to the battlefield in open order, carrying their hauberks and weapons, to prepare for battle. (The knights wore hauberks which had divided skirts to allow them to mount their horses. Foot soldiers on both sides wore hauberks with combined leggings providing protection for groin and inside leg.) William himself then donned his own hauberk and, inadvertently, put it on back to front, another evil omen which he hastily reversed by promptly reversing his hauberk, by laughing and saying that so he 'would be turned from a Duke to a King' that day.

The Poitevin, Count Aimeri de Thouars is credited with saying, 'Never has such a knight been seen under heaven. A noble Count will become a noble King'. Duke William was always scornful of omens. He then hung round his neck the relics upon which Harold was alleged to have sworn the famous (or infamous) oath, though the Bayeux Tapestry does not depict him doing so. Holding his position at the bottom of the hill, the Duke marshalled his men into three ranks and three sections. As he did so Vital, one of Odo of Bayeux's tenants, pointed out to the Duke the royal standard that showed where King Harold stood.

In the front line the Duke placed his corps of archers, the men of Evreux and Louviers, equipped with both bows and some crossbows, and possibly supported by lightly armed skirmishers with slings. In the second section came the heavy infantry, armed with swords or throwing spears, and shields, wearing helmets and hauberks. In the rear he marshalled his knights, armoured and mounted and with shields, swords and spears. These forces were divided into the usual formation of a centre and two wings. The Duke commanded his Normans in the centre, placing the Bretons and possibly the Aquitanians on the left, under Count Alan Fergant (Iron Glove) and the rest of his miscellaneous Frenchmen, under Roger of Montgomery, on the right.

William's banner, the gift of Alexander II, was carried by Toustain fitzRou, the White, from Bec. A knight, William Patry or Patric, from Lalande, who had received Earl Harold as his guest, swore to confront him face to face for his perjury. Before marching to the field of battle, Duke William had exhorted his men to remember the successes of the Normans in war as against the lesser fame of the English, reminding them of the infamous death of the Aetheling Alfred and of the Duke's own claim to the English throne. Harold's 'perjury' was again mentioned and the Duke held out to his men the prospect of the glory of victory and the rich spoils that would result from it. Lastly he claimed that God would fight with them.

King Harold had drawn his men up in the traditional shield wall or war hedge. A shield wall is exactly that, a line of shield-bearing men which, to the enemy, is like a wall. It could equally well be called a spear wall or war-hedge. It does not imply a line so closely packed together that the shields overlapped, as that would prevent the warriors striking out at the enemy. Groups of men within it can form a wedge-like column which would advance in loose formation and kill the enemy. The use of the phrase 'war-hedge' suggests that the shield wall resembled a hedgehog, with spears for spines. King Harold commanded the centre from a small mound just to the left of centre and several ranks back from the front line.

Earl Gyrth, who was to be involved in the fighting against the Bretons, clearly commanded the right wing, leaving the third brother, Earl Leofwine to command the left. King Harold distributed his seasoned troops, the Housecarls and the King's Thegns, among the shire levies, to provide professional stiffening and leadership among these less experienced warriors. The Housecarls and King's Thegns would have been fully equipped for war, indistinguishable in many respects from their Norman opponents. Other troops, the Fyrd levies would also have been well armed but some of those who fought were less so. At the least, fighting men had padded leather jackets, often covered in metal rings which were sewn to them, and carried convex shields of lime wood. Most of the trained warriors had helmets and chain mail armour, over a padded under-shirt, and carried shields. Some were armed with swords or battle axes, and spears, others had 'bills' long handled weapons with a hooked blade on the end like a halberd.

It is not really possible to estimate the length or depth of the English frontline, there are too many variables and the ground has been considerably altered since 1066. The area on which Battle Abbey stands has certainly been levelled and probably lowered.

To the Normans they appeared like a circular mass of men (densius conglobati), as the wings of the line were bent back somewhat at each end.

There were many banks and ditches scattered about the field of battle, some quite steep and Henry of Huntingdon reported that there was what he calls a 'fovea' (some kind of earthwork) in the centre, at some little distance down from the English line, which was an obstacle to a direct approach; it consisted possibly of an 'agger' or rampart with a ditch. There are also references to the hillock said to have lain someway down the hill off to the English right.[6]

The sources imply also that the English, perhaps by means of using a squad of picked warriors, had occupied that small hill off to the right of the frontline from which flanking attacks could be made on the Normans as they approached. Reports of the construction of field works such as ditches and walls probably reflect the pre-existing features of the battlefield rather than works made by the English army, although eleventh-century warriors were adept at constructing such defences quite rapidly. Wace, in saying that 'they made shields for themselves out of shutters and other pieces of wood', was probably confusing the actual shield wall with a barrier, an abbatis, of logs and tree trunks located in front of it. He reports that the shield wall itself was set firmly joined together, as keys are set into locks. This is a poetic image for an array in close order.[7]

The Kentishmen occupied their customary position in the front line, the men of Wiltshire, Devon and Cornwall behind them, while the Londoners formed round the English Standard, the battle flag. Other contingents took up positions grouped shire by shire commanded by their Sheriffs and within each shire contingent men from separate hundreds stood together led by their Hundredman. There is no reason to suppose that the English had no archers at all but if they did they made no significant contribution to the battle, though Norman attacks were repelled by showers of missiles of all kinds.

King Harold is reported to have remarked, concerning his absence in the North when William landed, 'But the mischance was the Will of Heaven and I could not be everywhere at the same moment.' He added that had he been on the South Coast the strangers would never have made good their landing but either been driven into the sea or have perished on English ground. But he now made his dispositions effectively. Like Byrhtnoth the ealdorman at the battle of Maldon, King Harold would have exhorted his men to fight well and hold the shield wall. He roused his men to battle by describing the horrors which would befall the land if they were defeated and they all, contrary to Norman allegations of desertion, swore they would die rather than acknowledge any King but Harold. He then probably rode up and down before the shield wall to ensure that men held their positions firmly, reminding them to hold their ground and have no fear, before dismounting and taking up his position by his battle flags, where he knew his most loyal troops were stationed.

All of the English had been ordered to leave their horses and these had been driven afar off for safety. King Harold had no need to place too many men in the front rank, only enough to occupy a position which could not easily be outflanked as long as the shield wall held firm. The contour lines to the east and west of the English position are close together, indicating a steep approach. Having observed Norman use of cavalry while he was in Brittany, Harold had chosen a position which allowed him to cancel out much of the advantage Duke William derived from having cavalry. He set out a close array of warriors armed with the dreaded two-handed battle axe, supported by swarms of lighter armed men equipped with javelins and slings and heavy throwing sticks. Henry of Huntingdon said that he built the battle line 'like a castle'. It faced downhill, turned slightly towards the south-east and towards Telham Hill. William of Malmesbury described the shield wall as like an impenetrable wedge. Marianus Scotus said the English were in seven divisions, suggesting seven wedge shaped formations closely ranked together. One severe disadvantage in this position was that the English had the sun in their eyes, but in early morning in October the mist obscured full sunlight and the sun remained faint and watery until long into the day.

The Church also provided units of the English army, so that, for instance, the Men of Peterborough Abbey were led by their Abbot, Leofric, as were the fighting monks of New Minster, Winchester, under Abbot Aelfwig. It is possible, given the size of his army now thought likely, that the English host extended out beyond the ridge bearing the plateau and so a little way down the slope. As they were to encounter horsemen, the English might well, at least in places, have hastily positioned hurdles, branches of trees and logs as an additional obstacle, an abbatis, and that they planted spears in the ground at a forward slanting angle, butt first, to provide a further deterrent to horses.

Naturally, the Duke is reported as making a speech immediately before battle was joined to encourage his men but what William of Poitiers says of it is his own idea of what the Duke might have said; reminding his men of past victories, telling them that 'if you fight like men you shall have the victory!' The writer says that Duke William warned them to avoid capture and that as no escape was possible by flight in hostile country, they would have to fight hard. He reminded them of the defeats suffered by the English at the hands of the Danes and concluded by saying that 'men inexpert in warfare can easily be crushed by the valour and strength of a few'. No doubt the author had spoken to survivors of the battle and based his speech on what he had been told. The Carmen de Hastinge Proelio also grants William a preliminary address to his men, in the form of 'Orders of the day'. He is said to have reminded them that they were chosen and favoured by God and addressed first the French, then the Bretons and the men from Maine, volunteers from Apulia and Calabria and even Sicily and finally his own Normans. The Norman front lay along the 125 foot contour line looking up at the English position another 125 feet above sea level.

So, at the third hour of the day, that is, 9.00 a.m., since the knights feared to attack the English line immediately, the Duke sent in a wave of archers, crossbowmen and lightly armed troops with throwing spears or slings, to soften up the English line with a barrage of arrows, some crossbow bolts, and other missiles hurled by slingers. As the poets put it, 'the bows were busy and bitter was the onset of war'. But in the main the Englishmen's shields protected them. The advance was almost certainly slowed by the soft wet grass, soaked in dew. These skirmishers advanced, rushing forward in short bursts as near as they dared to the English line to discharge their weapons or throw their javelins. They were greeted by a ferocious counter-barrage of missiles of all kinds, long throwing spears, shorter javelins (called the 'ategar'), rocks and stones and even heavy stones tied to sticks which could be whirled round the head and released with great force. Both sides gave vent to loud shouts, but that was 'drowned by the clash of weapons and groans of the dying'. The English, 'in their serried ranks, drove back those who dared to attack them with drawn swords'.

This attack went on until the Normans had exhausted their arrows and missiles and were driven back by the severity of the English response. They then retired, giving way to the advance of the heavy infantry, who composed in fact the largest part of the Norman army. They came pounding up the slope, shields locked together, in group formations, seeking to engage the English frontline, but impeded by the rough nature of the terrain. Their job was to open a gash in the shield wall to enable the Knights to penetrate it. They failed repeatedly. The Norman troops clashed bloodily with the shield wall, meeting the response of the Housecarls wielding the dreaded Scandinavian-style two-handed battle axe, capable of cleaving a man in two. The English issued their battle cries; Out! Out! Out!, Holy Cross! Holy Cross! and God Almighty! To which the Normans replied with 'Dex Aie! Dex Aie! (God helps!)[8]

The struggle between the English warriors and the Norman infantry must have lasted for the best part of an hour or more. It would have taken some time for the first wave of archers and skirmishers to advance, discharge their weapons and retreat, and for the infantry to charge laboriously up the hill, quite forcefully this time as they were fresh and in their full strength. The two front lines became locked in combat, thrusting forwards with shields and spears, but mainly slashing with swords and, on the English side hewing men down and chopping off heads, arms or legs with the fearsome battleaxes. The Bayeux Tapestry illustrates these stages of the battle in the lower border. The archers advance and dead men are shown, some without heads or limbs. But the unfortunate infantry are nowhere shown fighting as the designer concentrates on the feats of the knights. This is somewhat misleading but the fighting by the infantry would have been difficult to portray. The Tapestry does show the effectiveness of the axemen. So dreadful wounds and deadly strokes were exchanged on both sides until the Norman attack wavered and the effort to overcome a determined and well entrenched foe drained the infantrymen of strength and they disengaged to allow the knights to do their part.[9]

There is no need to assume that the English line was wholly static. At previous conflicts the English had made use of a manoeuvre involving counter-attacks by columns of attack in which two such columns of men might converge to form a blunt wedge which would drive back opposing infantrymen. At Fulford the Earls Edwin and Morcar had used it unsuccessfully against King Harald Hardrada, allowing him to outflank them. But a competent war leader and his Housecarls could repulse opposing infantry with thrusting spears, hacking away with swords or battle axes.

The 'killing zone' in front of the English line was about thirty yards deep, the effective range of a javelin. A wedge shaped column could cross it at walking pace in under a minute. So the shield wall, a line of men in close order protected by shields and equipped with thrusting spears and javelins, could mount an effective tactic of fire and shock; a barrage of missiles of every description, accompanied by a great roar, the 'war shout', and follow that up with a forward move, hacking away with swords and axes. Very little tight control could be exercised over this kind of fighting by commanders until the two sides disengaged. The aim of the attackers was, of course, to punch a hole in the shield wall, penetrate it and so cause its collapse. This the infantry signally failed to do. William of Poitiers describes none of this, he is concerned only with the exploits of the knights.

Then came the knights riding in full armour up hill on their well trained destriers or battle hardened horses. These were not the heavy cavalry horses of the later Middle Ages, ancestors of the Shire Horse, bred to carry a knight in full plate armour. The Norman horses were smaller and lighter, unprotected by armour, and certainly faster, possibly fourteen hands high, trained to react to the rider's pressure from his knees or the prick of his spurs, leaving his hands free to hold shield and spear or sword. As the charge was uphill, couched lances were quite useless and the knights had to draw their swords, possibly after throwing their spears at the English or jabbing at them with them until the spears broke. Riding uphill is not a problem, but doing so against steady, close order infantry, with secure flanks, is. Horses are easy targets for long spears and even for long handled battle axes, as the Normans found to their cost.

The shield wall braced itself to meet them, presenting a glittering hedge of spear points. There could have been no shock charge by knights riding full tilt against such an obstacle with couched lances. Their horses could not have made a sustained assault against naked steel blades. (As Waterloo was to demonstrate, with the failure of the French cavalry against the fixed bayonets of the British Squares, horses cannot face naked steel.) Instead the Normans charged up, relying on the advantage of height as they struck downwards from the backs of their horses. The Bayeux Tapestry shows them riding in with spears held overhead for throwing, the couched lance used only against individual Englishmen caught in the open. So they rode up, finding that the last few yards were very steep and that the English shield wall was virtually level with them. It is likely that the English had set their spear shafts into the ground to meet the advancing horsemen. The front rank turned the points towards the riders and those immediately behind set them against the horses' chests. The knights struck partly downwards and wheeled their horses to left or right, some horses striking out with their hoofs. Then they, as a natural consequence, retreated back down the slope. The Bretons in particular, on the Norman left, were terrified by the ferocity of the English response as they fought with all their might to prevent any breach from being opened in their ranks.[10]

One Norman, bolder or more rash, than the rest, Taillefer by name, with a talent for minstrelsy, had advanced uphill ahead of his particular troop (or conroi, a squadron of ten or more knights), strumming on his instrument and singing the Song of Roland to encourage the others. He juggled with sword and spear, throwing them into the air and catching them as he advanced. Before he reached the English line, one man, more rash than wise, rushed out to attack him. The Norman, with one tremendous blow, beheaded him and, seizing the bleeding head by the hair, turned and held it up for his comrades, still labouring up the slope, to see. Taillefer then made a single handed attack on the English shield wall which simply opened up as he approached, allowed him in and cut down horse and rider.[11]

So the Norman knights made their first attack, led into battle by Turstin fitzRou, the Standard Bearer, wheeling around before the English shield wall, striking out vigorously and suffering heavy casualties themselves as the impetus of their attack was absorbed. Then they turned and retreated back down the hill, leaving much slaughter and piles of men and horses in front of the shield wall. Cavalry tactics at this period derived much from the practices of the hunting field, particularly the hunting of wild boar. Men rode in at them, spears held aloft and threw or stabbed downwards with them, hoping to spear the target. William of Poitiers also emphasizes the tactic of slashing at the enemy with swords. He says the knights disdained to fight at long range and challenged the enemy sword in hand. Some knights might perhaps, on occasion, have attempted to use their spears as lances, thrusting them at the shield wall. The English, full of confidence, fought back with all their might.

The fog and confusion of war has led those who described the battle afterwards to vary in their recollection of the exact sequence of events beyond that first assault. An impression was left that this first attack was almost a disaster for the Duke and that the Bretons on the left wing panicked at the first contact with the shield wall, a type of opposition they, and the Normans, had probably never experienced before, and recoiled from the English line in disorder, so causing the less disciplined men among the English host to break ranks and pursue them.

It is unlikely that this happened quite so early in the battle when both sides were fresh and English and Breton discipline held. The confusion is understandable, since every Norman attack would have ended with the cavalry retreating down the hill. It is more likely to have occurred later when the English were growing weary of merely standing fast and taking punishment without counter-attacking, eager to revenge themselves on the foe. They are reported at one stage as having seized a hillock or tumulus from which they were able to repulse the Normans as they struggled to retake it. On this first occasion, then, the assault petered out and both sides took an opportunity to recover, reorganise, remove the wounded where possible and prepare for a renewed assault. Men on both sides would have been exhausted by their efforts, weighed down by the great weight of weapons and armour. This first phase of the battle must have occupied most of the morning and could well have been followed by a second phase which followed much the same pattern. The battle had become, in the words of William of Poitiers, 'a battle of a new type; one side vigorously attacking; the other resisting as if rooted to the ground'.

But during a third or fourth attack, the Bretons did break. The slope up which they had to ride was by now slippery with mud and blood and littered with the shattered bodies of the dead or dying. The air stank with the reek of blood and emptied bowels, resounding with the groans of the wounded. Many of their best men had been killed, they and their horses were tiring and the attack was probably not made as vigorously as it ought to have been. They had come to fear the unshakeable strength of the shield wall and recoiled. The Brevis Relatio put the number who fled at one thousand. The slope on the Breton wing was not quite as steep as elsewhere and they tended to hit the English line before the centre had come up, so their flank was exposed. The English now made a counter attack and the Bretons 'panic–stricken by the violence of the assault, broke in flight before the English'. The whole Breton line, and the auxiliary troops which formed part of it, recoiled in disorder and fled, rather than retreated, tumbling back down towards where the Duke was urging on his men. The English right wing broke ranks and charged down after the fleeing Bretons.

Alan Fergant's men had almost become a rabble of unhorsed knights and riderless horses all mixed up with those still on their horses and with infantry and archers. The panic extended even to the Normans attacking in the centre and they too recoiled. Their left flank had been exposed by the precipitate Breton retreat. For a moment it looked as if the whole Norman army might flee. Some commentators have suggested that had King Harold ordered a general advance then, the Norman host might have been swept away, but equally, the king could have seen the risk of leaving his strong position, surrendering the advantage of the high ground and opening his men to a mass charge by the entire Norman army, knights and foot soldiers together. He steadied his men and sent his brother, Earl Gyrth, to recall as many men as he could. That could have caused a problem for the English.

A rumour then spread like wild-fire among the Normans that the Duke himself had been killed and Norman hearts were struck by terror, so the Duke thrust himself in front of those in flight, shouting at them and threatening them with his spear. Staying their retreat he took off his helmet, standing before them bare-headed and cried "Look at me well! I am still alive and by the grace of God I shall yet prove the victor! What is this madness which makes you fly? What way is open for your retreat? You are allowing yourselves to be pursued and killed by men whom you could slaughter like cattle. You are throwing away victory and lasting glory, rushing into ruin and incurring abiding disgrace, yet by flight none of you can escape destruction!" With these words he restored their courage and leaping to the front (he had in fact been unhorsed, hence the rumour) and wielding his death-dealing sword, he defied the enemy'. As a result, some of his knights, wounded and streaming with blood, leaned on their shields and fought on in that manner.[12]

As a result of the Duke's intervention, supported by his half-brother, Bishop Odo, who rallied the younger knights, the Normans turned on the pursuing English, surrounding a large number of them, and rapidly cut them down so that few escaped. The Bastard himself seems to have led a charmed life during the battle, especially at this point. In all he is said to have had three horses killed under him. It was most likely during this crisis that the Duke encountered Earl Gyrth and sought to engage him in single combat. The Earl, undismayed, brandished a javelin and threw it, injuring the Duke's horse and forcing him to fight on foot. This bothered the Duke not one whit, instead he charged at the young warrior 'like a lion raging and furious', striking at him, saying 'Receive from me the only crown you deserve, if my horse is slain, I attack on foot'. The Duke appears to have thought he was fighting King Harold himself rather than Earl Gyrth. The Duke also encountered a warrior identified only as 'son of Helloc' who unhorsed the Duke who then slew him as well and, it is said, then encountered a 'Centurion' (that is a Hundred man) and slew him. It is barely possible that the phrase 'son of Helloc' somehow conceals the identity of Earl Leofwine, who is also said to have been killed during this affray, but it cannot be proven. So, striking out at heads and limbs, determined to exterminate the foe, Duke William sent 'countless souls into the darkness of death', or so says William of Poitiers. The Carmen de Haestinge Proelio says Earl Gyrth died at this point in the battle so it could be that it was deaths of Earls Gyrth and Leofwine that caused the English attack to stall and a retreat to set in.

The English desperately retreated back up the hill. Some, possibly a squad of hardened troops, held out on a little hillock some way up the slope towards the English right, until cut down by Norman knights, while the English shield wall reformed and repelled the attack, preventing the Normans from breaking the line. The English host as yet 'even after their losses scarcely diminished in number' still held out. The Duke and his men now realised that 'they could not, without severe losses overcome an army massed so strongly in close formation', as William of Poitiers says in his account, which explains King Harold's determination to hold the shield wall intact. Whether the King had actually ordered a counter-attack when the Bretons fled or whether he had been unable to prevent a spontaneous counter-charge remains uncertain. But the English beat off all attacks. King Harold could not, in fact, break off the engagement, that would have allowed the Normans to massacre his men, but he could stand fast and hope to survive until nightfall when the English could retreat under cover of darkness, leaving the Normans to lick their wounds and starve. King Harold could then have mobilised another army and resumed the war.

But it was now past the sixth hour, the hour of Vespers in the late afternoon. William of Poitiers insists that the Duke had recourse to the gambit of a feigned retreat. Having seen how the flight of the Bretons had been turned to Norman advantage, the Duke, so says Poitiers, ordered now one, now another conroi (as groups of ten or twenty knights were called), to pretend to turn and flee in panic, so tempting groups of Englishmen 'thinking victory within their grasp and issuing shouts of triumph' to break ranks and pursue the Normans, only for the knights to wheel round, in a manoeuvre which they are known to have practised, and slaughter them. So the war of attrition went on.

This matter of the 'feigned retreats' is a contentious one. The use of such a tactic is a common theme in reports of eleventh century battles and gives rise to the suspicion that the claim that retreats were an organised tactic was a means of disguising what were real failures of nerve, and used to explain them away. If the tactic had been used often, then armies would have been aware of it and would almost certainly not have been deceived by it. It is likely that the natural tendency of cavalry to wheel away and retreat as an attack petered out and failed to penetrate the enemy line, in order to regroup, led to the idea that this was a deliberate ploy. An orderly retreat followed by regrouping and a renewed attack would have looked much like a 'feigned retreat'.

In between these assaults by the knights, in order to give the English no rest, there were renewed attacks by waves of archers and crossbowmen, followed by determined assaults by the infantry. Their line remained 'formidable and very difficult to overwhelm', but the English were undoubtedly growing weary as 'if more movement was caused by the falling dead than by the living. Those who were lightly wounded could not withdraw because of the density of their formation but were crushed in the press of their companions'.

The English thegns were now suffering huge losses, confined to a defensive posture, repeatedly exposed to showers of arrows and faced with alternating assaults by infantry and cavalry, given scarcely any time to rest or recover. Towards the end of the day which now loomed upon them, the English suffered heavy losses. The bodies of Leofwine and his brother Earl Gyrth were to be found after the battle relatively close to the place where their brother the King was also slain, probably after moving to the forefront of the battle.

The struggle raged on and twilight approached. Casualties were mounting on both sides and the Bastard had as yet made no significant breakthrough. If he could not break the shield wall and night fell the Normans would eventually lose, unable to replace their losses.

Duke William now conceived of a final throw of the dice. He ordered his archers into the fray once more, encouraging them to advance as near as possible to the shield wall and to fire their arrows, over the heads of the advancing Norman knights and infantry, almost vertically upwards, to fall on the English lines from overhead. The English would then have had to choose between defending themselves from the attacks of infantrymen and knights coming at them from the front or raise their shields to ward off the arrows. Archers were capable of firing ten arrows each in a matter of a few minutes. The result was that more than one breach in the shield wall was opened, enabling the knights to ride up onto the plateau, possibly from the west, through the gaps, rolling up the English line and cutting down isolated groups of defenders. Duke William is said to have been struck on the head by an English captain of a Hundred, but was saved by his helmet, and beat off the attack. The English captain seemed unstoppable until laid low by the Norman baron Roger of Montgomery. Robert fitzErneis attempted to seize the English Standard and lost his life in the attempt. Then a conroi of twenty knights resolved to capture the Standard and succeeded in doing so.

In this last phase of the battle, King Harold, still hoping to hold out until nightfall, and seeking to rally his men for a last supreme effort, moved forward for the first time into the front rank of the shield wall and was seen by a Norman soldier who pointed him out to the Duke. The English King is described as fighting like Hector at Troy, against Achilles, or like Turnus in Italy against Aeneas. He was no longer at his command post, marked by the presence of the English standard, but with the remnants of his Housecarls. He now fought vigorously, often striking down any enemy within range. No one could approach him unscathed. He could lay low horse and rider with one blow. As long as he continued to triumph, the English continued to resist. Then King Harold was attacked by a determined group of four knights and slain. When he was killed, the cry 'Harold is dead!' spread through the English ranks and they broke and fled. His companions no doubt thought of what Byrhtnoth's men said after Maldon, 'Here lies our Lord, hacked and cut down, a brave man in the dust.' There are no reports of the Normans taking any prisoners, only of slaughter. So that it was said that the parched earth drank the blood of the dead.

Later reports that Harold was struck in the eye by an arrow (and according to some actually killed) are not contemporary. Neither William of Jumièges nor William of Poitiers reports the details of Harold's death, possibly because there was something shameful about the manner of it. William of Poitiers ignores the manner of his death completely. William of Jumièges reports only that he fell 'pierced with lethal wounds' and, erroneously thought he had been killed during the first Norman attack (in primo militum congressu) which is contradicted by several other sources. The Carmen de Hastinge Proelio has its own account. It concludes that the report of Harold's death led the English to refuse to continue the fight. The famous scene in the Bayeux Tapestry has been heavily restored and cannot, by itself, be entirely relied upon. The eighteenth century copies of the Tapestry show what could be a spear rather than an arrow. If it was an arrow, the flights seem to have been added during restoration. The earliest source to suggest that Harold was killed by an arrow was the chronicle of Amatus of Montecasino, written circa 1080, but it does not name the king so killed and survives as a French translation from Latin made in the fifteenth century. Then Baudri of Bourgeuil, *c.*1096-1102, said that he was wounded (pierced) by an arrow. Only later does this become the tale of an arrow in the eye. But, since the figure attempting to remove an arrow is clearly labelled 'Harold' and that in six other scenes Harold is clearly so labelled with his name above his head, boarding his ship, where he and Guy converse, where Guy conducts him to Duke William, where William enters his palace with Harold, where William bestows arms on Harold, where Harold is informed of the coming of the Comet, and where he is told of the coming of the Duke's army, it is difficult to say that the figure with the arrow is not King Harold.[13]

The solution would certainly appear to be that, although reports that he was *killed* by an arrow are late, he *is* shown struck by an arrow and is reported to have been so struck, that he must have been severely wounded by one, possibly almost blinded by blood and pain, and so fell easy prey to his attackers.

Duke William, seeing his hated rival in a conspicuous position, had ordered a group of four knights to lead an assault aimed directly at King Harold's position. He is unlikely to have led such an assault himself. The King could well by now have moved into the front line, to encourage his men, and that would account for phrase in the account by William of Jumièges which now reads as if Harold was killed early in the battle. So 'in primo militum congressu' means in the front line rather than during the first assault. ('primo' here meaning 'in the first place'.) Count Eustace of Boulogne led three others who fought their way into a breach in the shield wall to attack the King himself. With Eustace rode Hugh II, of Montfort-sur-Risle, Walter Giffard I (their presence at Hastings is confirmed by William of Poitiers) and the 'noble heir' of Count Guy I of Ponthieu, called Enguerrand. Of this man all that is otherwise known is that he was dead before 1087. His name could have been omitted out of a sense of shame, because one of the four attackers mutilated King Harold's body in a repellent manner and was dismissed from the Norman army in disgrace. Bishop Guy of Amiens was his uncle, and is probably author of the Carmen de Hastinge Proelio, so the poem refers to Enguerrand as 'noble heir of Ponthieu' without giving his name. Duke William himself cannot have participated in the attack since had he himself been responsible for killing King Harold the fact could not have been concealed, nor would he have wanted to conceal it. One might suspect that contemporaries would never have heard the last of it if Duke William had actually managed to kill King Harold.[14]

When the four knights attacked and slew the king, the first speared his chest through his shield, the second beheaded him with his sword, the third disembowelled him with another spear thrust and the fourth hacked at his thigh, or perhaps his hip. That could have been a euphemism for cutting off his genitals. The Carmen uses the word 'coxa' and William of Malmesbury uses 'femur', both referring to the groin area, the very top of the thigh. The Bayeux Tapestry shows a figure in armour, which may be Harold, falling to the ground as a knight on horseback strikes with his sword; above this figure the statement 'interfectus est', he was killed. Although some argue that the original read rather 'in terra iactus est' or something similar, that he died cannot be disputed. The body, in common with those of the rest of the slain, was stripped of all insignia and clothing. After the fighting was over the royal armour and the two Standards, the Dragon of Wessex and Harold's Fighting Man, were taken to the Duke. But so mutilated was Harold's body that when Duke William ordered it to be found so that it might be buried, it proved impossible to identify him. He was eventually recognized by certain 'secret' marks on his body known only to his long-standing wife, (*more Danico*), Edith the Swan-necked.

When news spread of the death of the King of the English, all resistance collapsed as the men broke and fled, back along the narrow neck of land by which they had reached the field of battle. All was chaos and confusion in the gathering gloom. It was probably then that Robert fitzErneis had tried to burst through the English line and seize the Standard, only to be killed. Many men lay on the ground bathed in blood, too weak to escape. Others died in the forest of the Weald as they struggled to escape, some from their wounds, others slain by the Normans who eagerly carried on the pursuit. Some were even trampled to death by runaway horses.

There are confused accounts of desperate last stands by groups of thegns and Housecarls and the Duke called on Eustace of Boulogne who, with a conroi of fifty knights was about to give the order for them to retire from the field, to stop the pursuit. Eustace turned to the Duke to warn him to retire as it was becoming too dangerous with the visibility declining, but was struck from behind between the shoulders so forcefully that blood gushed from his mouth and nose and he, half dead, hastily made his escape with the aid of his knights. The Duke rallied the remaining Normans and beat off a last attack before returning to the battlefield proper.

Reports came in of a group of knights who fell into a wide and deep ditch (later called 'Malfosse' or evil ditch by the monks of Battle Abbey) where so many men and horses died that the ditch was full of corpses. Engenulf de l'Aigle, (one of the very few Norman casualties to be named), and many others died there. It is most likely that this is the vast chasm, now concealed by the present day road, where Battle High Street meets Virgin Lane, which is known as Oakwood Gill, though several other locations are possible. However, this was not the only disaster of the closing stages of the battle and there are other reports of men falling into ditches and being trapped by the English. Even in good conditions it is hazardous to ride round the field of Hastings in October even today and in the evening it rapidly becomes impossible.

So night finally fell and the battle ended. Sunset that day was at 4.54 p.m. and twilight ended by 6.25 p.m. Norman scavengers roamed the battlefield, stripping the bodies of the slain of clothing, possessions and weapons, all too valuable to be left to rot. Some of the Norman warriors were little more than bandits. Others had painted their faces black, using lampblack (which provides the surname of one Norman family, 'Talbot'). Far and wide the earth was covered with the flower of English nobility and youth, drenched in blood. The Duke ordered that the bodies of his own men slain in the conflict be collected and buried but for the time being the bodies of the English were left at the mercy of the elements and wild animals. A tent was erected on the battlefield for the Duke. He had ordered his banner to be carried to the place where the English Standard had been and had his own banner raised high there. There he ordered his food to be prepared and brought to him and sat and drank 'champagne' (not the sparkling wine, the méthode champenoise had not been invented, but the white wine of the region). The Duke had Harold's body found and brought to him and, discovering the despicable action of the fourth knight, had him expelled from the army in disgrace. The Carmen implies that this was the knight 'Gilfard', thought to be Giffard, (either Walter or his son Robert), but the text is confused and unpunctuated, so the identity of the man responsible for the mutilation remains uncertain.

The Battle Abbey tradition, according to its Chronicle, was that 'the fields were covered with corpses and all around the only colour to meet the gaze was blood-red. It looked from afar as if rivulets of blood, flowing down from all sides, had filled up the valleys, just like a river'.

The verdict of William of Malmesbury was to be that King Harold and his men had engaged William 'with more rashness and precipitate fury than military skill... and so... doomed their country to slavery by one, and that an easy, victory.' But that Hastings had been an 'easy' victory is belied by the facts. It had not been a foregone conclusion; one might say of it what the Duke of Wellington said, of Waterloo, that it was 'a damned close run thing'. The Normans themselves admitted that so heavy were their losses that victory could only be attributed to the intervention of God Himself. It was said that God granted victory to the Normans because of the sins of the English people. But William of Poitiers thought it proved that Harold was in the wrong; 'Your doom proves how lawfully you were raised up by Edward's dying gift' he says, implying that it was not lawful at all. In so doing he testifies to the fact that the English saw Harold's rule as lawful and that Edward did designate Harold.

From Victory to Kingship:
Sunday 15 October to Monday 25 December 1066

William of Malmesbury's verdict on the battle of Hastings was that Harold and his men, by engaging William 'more with rashness and precipitate fury than military skill, had doomed their country to slavery and that by an easy victory'.

To say that Hastings was an easy victory is belied by the facts. It had not been a foregone conclusion and, had King Harold not been struck down in the closing stages of the day's fighting, the English could well have continued the struggle under his leadership. But it was not to be.[1]

The Chroniclers tried to provide reasons for the defeat. They say that he fought 'before his army was drawn up in battle array' or 'before a third of his army was in order for fighting' and even 'before all the army had come'. They summarize the battle in these words, 'but in as much as the English were drawn up in a narrow place, many retired from the ranks, and very few remained true to him; nevertheless, from the third hour of the day until dusk he bravely withstood the enemy and fought so valiantly and stubbornly in his own defence, that the enemy's forces could hardly make any impression. At last, after great slaughter on both sides, about twilight, the King – Alas! – fell. There were also slain Earl Gyrth, his brother, and Earl Leofwine and nearly all the nobility of England'. If that was the battle of the 'few', what might a battle by the many have been like? But of course, the English army cannot have been that much smaller than the Norman.

The casualties had been catastrophic, especially on the English side, though the numbers involved remain unknown and unknowable. That they were high is suggested by the Annals of Nieder-Altaich, on the Rhine, which claim that Norman losses were 12,000 men. That reflects how the battle was seen in Europe. It is probably too high a total even if taken to mean the total slain and mutilated on both sides. Few of those who fought in the three battles of 1066 are known by name. No names survive of those who fought at Fulford, and, on the English side, at Stamford Bridge there is record only of an unnamed uncle of Abbot Aethelwig, a leaseholder from

Witton, Worcestershire, who 'died subsequently in Harold's battle against the Northmen', and of two other thegns, also unnamed, from Essex and Worcestershire.

The roll of honour for Hastings is a little better. King Harold and his brothers Gyrth and Leofwine, Aelfwig the Abbot of New Minster, Winchester, and twelve of his monks, Abbot Leofric of Peterborough, who escaped from the battlefield and died after returning home, an unknown number of thegns in the service of the Abbey of Bury St Edmunds, and a handful of men from Norfolk, Suffolk, Essex, Bedfordshire, Hampshire, Cambridgeshire, Huntingdonshire, Sussex and Lincolnshire. These were all men of whom King William was to say that they 'stood against me in battle and were slain there'.

The Normans recorded few of the names of their slain or wounded, naming only the minstrel Taillefer, and Robert fitzErneis to whom can be added Robert de Vitot who, while lying at Dover, gave land to the Abbey of St Evroul 'after the English war in which he was wounded in the knee'.

Duke William of Normandy was to date his reign not from 14 October 1066 but from 'the day King Edward was alive and dead'. The Normans did their best to eliminate the record of Harold's reign and he is rarely accorded the title of king, except on the Bayeux Tapestry.

The Bastard had spent the night after the battle encamped in a tent on the battlefield. He asked for his banner to be carried to the place where the English Standard had been raised, and had it raised on high to replace Harold's. He had his tent set up among the dead and had his food brought to him and his supper prepared. The story goes that Walter Giffard rode up and finding him about to eat, cried out, appalled, 'My Lord, what are you doing? It is not fitting for you to remain here with the dead.' He warned the Duke that although there were many dead Englishmen there, covered in blood, some might be unhurt or merely wounded and pretending to be dead, having smeared themselves with blood. They might rise up in the night and seek to avenge themselves before escaping. 'They do not mind if they die,' he said, 'so long as they have killed a Norman.' Yet William stayed nonetheless, while his men, the servants of his knights, the common soldiers, and others, scavenged the battlefield, stripping the dead and recovering all useable arms and equipment. Next day, Sunday, the Normans buried their friends while noble English ladies came looking for husbands, brothers or sons and were allowed to carry them off to their towns and bury them in their churches. Some were taken away and placed in mass graves, but many whose bodies were unclaimed were left to rot. Yet, since then, almost nothing has been found to indicate that a battle was ever fought there, only the head of a single battle axe. No burial pits have been found anywhere. Perhaps during the building of Battle Abbey, the area was carefully cleansed and most of the dead removed from the area by the monks.[2]

The removal of English bodies did not take place quickly, and the Normans contemplated leaving the bodies there to be eaten by wolves, vultures or dogs. Naturally William of Poitiers attributes the permission to remove the bodies to the clemency of his master. But the legend at Battle, still current in the nineteenth century, was that, as William of Newburgh in 1198 reported, the blood of the slain could still be seen welling up from the ground. The writer wrote that it was the voice of Christian blood crying out to God and that the ground was opening to reveal blood and bones.

A monk, William Faber, from Marmoutiers, is reported to have suggested to Duke William that an abbey dedicated to St Martin of Tours should be built on the site of the battle, if he won. This might only be part of the Abbey's foundation legend rather than fact. The decision to build an Abbey could well have been made in 1070 in response to the Legate Ermenfrid's imposition of public penance for the killings at Hastings. What is certain is that the high altar of the Abbey church was placed on the exact spot where King Harold was killed. In order to build the Abbey the ground on which the English shield wall had stood was levelled and lowered. The thirteenth century buildings extended over a wider area and are supported on immense buttresses to compensate for the steep slope. Then after the dissolution of the monastery in Henry VIII's time, the outer courtyard was levelled and extended, so building up the hillside. It must have been much steeper in 1066. All this makes any detailed location of the English army quite speculative.[3]

The Norman Duke certainly ordered the recovery and burial of the bodies of his own men, but, at least for some days, left the bodies of some the English to rot, a prey to wild animals. He did, however, insist on the location and identification of Harold's body. He did not want it secretly removed, fearing that its burial place might become a place of pilgrimage and a focus for rebellion. Even worse, the English might claim that he was not really dead. A legend to that effect did develop, but not until late in the twelfth century.

The exact sequence of events dealing with Harold's body is confusing. The Duke is reported to have been approached by Harold's mother, Countess Gytha, the widow of Earl Godwine, who is said to have offered the Duke the weight of her son's body in gold for permission to remove and bury it. The Norman Bastard refused on the grounds that King Harold's alleged avarice had led to the deaths of many men who remained unburied. Those with the Duke coarsely jested that 'he who guarded the coast with such insensate zeal should be buried by the seashore'. So Duke William, at first, gave charge over the body to William Malet, with instructions to see to its burial.

The author of the Carmen de Haestinge Proelio concluded from this that William Malet (though he identifies him only as 'a certain compater (companion or intimate friend) of Harold's, part Norman, part English') was actually instructed to bury Harold on the cliff top, presumably at Hastings, under a cairn and that it was said that 'by the Duke's command, O Harold, rest here a king, that you may still be guardian of sea and shore'. But later sources, especially William of Poitiers, insist that the Duke was induced to change his mind. It is thought that the author of the Carmen based his account of Harold's burial on the format of a Viking funeral rather than on reality.

William of Malmesbury recorded that the body was sent, after it had been identified, to his mother Gytha, without a demand for its ransom, and that she buried it at Waltham Holy Cross, his collegiate foundation in Essex. The Waltham Chronicle confirms that the body was taken there, and names two of its brothers Osgod Cnoppe and Aethelric Childemaister who had come to find it. At first, they were unable to identify the body as, because of its many wounds, it was quite unrecognizable. They therefore prevailed upon Harold's wife, more Danico, Edith (that is Eadgyth) Swanneshals, the Swan-necked (rather than his recent Christian wife Ealdgyth, the sister of Edwin and Morcar) to seek him out and identify him by certain secret marks on his body known only to her since she was 'privy to the secrets of his bedchamber' and had seen him naked. Eadgyth Swanneshals is the Cambridgeshire land owner known variously as Eadgyth the Rich, the Fair or the Beautiful. They then journeyed to Waltham with the body on a cart, travelling by way of 'Pontem Belli' or Battlesbridge, in Essex (near present day Billericay), and at Holy Cross it was interred.

Early in the twelfth century when the grave was opened, so that the body could be moved to a new tomb, the sacristan, Turketil, who had been there since early youth, witnessed this and told those present how he remembered King Harold's triumphant return from Stamford Bridge. Other older members confirmed that they were present when the body was first buried.[4]

Duke William had certainly changed his mind about how the English dead were to be treated, and allowed 'all those who wished to do so to collect the bodies for burial'. All this post battle activity took several days and, uncertain whether some new challenger would present himself to renew the struggle, while hoping that the English would see sense and submit, Duke William remained in the vicinity of the battlefield and of his fleet at Hastings. The area around the battlefield was comprehensively ravaged to supply the army with provisions and intimidate the local population. The Norman army also went in search of supplies to the west of Hastings. The signs of Norman visitation are revealed in Domesday Book by reductions in the immediate post conquest value of the estates. An area as far west as Lewes and as far north as Uckfield was despoiled.

But neither a new challenger nor any submissions of consequence materialised. It became clear that it was by no means certain that those in London would accept the verdict of Hastings, let alone the men of the Danelaw further north. The Northumbrians could maintain their independence still until forced to concede it and the Danelaw might make overtures to King Swein of Denmark who still harboured pretensions to the succession. But in fact the Danish King dithered and made no real effort until 1068.

The remnants of the Witan, gathered somewhat panic-stricken in London, were considering their options. One party spoke up for the possibility of electing Edgar the Aetheling as King. Unlike King Harold, the Aetheling had no obligation to recognise any claims put forward by the Norman Duke and he had not been condemned by the Papacy. He was seen by some as having undoubted hereditary right to the crown. The Chronicle of Hariulf of St Riquier in 1085 accused King Harold of using the power and insignia of his Kingdom unjustly because he had expelled King Edward's 'cousin Aelfgar' (an error most likely for Edgar, his nephew) whom Edward had intended to be his heir. On the other hand, Edgar had been born to an exiled father, in Hungary, and, like his father Edward the Exile, had no natural allies in England. He had little property and few clients. He was only a youth of about fourteen years of age, probably the youngest child of Edward the Exile's belated marriage. Many of the bishops were arguing that the defeat was God's Will as a punishment for sin.

Archbishop Ealdred of York and a substantial element among the London burgesses supported the Aetheling Edgar but others, notably the Earls Edwin and Morcar and probably Archbishop Stigand of Canterbury were more reluctant. King Edward's widow, Edith, still watching in trepidation from her vantage point in Winchester, had no reason to support the Aetheling. There was support elsewhere in the country, as time would show, especially in the Fens. When Leofric of Peterborough finally died, on All Saints Day, Wednesday 1 November, the monks elected one of their number, the provost or prior, Brand, scion of a rich Lincolnshire family and brother of the wealthy King's Thegn Asketil (recently dead either at Stamford Bridge or

Hastings). Abbot Brand, much to the outrage of the incensed Norman Duke, chose to approach the Aetheling for recognition, 'because the local people thought that he ought to become king' and the Aetheling 'gladly assented to it', no doubt flattered at this recognition of his royal pretensions. By then the Norman was in control of London and in no mood to brook opposition. However, 'good men' interceded for the abbot with the Duke, because the abbot 'was a rather good man', and he was persuaded to offer the Norman forty marks of gold that he might be recognised as abbot, and so it was done. But the scribe noted sadly, 'afterwards there came calamity and all evil on the minster. God have mercy on it!'

Then, in the fortnight after Hastings, from the 15-30 of October, nobles and clergy in London dithered in confusion and the Chronicle notes sarcastically that 'always the more it ought to have been brought forward, the more it all got behind'. Meanwhile, no Englishmen of repute submitted to the Duke, so he decided on action not words.[5]

Informed of the fate of at least two of his ships which had lost touch with the rest of the fleet, either during the crossing or perhaps during the move from Pevensey to Hastings, Duke William ordered reprisals. The Norman ships had ended up at Romney, having become separated from their comrades near Dungeness. There they had beached their ships and had immediately found themselves 'attacked and scattered with great loss by the fierce people of the region', the men of Romney Marsh. The Duke therefore ordered his men to inflict 'such punishments as he thought fit for the slaughter of his men who had landed there by mistake'. Villages and houses were burnt and the occupants slain, for daring to defend their homes from an invader.

This had the desired effect. As the Norman army moved along the coast, ravaging as it went, estates north of the Marsh were sacked, and Folkestone was ravaged. It was valued in total in King Edward's day at £110 but when passed to its new Norman owner, William d'Arques, only at £40. Dover, then as now a major cross-Channel port, surrendered without delay. Despite the surrender, the 'vill' was burnt down so comprehensively that it could not be given a valuation of what it was worth when the Bishop of Bayeux was given possession of it and even in 1086 was still only valued at £40. Nonetheless the Duke moved the whole of his fleet there as it provided a much more secure haven. The inhabitants had been terror-stricken at his approach, they 'lost all confidence in the natural defences and the fortifications of the place and its multitude of men'. The areas of destruction along the Norman line of march are about twenty-five miles apart, marking a day's march on alternate days, with a halt during which the men scavenged for food and plunder.[6]

The garrison offered to surrender but before it could do so, William's squires set fire to the 'castellum', that is the burh or fortified enclosure on the cliff top within the ruins of the Roman Fort, just to speed up the surrender. William's disciplinary control over his men left much to be desired.

News of the treatment meted out to Dover reached Canterbury and the citizens there promptly offered hostages and oaths of fealty as 'the mighty metropolitan city (seat of an archbishop) shook with terror'. But Duke William did not at first come to the city. Instead he was delayed for at least a week at Dover when his men were stricken by an outbreak of dysentery brought on by over indulgence in rich food, especially meat and by the local water. The Duke, possibly mortified by his men's lack of discipline, or fearful that the illness was an indication of divine wrath, compensated the citizens for the damage caused by the fire. This did not prevent him from driving out a number of the citizens and replacing them with his own men. That pattern was to be followed in other towns and cities following their surrender.

At length, feeling time was passing to little benefit, he decided to move to Canterbury, leaving his sick and wounded at Dover as he had now received some reinforcements from Normandy. By Sunday 29 October he was at Canterbury, and no doubt celebrated All Saints Day there on the Wednesday. In order to accommodate his army, he encamped at a place referred to only as 'Turris Fracta' or Broken Tower (not now identifiable) where he himself contracted dysentery. In consequence he was forced to remain there for a month, until 1 December, a Friday, and by then he had recovered. It seems that during this enforced delay messengers were sent to Winchester to secure its submission and that of Queen Edith.

Duke William now resumed his march on London. Much of Kent between Dover and Canterbury had been thoroughly ravaged, and the army had sought supplies also from an area covering all the estates from Sandwich to Dover by way of Deal. The Duke therefore now marched his men due east towards Maidstone, ravaging as he went along a broad front between Faversham and Challock. The army's progress was marked by more ravaging and slaughter. A force of 500 knights was despatched to probe the defences of London while the main army seems to have continued along a line between Orpington in the north and Oxted to the south, heading towards Epsom.

London was found to be heavily defended by men commanded by the wounded Staller, Aesgar, apparently carried on a litter since he could not walk. Messages were exchanged between the Staller and Duke William, who made various specious promises (as he was to do in future to other leading Englishmen) guaranteeing to the Staller his continuance in office and possession of his estates, even promising that he would be one of the Duke's councillors when he became king, if only London would surrender.[7]

The talks seem to have come to nothing, since the knights continued their advance, penetrating through Southwark as far as London Bridge before being forced to retreat. Proving unable to hold the bridge, they withdrew and contented themselves by burning Southwark. The opposition had been mounted by those magnates still in London who favoured continued resistance. They could have been led by Archbishop Ealdred and the Earls Edwin and Morcar, with other lesser nobles, since William of Poitiers claims that they threatened to give battle. He says that London was capable of raising a 'numerous and formidable force' because the Londoners 'had been joined by so many troops that they could hardly be housed even in this large town'. Some attempt must have been made to levy a third muster of the Fyrd.

This group of nobles were prepared to put forward the claims of Edgar the Aetheling since 'their highest wish was to have no lord who was not a compatriot', and, at this point, certainly not a Norman. But other magnates, lay and ecclesiastical, were developing cold feet and support began to ebb away as the Normans continued their advance. The most that could be achieved had been to refuse entry to the city to William's men in the skirmish at London Bridge.

It proved to be enough to persuade the Duke not to attempt to take London by storm across the river. Other crossing points of the Thames seem to have been defended also, since the Normans continued their march through Surrey and southern Berkshire, even into northern Hampshire, so cutting London off from supplies coming from south of the Thames. The conrois of knights sent to Southwark returned to join the main body of the army, passing through Lambeth, Battersea, Fulham and Mortlake and on towards Walton-on-Thames, while the main army came up by way of Esher. The line of march curved around Reading to the south (the borough was untouched) and swung in an arc to Wallingford where, with the connivance of the King's Thegn Wigot, the Normans were able to cross the Thames, by means of a ford and a bridge, and Archbishop Stigand came in and made his submission to the Duke.

While Duke William was at Wallingford an embassy also arrived, at Queen Edith's instigation, from Winchester offering the submission of that ancient city, home of the Kings of Wessex. The Queen herself sent gifts and formal confirmation of her submission. This won her the praise of William of Poitiers who describes her as 'a woman of manly wisdom, loving good and shunning evil, who wished to see the English governed by William'.

He alleges that she admitted that the Duke was King Edward's chosen heir and that she had opposed King Harold's ambition. Duke William graciously allowed her to continue to occupy the royal palace at Winchester (he had a new one built for his own use) and to retain a respectable quantity of land, suitable for a royal widow. There is no confirmation for any of this in the work commissioned by the Queen and known as the 'Vita Edwardi Regis'. It also looks as though, while at Wallingford, the Duke sent men to ravage further west to the south of Newbury and Hungerford, and the area around Andover was heavily affected.

As for Archbishop Stigand, he no doubt hoped to hang on to his See and the rich pickings of its estates. He renounced all allegiance to the Aetheling, saying that he repented of having 'rashly nominated' him as king. He was the first of a succession of Churchmen, bishops and abbots, who confirmed their fealty to Duke William on oath, also out of concern for the preservation of their estates and out of a desire for a strong king who would guarantee their possession of them. William was to demand a heavy price for his concessions. The Churches had to accept Norman barons and knights as their tenants and provide the Norman king with the service of large numbers of knights and other soldiers to provide castle-guard.

Having crossed the Thames at Wallingford, the Duke continued to approach London, now heading broadly eastwards, proceeding well north of the river and possibly dividing his army into two divisions. If the pattern of ravaging can be trusted, one part proceeded along the line of the Thames touching such places as Sonning, Wargrave, Maidenhead and Chalfont St Peter, while the other, commanded by the Duke himself, went much further north, staying south of Aylesbury, through Wendover to Berkhamstead where in time a formidable motte and bailey castle was constructed. There the leading citizens of London eventually came out to meet the Duke and make their submission, 'out of necessity'.

During the whole of this march, people of all ranks had been flocking in to submit, terrorized by the advancing Norman army, ravaging as it came. The Normans gleefully rejoiced to see that they 'flocked to submit like flies to a running sore'. Yet, until the Duke had completed his circuit of the beleaguered city, so completing a blockade which cut it off from its economic and agricultural hinterland, upon which it depended for vital supplies, many men still hesitated to surrender. William of Poitiers insists that 'no one meant to come to him' and that was why he 'had gone inland with all his army that was left to him and that had come to him afterwards from overseas' (a clear admission that casualties at Hastings had been far from light). The Duke had preferred the economy of effort involved in a slash and burn approach to the risk involved in remaining in Kent and inviting another pitched battle.[8]

As the Duke approached London, after the crossing of the Thames at Wallingford, another advance party of knights went on ahead into the city itself where they found a large force of 'rebels', as they were to the Normans, determined on making a vigorous resistance. But the knights at once engaged them in battle and inflicted 'great sorrow upon London by the death of many of her sons and daughters'. It was perhaps this that finally moved the leading citizens of London, seeing that they could resist no longer, to give hostages and to submit themselves 'and all they had, to their noble Conqueror and hereditary lord', as William of Jumièges puts it.

The Earls Edwin and Morcar were reported to have withdrawn to their earldoms to await further developments and yet they submitted at Berkhamstead. One suspects that they did this through intermediaries (as Earl Cospatric was to do several years later), since they also submitted in person when the Duke, not yet a King, took up residence in Barking. Thus they joined the leading citizens of London and thegns from Middlesex and Hertfordshire in submitting after those areas had been ravaged. Again, Domesday Book shows a pattern of depreciation in the values of estates over many parts of Middlesex and north of London into Hertfordshire, as far north as Hatfield and Hoddesdon. The Abbot of St Albans also made his submission. The reports state that 'they sought pardon for any hostility they had shown (the Duke) and surrendered themselves and all their property to his mercy' and he, in his turn, graciously no doubt, 'restored all their possessions and treated them with great honour'. How magnanimous![9]

The surrender party was conducted to the Duke by the Norman Bishop of London, William, by Walter, Bishop of Hereford, Wulfstan, Bishop of Worcester and various other bishops, especially those from Lorraine, like Bishop Giso of Wells. These clerics preferred discreet submission to open rebellion and set a pattern of collaboration with the Norman. They begged Duke William 'to take the crown, saying that they were accustomed to obey a King and wished to have a King as their lord'. The Londoners sought confirmation of their existing customs and, after the Coronation, these were confirmed. Other boroughs also, in due course, sought and, for the most part, received such confirmation. So the 'Lawmen' of Stamford and Cambridge, the 'Judges' of York and Chester, (who sat in judgement over the borough courts), joined the burgesses of London and were allowed to continue in office, often with the addition of Normans to their ranks. The folkmoots and hustings of London and Southwell were also allowed to continue to meet.

Then the Aetheling Edgar, who had been 'proclaimed King by the English', now 'hesitated to take up arms and humbly submitted himself and the kingdom to William', as Orderic Vitalis puts it, and the Bastard then 'treated him as long as he lived like one of his own sons'.

So the magnates and princes of the Church came in to make their submission and men like Aesgar the Staller, the great thegn Siward son of Aethelgar and his brother Ealdred (cousins of the Shropshire thegn Eadric the Wild, a collateral descendant of the mighty Ealdorman Eadric Streona) and the West Midland thegn Thorkell of Limis (who was most likely the thegn of Arden) followed suit. Aesgar was alleged to have been offered confirmation in office, but if the offer was made it was never confirmed, possibly because he had died of his wounds.

Others who must have submitted then or some months later went on to become real collaborators, delivering their cooperation willingly and benefiting from it. The Bastard made some generous grants to those who aided his accession. But the number of laymen who prospered proved to be remarkably small. There was the Staller, Eadnoth, with lands in the West Country, another staller, Bondi, Ulf, son of Tope (a relative, possibly cousin, of Abbot Brand of Peterborough), Tovi, sheriff of Somerset, Thorkell of Arden, Eadric the sheriff of Wiltshire, Maerleswein, sheriff of Lincolnshire, Gamall son of Osbert sheriff of Yorkshire, and Saewold and Northmann the sheriffs of Oxfordshire and Suffolk. They are found witnessing King William's writs in the early years before the revolts began.

Only Eadnoth, who led the Somerset levies against the sons of Harold and was killed along with sheriff Tovi at Bleadon, and Thorkell of Arden really prospered. Thorkell acquired a great fief made up of the lands of other dispossessed Englishmen and worth over £120.

Another collaborator was Earl Tostig's factotum, Copsige, who submitted at Barking. He was said to have much favoured the King's cause and other, rebel Englishmen, tried to win him over to the revolt, unsuccessfully. Instead Duke William gave him the earldom of Osulf of Bamburgh and Osulf slew him. Other collaborators were Colesuen of Lincoln, Edward of Salisbury and Cospatric son of Arnkell. Those three, together with Thorkell, were the only survivors in 1086 with lands of baronial extent. Clearly collaboration was only rewarding for a few. There was, of course, a much larger number of men (and some women) with smaller estates who survived as the tenants and vassals of Norman Lords, a few of whom held directly of King William.

Of Aesgar the Staller the Carmen de Haestinge Proelio relates a strange tale. It maintains that the Duke had intended to bombard the defences of

London, presumably using siege weapons such as ballistae to catapult rocks against its walls, but that Aesgar avoided that by offering to negotiate a surrender, hoping to deceive the Duke, and that the deceit failed, since the Staller was in fact dismissed from office. The story reads like a confused account of a last despairing effort to resist on the part of some of the Londoners, a sort of eleventh century version of 'London can take it!'[10]

But a large party of collaborators, especially bishops, had now formed among men who were determined to accept Duke William as King and by doing so, to legitimize his rule and persuade him to observe what became known as the 'Law of King Edward', that is, English Law as it was on the day King Edward 'was alive and dead'. Orderic summed up the situation thus; 'by the grace of God, England was subdued within the space of three months and all the bishops and nobles of the realm made their peace with William, begging him to accept the crown according to English custom'.

From Berkhamstead, the Normans advanced on London, down through Stanmore, Hendon, and Hampstead to Marylebone and so, as William of Jumièges asserts, reached the central square of the City where they found, and were opposed by, a large crowd of young men and citizens, who were immediately attacked and killed. The rest of the city fell into great mourning after this massacre as the majority of Londoners now realised that resistance was futile, so the remaining citizens offered hostages and made their submission. It had been only the wealthier burgesses who had gone with the nobles and bishops to Berkhamstead. The Norman writer concluded that William became 'their most noble *conqueror*' (which might well be the first application of this word to William).[11] Of all this the Waltham Chronicle was to remark coldly that 'Londoners were accustomed to obey a king and wished to have a king as their lord'.

Submissions continued and gradually other leading men came to submit over the next few weeks, such as the other Stallers, Bondi and Eadnoth, the Breton Staller, Ralph of Norfolk, and Aethelwig, Abbot of Evesham, who proved to be staunch supporters of the Norman king, most of the sheriffs, who were retained in office for the next few years, until gradually replaced by Normans, and, of course, all but one of the bishops. (The exception was Aethelwine of Durham). So they all submitted, as the Worcester Chronicler put it, 'out of necessity after most of the damage had been done!... and swore oaths and gave hostages' to the Norman Duke.

The Bastard himself, in a most facile manner, promised to be a gracious lord to them. Yet, after the coronation, they discovered that they had to pay heavy taxes and to redeem or buy back their lands from him for considerable sums of money. One of William's most prominent characteristics turned out to be avarice. So 'renouncing allegiance to Edgar, they made peace with William,' in true quisling fashion, 'acknowledging him as their lord, and were graciously taken under his protection and reinvested with all their former offices and honours'. As Robert Burns was to say of those Scots who agreed to the Act of Union, 'such a parcel of rogues in a nation!'

Collaboration became the fashion, and many were the quislings and collaborators who crawled out of the woodwork. No doubt many thought they were doing what their predecessors had done in Cnut the Great's time (and that of his sons, Harold Harefoot and Harthacnut). Men had accepted Cnut as king and as their lord by commending themselves to him, by 'bowing' to him and swearing a hold oath, pledging to 'shun all that he shunned and love all that he loves, on condition that he will keep me as I am willing to deserve, and all that fulfil that our agreement was when I to him submitted and chose his will'. This is commendation to a lord not vassalage.

There was no question in their minds of vassal status (as understood on the Continent). They were not invested with a fief, nor did they do homage by 'immixtio manuum' with their hands between those of their lord. But, as Conqueror, William simply claimed the whole of England as his own, seeking to dispossess all but a handful of English lords in order to give lands to his own men. So, after the Coronation the English thegns found themselves required to buy back their lands, which in effect then became fiefs held in return for doing service. Everyone was now a tenant, doing service or paying rent. As Florence of Worcester pointed out, William had made a treaty with those who surrendered and they, as they thought, had made a bargain with him. But to the Norman king, commendation was a form of homage and the hold oath an oath of fealty. He regarded all English landowners as vassals who could forfeit their lands if they rebelled against him or offered any resistance to his will. Their lands could also, as fiefs, be restored to them again if they were able to make their peace with him and, after participation in a rebellion, were received back into his favour. No doubt at a price, of course. Even the bishoprics and abbeys became Crown tenants and had to provide military service. William was both King and feudal lord and England became a feudal military monarchy. This application of feudal law is clear from the terminology adopted. Land which before the Conquest had been held 'sub' (under) a lord, by commendation, and land held 'de' (from) a lord under the terms of a lease, became land held 'of' such and such a lord as vassal in return for service, whether military or other honourable service.

But the English saw themselves as placing themselves under King William's protection by taking him as their lord in the English manner, and were to be gravely disappointed when that protection did not materialize. Nonetheless, wherever the Conqueror now went men 'laid down their arms' and flocked to submit or negotiate surrender.

The Aetheling, Edgar is described as having been given wide lands but if so, he lost them by subsequent rebellion, as there is now little evidence that he held very much. He is assigned only a modest amount of land, as recorded in Domesday Book. He had a total of eight hides and one virgate worth ten pounds, in Barkway and Great Hormead in Hertfordshire, previously the property of Aesgar the Staller. But many others, particularly Churchmen, who gave their full cooperation, did indeed receive quite generous gifts of land which they had not held in King Edward's day. Others, who were not so fortunate, were to become aggrieved when the Norman King demanded payment for restoring to them the estates they no doubt considered were their own property.

The Peterborough Chronicle, commenting on William's avarice, explains what he did. He was prone to pass the land to the highest bidder. 'The king sold his land on very hard terms, as hard as he could. Then came someone else and offered more than the other had given, and the king let it go to the man who offered him more. Then came a third and offered still more and the king gave it into the hands of the man who offered him most of all.'[12]

In the end such fundamental misunderstandings and misgovernment fuelled rebellion. This arose especially because the Norman assumption now was that Duke William was the rightful heir of King Edward and that therefore all those who had fought against him, or even who had accepted Earl Harold as King, were rebellious vassals whose lands were forfeit.

The Kingdom, immediately after Hastings, was still in a strong position, in theory at least. The Aetheling and the Earls Edwin and Morcar had not been involved in the battle; London, a great city by the standards of the time, with a population of twenty or thirty thousand, could have been held against the Normans and the ships of the late King Harold could have blockaded the Channel and prevented reinforcements from reaching the Duke, but did not. Another army could have been raised, from the North and from the South West, from shires which had not yet even seen a Norman let alone been occupied. What was lacking was unity of purpose and leadership and too many were prepared to collaborate.

The collaborators favoured accepting the Duke as King and after he had accepted the offer and been crowned, he ruled with the assistance of these collaborators. The Aetheling Edgar was not a charismatic figure, as Harold had been, and men simply failed to rally round him. His claim had been set aside once already, in Harold's favour, and now the Witan of magnates and clerics turned to another strong contender, the Duke, and made the best of a bad job. William therefore retained the bishops and abbots in office, and, during his first three years as King, appointed only one bishop, the Norman Remigius, to the See of Dorchester, and only two abbots, Brand to Peterborough and Turold, a Norman, to Malmesbury. The group of mainly Lotharingian English bishops were acceptable to the Norman, inclined as they were towards reform of the Church on Continental lines. The rest of the monasteries remained in English hands for the time being, until Lanfranc, appointed by King William to replace Stigand in the See of Canterbury, began to purge the monasteries after 1072.

After the early submissions, came the coronation. William had been in no apparent hurry to be crowned while the situation was still so fluid and uncertain. Rebels were reported to be already lurking around 'to disturb the tranquillity of the realm'. The Duke would also have preferred to wait until it was safe enough for his wife, the Duchess Matilda, to be crowned queen at the same time, or so it was said. Perhaps in fact he was acting cautiously now that he was so near to the summit of his ambition. He waited, in fact, until the English themselves made the offer of the crown and then had to test the reaction of his followers.

In the end the army made up his mind for him. The Poitevin Vicomte, Aimeri de Thouars, made the decisive intervention, pointing out that it was not a matter for knights to give any opinion on such a grave matter and that it was unnecessary to discuss further something that everyone wanted done as quickly as possible. The Duke's wise counsellors, he argued, would never seek 'to raise you to the peak of monarchy if they were not assured that you were in every way suited to discharge the duties of a king'. William then bowed gracefully to public opinion thus expressed, hoping that once he had been crowned king, the English would hesitate to rebel against him and that if they did 'they would be the more easily crushed'.[13]

He now sent men into London to build him a fortress in the city and prepare for his coronation, and while that was being done, he went hunting. The coronation was set for Christmas Day, Monday 25 December and was conducted according to the established ritual which had been used for King Edward and for King Harold. It was a magnificent occasion designed to expunge from men's minds all recollection of Harold's kingship. Once crowned and anointed William would be able to demand that all freemen swear the hold oath and recognize him as king.

So, on Christmas day he was conducted solemnly in procession to Westminster Abbey, chosen to emphasize his claim to be King Edward's heir, so that he would be crowned, as it were, in the King's presence, where Archbishop Ealdred of York, an archbishop in full communion with Rome (unlike Stigand), assisted by Bishop Geoffrey of Coutances, waited for the ceremony to begin.

It followed much the same lines as that originally devised for the coronation of King Edgar by Archbishop Dunstan at Bath in 963, full of splendour and packed with political and religious meaning. The Duke prostrated himself before the High Altar, and a Te Deum was then sung. Archbishop Ealdred made a 'fitting oration' requiring the Duke to take the Coronation Oath, called 'Promissio Regis'. That was a threefold promise to provide peace for the Church, put an end to rapacity and unrighteous deeds, and give equity and mercy to his people. William had to swear the oath before Archbishop Ealdred would agree to place the crown on his head. He was then anointed with Chrism and a ring was placed on his finger. He was girded with a sword and the Crown was placed upon his head by the Archbishop. Then he was invested with the Sceptre and the Rod.

The Archbishop accompanied by Bishop Geoffrey, then presented the new King to the congregation and demanded, Ealdred in English and then Geoffrey in Norman French, whether it was their will that William should be their King, 'and all without the least hesitation shouted their joyous assent', and, at that point, the whole ceremony went wrong.

So loud and enthusiastic was the response, particularly no doubt from the Normans, that the Guards set outside the Abbey, armed and mounted, and there in case of trouble from the London citizens, concluded that some English mischief was brewing. They panicked and set fire to the houses around the Abbey. Some began to fight the fire, others began looting. The noise of the fire and the billowing smoke panicked the congregation and everyone rushed out of the Abbey pell mell, leaving King William alone and fearful, quaking in his boots. A handful of remaining clergy hastily completed the ceremonies, that is the closing prayers and a blessing from the Archbishop. Order was then gradually restored.[14]

But William was now an anointed King. His crown, specially designed for the occasion by a Greek craftsman, was of imperial style with an arch and hung with twelve pearls. It is likely that at some point in the ceremony the Laudes Regiae had been sung, with a Litany and the invocation 'To the most serene William, the great and peace giving King, crowned by God, life and victory'. It was a salutation accorded to no other ruler in Western Europe other than the King of France and the Emperor of Germany.

Whenever he was in England on the appropriate days, Christmas Day, Easter Sunday and Whitsun, King William was accustomed to hold solemn Crown-wearings, at which these Laudes were sung, so underlining the Norman King's supremacy.

William the Bastard, Duke of Normandy, had now made himself King of England. He had done so by trampling on both hereditary right (in rejecting out of hand any claims on the part of Edgar Aetheling) and on right by election, for he was not a member of King Edward's royal kin from among whom the Witan usually made its choice. Harold Godwinson, the King's brother-in-law, had been commended to the Witan by King Edward, the Witan had accepted his choice, and Harold had been duly crowned and anointed as King. William had now overthrown Harold by force and imposed himself on the remains of the Witan also by force.

There is evidence that William had a rather murky track record for this kind of behaviour. There is a distinct resemblance between the diplomatic tactics used to justify the attack on England and Duke William's earlier seizure of the County of Maine. In both cases William had taken possession of the land against the will of the inhabitants and in both cases he had done so to the extreme prejudice of the reigning family. In both cases he had used deception, contriving to give his own claim to rule a veneer of legality, in both cases alleging (after the donor was safely dead) a bequest by the reigning sovereign and alleging an act of homage to himself on the part of a rival. In both cases more than one marriage alliance was projected (but unrealised) to connect William's House to that of his rival who was thus intended to become his vassal.

King William Has
His Triumph & England Rebels:
January to December 1067

Following on from the coronation and into January 1067 the submissions of the English continued. A further round of such acts of submission was arranged at Barking, at the Abbey of St Mary. There King William had installed himself and his entourage while awaiting the completion of the fortress in London. He had retired there because of the hostility of the Londoners. Among those who submitted in person were the Earls Edwin and Morcar, which suggests that they might not have been present at the coronation.

King William now held a Council, still termed in English sources a Witan, at which, among other things, he issued a writ in favour of Abbot Brand of Peterborough which confirmed him in the possession of his lands in their entirety, that is 'the lands that his brothers and kinsmen held hereditarily and freely under King Edward'. The writ is witnessed by the Lincolnshire thegn Ulf Topesune (who was related to the Abbot), and by Archbishop Ealdred and Maerleswein, Sheriff of Lincolnshire and even William fitzOsbern. These were the 'good men' who interceded with the King on the abbot's behalf.[1]

But the major decision of that Council was the levying of a heavy geld, probably, like most of the Conqueror's gelds, at two shillings on the hide. It was found to be very burdensome especially if the Domesday record of the geld paid (in Berkshire) under King Edward can be taken to suggest the level of that King's gelds over the country as a whole. Berkshire paid only seven pence per hide, half at Christmas and half at Pentecost. But William was now demanding gelds in shillings. Furthermore men now found themselves faced with the demand that they buy back the estates which previously they had owned. Failure to pay the geld resulted in forfeiture and the land was then sold to anyone who was prepared to pay the geld due on it. (Ralf Taillebois, who became sheriff of Bedfordshire, for example, paid the 'gafol' [which the Normans called Danegeld] due on the lands of Tovi the Housecarl at Shambrook and then gave the land to his own knights as a fief. Some Normans did not deign even to go through the process of obtaining the King's grant before seizing land. Walter of Douai, for example, in Wallington Hundred in Surrey, 'held two hides of land of the King, as he says, but the men of the Hundred say they have never seen the writ or the King's commissioners who had given him seisin [possession] of it').[2]

William of Poitiers reports that shortly after the Coronation, that is, during the Christmas Witan, King William 'distributed liberally' what King Harold 'had avariciously shut up in the Royal treasury' (probably including the spoils of his victory over the Norwegians) and used it to pay his mercenary soldiers their wages, that is those who 'had helped him in the battle'. But he used most of it to enrich the Norman monasteries. To it he then added the 'gafol' or tribute he was extracting from the English, by means of a heavy geld, that is the money which, as William of Poitiers puts it, was 'that which rich men and cities everywhere offered to him'. The Chronicle complains at the same time that the King robbed the monasteries and that 'all that they (the Normans) overran, they caused to be ravaged'.

As a result, the English, or many of them, began to have second thoughts about the wisdom of accepting William's rule. The near riot and the firing of houses during the coronation was reported to have persuaded many Englishmen, 'hearing of these evil events… to decide… never again to trust the Normans' because 'they seemed to have betrayed them' and so they 'nursed their anger and bided their time to take revenge'. The Normans complained that 'neither fear nor favour could so subdue the English as to prefer peace and tranquillity to rebellion and disorders'.

King William was now an anointed king with all the power and authority that that conveyed. His anointing added force to his unctuous claim that he had received the kingdom 'by the Grace of God' (rather than by force of arms). Such royal anointing in the eleventh century was, for a time, almost recognized as an eighth sacrament of the Church. The concept, also, of the monarch as a 'priest-king' was a Norman motif. (That the hallowing of kings did not reach that status was probably due, in practice, to the quarrel between the Papacy and the Empire over Investitures.) But the aura of ecclesiastical blessing contributed to the consolidation of King William's power.[3]

This enabled him to claim the loyalty inherent in the English concept of kingship. He could tax the whole kingdom and his writ now ran through every shire. He was, in England, more truly a king than Philip I was in France. King William avowed an aim to rule as the direct heir and successor of King Edward, effectively cancelling out and annulling Harold's reign and his acts as though he had never been king. Bishops and Magnates therefore sought confirmation of any grants of land made during Harold's nine months.

For the first few years of his reign, King William affected a desire to rule with Englishmen in positions of authority, an Anglo-Norman Kingdom, though this proved to be illusory and by no means acceptable to his Norman followers, as became clear during 1067 when William, needing to return to Normandy to reaffirm his rule, left William fitzOsbern and Bishop Odo of Bayeux to govern the realm in his absence. Nor was it clear, even so, how long William intended to rule in this way. Those Englishmen whom he had left in positions of authority during his return to Normandy, found that it meant little to William's regents. Odo and fitzOsbern were given quasi-regal powers over the occupied area of the country.

Nonetheless, the claim to be King Edward's lawful successor was essential if William was ever going to be able to dispense with his dependence on the Norman army which had put him into power. He therefore retained in his service a sufficient number of leading clerics and nobles, such men as the Earls Edwin, Morcar and Waltheof, the Archbishops, Stigand and Ealdred, several Stallers, most of the bishops and abbots, especially his fervent supporters such as Bishop Giso of Wells and Abbot Aethelwig of Evesham, along with a number of leading thegns, to give enough colour to his Council for the Chronicle to continue to call it his Witan. These men continued to endorse the King's acts and to witness his charters. Several Englishmen, and most of the Bishops, were prepared to 'act in the King's interest'. It was reported that the citizens of some towns were ready to rise 'unequivocally on the Norman side against their fellow countrymen'.

Archbishop Stigand was allowed to continue to occupy the See of Canterbury, despite his anomalous ecclesiastical position, and to reap the benefits of its considerable estates until he was finally deposed, and imprisoned, by the new Archbishop, Lanfranc, and the Roman Legates in 1070. One Norman, Remigius, appointed to a bishopric (Dorchester) in England even went to Stigand for consecration, and had to make his peace with Lanfranc later.

The Household Officials, such as Robert fitzWymarc and Regenbald (a priest who had acted in fact if not in title as King Edward's chancellor), remained in office (though Regenbald was eventually replaced by the Norman Herfast, who was then granted the title of chancellor). All such men were confirmed in office, after submission, and, for the most part remained loyal.

As William had invaded with the blessing of the Pope, Alexander II, the clergy were ready to use their influence to ensure the obedience of their flocks to the new government and their example was followed by the stallers, sheriffs, geld exactors and many leading thegns. During 1067 England south and east of a line from the Wash to the Severn, but excluding the south western shires of Devon and Cornwall, became an occupied zone.

At this stage there was little sign of overt or spontaneous rebellion, although not all Englishmen can have been as ready to accept William the Bastard as King as the collaborators seeking to hold on to lands and office. There was a long standing tradition, going back to the Synod of Chelsea in 787A.D. that only fully legitimately born claimants could be recognized as king 'by the bishops and elders of the people' (that is, the Witan) and that no one should be chosen who came from an 'adulterous or incestuous procreation'. King William had won his way to the throne over the dead bodies of English thegns, yet nevertheless he claimed to be King by hereditary right and to be 'King of the English by the Grace of God'. These were powerful arguments invoking both English tradition and Christian teaching.

William of Poitiers, his secretary, put it as follows:

> If it be asked what was his hereditary title, let it be answered that a close kinship existed between King Edward and the son of Duke Robert whose paternal aunt, Emma, was the sister of Duke Richard II, the daughter of Duke Richard I and the mother of King Edward himself.

Emma, of course, had not a drop of English blood in her veins and neither did her great nephew, William, but the Archdeacon of Poitiers simply omits that inconvenient fact. Nonetheless the Normans claimed, as one source puts it, that 'William, Duke of the Normans, acquired by inheritance the English Kingdom and imposed his right by force of arms upon that rebellious realm'.[4]

So during January and early February 1067, King William simply took over the existing administrative system as it had been under King Edward, though Regenbald did draft an early Writ in which the estate at Latton and Eisey in Wiltshire was conferred upon him by King William, 'as freely as it had belonged to King Harold', a rare and early instance of recognition of Harold's status and title. It is addressed to Count Eustace of Boulogne and other office holders, the Bishops Herman, of Sherborne, and Wulfstan, of Worcester, the Stallers Eadric and Brihtric, 'and all the king's thegns in Wiltshire and in Gloucestershire', and illustrates the King's attempt to show himself ruling an Anglo-Norman realm. It was issued just before William returned to Normandy in the Spring of 1067.

But, despite this assumption of the usual royal powers and the continuation of regular administration, it is clear that the transfer of estates from English into Norman hands had already begun. Shortly after the Coronation, and before the king returned to Normandy, Geoffrey de Mandeville I received the lands of Leofsuna at Moze in Essex and 'this manor King William gave when he stayed in London'. (Geoffrey was the successor everywhere in Middlesex and Essex of Aesgar the Staller).

De Mandeville may be the Gosfrith the Portreeve who is addressed in a writ along with Bishop William of London and all the burgesses of the city early in 1067. It grants that the citizens of London shall be 'worthy of all the laws you were worthy of in the time of King Edward. And I will that every child shall be his father's heir after his father's day. And I will not suffer any man to do you wrong'.[5]

Earl Edwin of Mercia had come to an agreement with King William, or thought he had. He received authority in northern England, even over his brother Earl Morcar, with an area amounting to over one third of the kingdom, and, he believed, was promised the hand of one of King William's daughters in marriage. William was remarkably ready to dispose of his daughters in this fashion. All of the Earl's known associates were northerners, men like Copsige, who had been Earl Tostig's right hand man, Ealdred son of Uhtred of the House of Bamburgh, and others. All were men who had thrown themselves on William's mercy and begged pardon for any wrong they had done him or even thought against him. The whole atmosphere is that of a series of impromptu show trials during which King William was accustomed to demonstrate how magnanimous he could be.

The English would have been intimidated and overawed by William's reputation in war. According to Guibert, Abbot of Nogent, William had a reputation for treating those captured in war with great severity. The Abbot's father had been present at the battle of Mortemer, and had himself been a prisoner of war. He told his son that captives were treated with a degree of severity hitherto unknown in Northern France and that William was known for refusing to ransom captives and for keeping them in prison for life. One tale circulated to the effect that William ordered the limbs of at least one captive to be crushed. But in England King William more often preferred to extract money from his opponents and to confiscate their lands. In time, several of those who offended him ended up in durance vile.

King William knew full well that he would have to reward those who had fought for him so the lands of all those who fought at Hastings were confiscated and the process of the distribution of the spoils of war began. The estates were confiscated on the grounds that these men could be deemed to have committed treason by opposing in arms the rightful heir to the throne. All the lands of the Godwines were taken and incorporated into the royal demesne, so vastly enriching the monarchy.

Those who actually still lived on and farmed these lands became tenants of the Norman King, or of those to whom he was pleased to give land. Many Englishmen became impoverished in the process since they could not inherit their fathers' lands if they were forfeit to the crown. Former free men and ceorls (peasant farmers) found themselves virtually tied to the soil, no longer able to change lords at will, and lesser men, the 'bordars' and 'cottars', holders of various kinds of small holdings with or without a cottage, were gradually reduced to dependence upon their Norman lords and came to be known as 'villani' (those who lived on the 'vills' which formed the estates, the manors) and in the course of time became 'serfs' or 'villeins'.

Some of the landowners who were allowed to retain possession of their estates, even bishops and abbots, had to pay to redeem them. The Abbot of Bury St Edmunds, Baldwin (who had been King Edward's doctor) paid eleven marks of gold 'when the English redeemed their lands'. He paid a further two marks for Stoneham in Norfolk, and five pounds for Ixworth Thorpe. Abbot Aethelwig of Evesham retained thirty-six estates by 'paying the appropriate price'. Such prices ran from as low as two gold marks to as much as ten pounds in silver coinage. A number of commissioners were appointed to deal with these redemptions and collect the cash. For Norfolk, Suffolk and Essex, for example, they were, respectively, Ralph the Staller, William Bishop of London and a man called Engelric, a priest of the royal household.

Landowners who redeemed their lands were well advised to obtain writs confirming the fact, such as that issued at Windsor to the Berkshire thegn Azor or the one that commended the Bedfordshire thegn Augi to the Norman sheriff, Ralf Taillebois, 'so that he should protect him (Augi) as long as he lived'. Without such evidence a man could be deprived of his lands. So Alric Bolest of Soulbury, Buckinghamshire, was deprived 'because of King William's arrival' or Alwig son of Thorbeorht of West Tytherly, Hampshire, who was challenged because he could not produce evidence of his right of ownership as his two predecessors had been killed at Hastings. A thegn called Eadric who held a single carucate under Archbishop Stigand 'after the King came to England' had to mortgage it for one mark of gold and for seven pounds in silver in order 'to redeem himself from capture by Waleran (the Crossbowman). Osbern the Fisherman, with half a hide in Sharnbrook, which had belonged before 1066 to Tovi the Housecarl, claimed another one and a quarter virgates but 'after King William came into England he (Osbern) refused to give rent from this land and Ralph Taillebois gave the rent (in his place) and took possession of the land itself in forfeiture and gave it to a certain knight of his'. Such actions were by no means rare.[6]

Some men who had readily submitted in late 1066 or early 1067 soon regretted doing so. One example is Abbot Ealdred of Abingdon. He readily 'swore fealty to the King' as a member of the 'party that agreed to submit'. But according to the Abingdon Chronicle he changed his mind when many, including Countess Gytha, 'the mother of the slain king, changed over and joined the latter party', of those preferring exile, so the Abbot left England. When he had left, everything which he possessed was taken into the hands of the king 'since he was held to be a renegade'. That precedent allowed Henry de Ferrières to seize the lands at Kingston of a thegn called Turchil who had fallen 'in the famous battle', despite the protests of the new Abbot and despite the fact that Turchil had given the lands to the abbey long before the battle was fought. Similarly, de Ferrières added the village of Fyfield, which had belonged to Godric the Sheriff who had fallen at Hastings, to his possessions despite the fact that the lands were held by Godric on a lease of three lives. These were examples of the sort of seizure of land that went on in 1067 during the King's absence in Normandy.

Accordingly, as the Dialogue of the Exchequer was to put it, in its historical excursus explaining the origin of the 'murdrum fine', the English made a general complaint, which came to the ears of the King, that 'since they were hated by everyone and robbed by everyone, they would be forced to take service overseas'. But others resolved instead to offer resistance.[7]

The process of the distribution of lands was not recorded in writing but left to the members of the Courts of Shire and Hundred to remember what had been done. So, how were the estates of fallen thegns identified? There must have been records of estates and their possessors which were used in the collection of the geld. One example of what these lists were like has survived, though only a post-Conquest example, and that is the Northamptonshire Geld Roll. This document records the collection of a geld taken after 1068 and before 1083 (that is while Queen Matilda still lived). Though the exact date cannot be established, it can possibly be dated as from the period 1072 to 1078. This is because it mentions 'Osmund the kynges writere'. If this is Osmund the Chancellor, then the Geld Roll must be earlier than 1078 when he became Bishop of Salisbury. The document also mentions land owned by the king in Scotland, which suggests a date after 1072. There was also available to the King the oral testimony of those who had a duty to attend the courts of shire and hundred who could be made to give evidence on oath.

The expropriation of estates and the reduction in status for survivors to that of vassals holding their lands from Norman lords, must have bred resentment which led in turn to a spirit of dogged resistance, though most people preferred surrender to starvation. It was dawning on the English, from early 1067 onwards, just how insignificant they really were in the Norman scheme of things and in the sight of other rapacious foreigners upon whose support King William really relied. When this sank in, rebellion became inevitable. But defeat of the rebellions, when they came, itself led to an intensification of Norman dominance as the lands of the rebels were also confiscated and granted out to Norman lords.

The offence given to the English was compounded when Norman lords sought to marry the widows or daughters of deceased or exiled thegns. This was done to provide a somewhat spurious air of legitimacy to their possession of the lands of those they called their 'antecessors' (so claiming to be the heirs of deceased or exiled thegns). This began early and went on throughout the reigns of the three Norman Kings. Thus, Geoffrey de la Guerche married Aelfgifu, sister of the thegn Leofwine Cild son of Leofwine, with lands in Warwickshire, Leicestershire and Lincolnshire. Richard Iuvenis married the widow of Alwine, sheriff of Nottinghamshire. Bishop Wulfstan of Worcester gave the daughter of his former thegn Silgrefr of Croome to one of his own knights, together with the land she had inherited. The knight was required to support his wife's mother. Even when the land held by women, or simply seized from the dispossessed holder was 'loan-land', leased from the Church (and, in former times held variously for a period of one, two or three lives), when the time came for renewal only a niggardly amount of land was left to support widows and orphans, and the Church had to accept the new Norman lord as its tenant, usually in perpetuity.

Some women probably married more or less willingly (and might have been seen as 'consorting with the enemy'), but by no means all. Orderic comments that 'noble maidens were exposed to the insults of low-born soldiers and lamented their dishonouring by the scum of the earth'. He adds that some thought it better that they should die rather than live under such oppression.[8] Archbishop Lanfranc records in his letters that some women took refuge in nunneries and wore the veil 'not from love of the religious life but from fear of the French' in order to avoid such a marriage. Norman objections were raised to this on the grounds that the estates held by these women might fall into the hands of the Church. Lanfranc's judgement was that such women did not necessarily become nuns by taking refuge in this way and that they were free to leave the nunnery if they chose to do so. Nonetheless, the English complained that forced marriages meant the 'usurpation of the inheritances of Englishmen'. English objections rested also on a principle established in the Law Codes of earlier kings (see II Cnut. 74.), that 'no woman or maiden shall ever be forced to marry one whom she dislikes, nor be sold for money'. The Normans married English women, when they could, because it seemed to them to confer a greater degree of legitimacy on their possession of the estates of deceased Englishmen.

Most of these grants by King William seem to have been made by word of mouth and the language used was of the form, 'I will give you the land of (name). Go and take possession of it'. William of Malmesbury comments that Norman lords were told that they would therefore have 'the lordship in castle and in tower'. In strictly legal terms they were being given the same rights over their estates as their English predecessors (the Norman term was 'antecessor'); this meant, as another example shows, the grant of three manors, which had been part of the fief of Geoffrey de Mandeville, to Eudo, the King's Dapifer, that the new owner received the lands 'with the same customs with which Aesgar the Staller best held them in the reign of King Edward, that is, with sake and soke, toll and team and infangenetheof, and as Geoffrey de Mandeville most quietly held them'. The Old English jingle refers to rights of lordship and jurisdiction, rights over trading in markets and the right to hang a thief caught red-handed. The justiciable rights of an English thegn.

While he was still in England, King William laid restrictions on his soldiers regarding their conduct so that law and order might be maintained among them during his absence. They were to refrain from the use of violence against the English, especially women, and from plundering them, offences 'indulged with the consent of shameless women were forbidden.' Military courts were to deal with offenders and the judges 'were appointed to strike terror into the mass of soldiers'. He scarcely allowed his soldiers to drink in taverns because drunkenness could lead to quarrels and murder. This was a matter of enlightened self-interest on King William's part as he could not afford to relax his grip on his own men. As far as the general population was concerned, the King forbade all brigandage, thefts and other 'evil deeds' and merchants were given the freedom of harbours and highways. However, Bishop Odo and William fitzOsbern proved to be less strict than the King and relaxed discipline in his absence.

But this is not the complete picture. There were plenty of Englishmen ready to collaborate with the Norman King, especially among the clergy. The lists in Domesday Book near the beginning of each shire's account of Church lands is witness to the success of the clergy, both Bishops and Abbots, in retaining the lands of their churches. They did so by submitting to the Norman king and then serving him faithfully. Orderic accuses some of them, and laymen also, of being 'covetous of high office' and says that they 'shamelessly pandered to the King' in order to secure bishoprics and abbacies, provostships, archdeaconries and deaneries. Some did so because they were eager for the reform of the Church along continental lines. Indeed only one bishop, Aethelwine of Durham, eventually joined the ranks of the rebels. But for the nobility there was only catastrophic downfall as the defeated survivors of a lost cause, now dependent on royal favour. Some 200 King's Thegns had fallen in battle and some 2000 thegns of median rank. They were replaced by about 180 major barons and their dependent vassal knights.

As the legal successor of King Edward, and now duly crowned and anointed, King William controlled the distribution of lands by utilising English precedent and his power to ban men as outlaws while confiscating their lands. In that way he managed to avoid major disorder in the early stages of the Norman takeover. Compact blocks of estates were given to a select few, men like Bishop Odo, Robert of Mortain, or William fitzOsbern, and earldoms were granted for a time to collaborators like the Staller Ralph who held East Anglia.

The office of sheriff became more important, especially after Normans began to be made sheriffs, as they tended to treat the office as the equivalent to that of a Norman 'vicecomes' or Vicomte, and the word 'Comitatus' (County) replaced 'shire'. These men became the lynchpin of Norman administration, the vital point of contact between the shire and the central government. 'Earl' tended to become a title of honour rather than a sign of real power. So Normans began to replace Englishmen in positions of authority quite rapidly, not merely by natural wastage as the English aged and died but as a result of forfeiture for rebellion. The question which arises is that if William really was only trying to rule as King Edward's legitimate heir, why did the English rebel? They were in a better position than modern historians to judge how much King William's fair words were worth.

Early that Spring, and at the beginning of Lent (21 February), King William decided that he could delay his return to Normandy no longer. He had to go back partly in order to reassert his authority over the duchy, and partly because he now wished to enjoy a 'triumph'. He set off from Pevensey, where he received even more submissions before his departure, though no names are recorded. The ship he sailed in had white sails, signifying victory. He took with him, in order to display his superiority over the English, Archbishop Stigand, Aethelnoth, Abbot of Glastonbury, Edgar the Aetheling, and three Earls, Edwin, Morcar and Waltheof as well as many other prominent Englishmen such as Aethelnoth the Kentishman. His motive was also a practical one, these men were in effect hostages, and as they were kept in the King's company, they could not, as they might have done if left behind, foment resistance against him.[9]

Once in Normandy, he set out on a ducal and quasi royal progress through the Duchy. He went first to Caen, and more gifts were now distributed, in addition to those already sent from England, to Churches in Normandy, and the rest of France. Pope Alexander had already been sent King Harold's Banner of the Fighting Man. There were many rich gifts of gold and silver, jewelled crosses and richly ornate vestments, and jewelled books and chalices. Some of these gifts had been made during January when William had sent word to his wife Matilda, no doubt warning her to expect to see him soon.

So that Easter, 8 April, he was at Fécamp, as that was where the Dukes usually celebrated Easter. Then on the Feast of St James, 1 May, the Church of Our Lady and St Peter at Dives was consecrated in King William's presence followed on 1 July by the Abbey Church of Jumièges. 1 May had seen the issue of ordinances 'for the common good', to restore peace, that is, law and order, to Normandy. Prior Lanfranc, (whom William was probably already intending should be his Archbishop of Canterbury) was then sent to Rome to obtain a pallium, not for himself but for John of Avranches, promoted by William to be Archbishop of Rouen. Lanfranc no doubt profited from his sojourn in Rome as he returned accompanied by Roman legates.

The Norman sources congratulate William on the manner in which he restored and maintained order in Normandy, by means of Ducal Ordinances, lauding him as a wise lawgiver and firm administrator. Charters issued in Normandy boast that William was 'Duke of the Normans who acquired the Kingdom of England by war' and that he was 'Lord of Normandy, and, having been created so by hereditary right, Basileus (King) of the English'. All this propaganda is in itself revealing, suggesting that all had not been as peaceful in Normandy as he would have wished. He was in fact forced to spend over six months in the Duchy, entrenching his popularity there. In so doing he was probably demonstrating the extent of his control over England, as to hurry back would have implied a loss of confidence. From March to December England had been left to the tender mercies of Odo of Bayeux and William fitzOsbern. They were left in charge of what was already a divided kingdom, with an occupied zone and unoccupied zone, and, in the latter, government was still in the hands of English Earls who, in name at least, represented the King in some two-thirds of the country. Earl Edwin still had authority in Mercia and his brother Earl Morcar in Yorkshire (though in a sense under his brother's supervision), and various writs addressed to the Earls reveal this arrangement. Earl Waltheof had been left with his earldom centred on Huntingdonshire, and the King had sent Copsige (who had been Earl Tostig's deputy) to Northumbria. Further north, Cospatric son of Maldred still ruled from Bamburgh. But no one had been appointed to rule in the areas governed previously by Harold and his brothers, though Ralph the Staller seems to have had authority in Norfolk and Suffolk.

Bishop Odo and William fitzOsbern had been given special responsibility for the occupied areas of England, Odo for the area south of the Thames, fitzOsbern for those shires north of the Thames between Herefordshire and Hertfordshire together with the whole of East Anglia. Dover was left under the watchful eye of Hugh de Montfort, much, it would seem, to the chagrin of Count Eustace of Boulogne. Hastings was held by Humphrey de Tilleul, a brother-in-law of the powerful Norman magnate Hugh de Grantmesnil. Hugh's son, Robert, who had been in England at King Edward's court before the conquest, sent from Normandy to complete his education, was to become a castellan and is known as Robert of Rhuddlan. Under King Edward he had, it was believed, been the king's 'armiger' or squire, or more likely only his personal page. Hugh de Grantmesnil himself was given charge of Winchester and Hampshire. So, even where English stallers and sheriffs were still in office, they found themselves under the supervision of Norman lords. The new Abbot of Evesham, Aethelwig, was to rise high in William's favour and was probably already charged with some supervisory powers in the West Midlands.

So, having made, as he thought, suitable arrangements for the government of the conquered English during his absence, King William went off to Normandy. He was there well before Easter of 1067 (8 April) and remained there for the next seven months. Some Norman lords also now chose to return home, some perhaps travelling with the King. A few of them were replaced by other Norman lords, such as Roger of Montgomery. Among those who went home were Gilbert of Auffray and the Poitevin lord, Aimeri de Thouars. Casualties at Hastings had been heavy and not all of the returnees were easily replaced, so King William had already begun to enlist Englishmen in his service for military duties.

During the King's absence, castle building continued. London saw not only work on the royal castle (the Tower, which was eventually rebuilt in stone later in the reign) but one by the river, Baynard's castle, and another to the north, well outside the city, at Montfichet. But as soon as King William was safely overseas, fitzOsbern saw to it that castles were multiplied, a policy which must have had the King's endorsement. fitzOsbern had been 'set up… in the marches with Walter de Lacy and other powerful warriors, to fight the bellicose Welsh', as Orderic reports. A royal castle was built at Winchester and fitzOsbern himself went on to build one at Norwich and, until he left England in 1071, others all along the Welsh border at Berkeley, Chepstow, Clifford, Monmouth and Wigmore, while Ewias Harold (named for the son of Earl Ralph of Hereford) was rebuilt. Elsewhere, other Norman lords were busily building their own castles. The Chronicle complained bitterly that the Normans now 'castles built here far and wide throughout this country and distressed the wretched folk, and always afterwards it grew much worse. May the end be good when God wills!' The wretched folk were distressed not only because of the oppressive behaviour of the garrisons of these castles but because they were pressed into service to build them. This burden was regarded as particularly shameful and now the English 'groaned aloud for their lost liberty'.[10]

Quite rapidly the castles spread through south eastern England until all the major river estuaries of Sussex were controlled by them. They became the centres of 'castleries', known there as 'Rapes', which controlled a sphere of influence around each castle which contributed to its maintenance. They contained planned enfeofments to support the knights. Ships were stationed in the Channel to provide secure lines of communication between English castleries and the lands of their Norman holders in the duchy.

Most of these arrangements were made by verbal directions from King William so that the exact manner in which estates were distributed and authority devolved remains virtually undocumented. Few Writs and even fewer Charters have survived recording the King's grants of fiefs. Domesday Book testifies that although some estates were granted 'by the King's writ and seal', others were relayed by the King's Officers rather than in writing. But it is also recorded that in many places lands were seized and the jurors stated that they had never seen either writ or seal nor heard the word of the King's officer.

King William, having returned to Normandy, then sent chosen men back to England and, as William of Poitiers testifies, 'in the castles he placed capable custodians, brought over from France, in whose loyalty no less than their ability he trusted, together with large numbers of horse and foot'. To these men it is said that the King 'distributed rich fiefs amongst them, in return for which they would willingly undertake hardships and dangers' (an indication, perhaps, that everything in England was not as calm as it appeared to be on the surface). As William of Malmesbury wrote, King William's men were told that they would 'have lordship in castle and in tower'. And so the indelible imprint of the Norman conquest was placed upon the land.

Bishop Odo and Earl William fitzOsbern are described as loyal servants of their master, King William, and as being, in their turn, loyally served by their castellans. But some sources tell a different tale and complain of oppression and lack of discipline. Orderic Vitalis contrasts King William's own rule with that of his haughty deputies who despised his strict orders and proceeded to tyrannize the people. They allowed women and property to be attacked by their followers and made no attempt to provide any redress. These were the kinds of evil which William, as Duke, had tried so hard to stamp out in Normandy itself. Orderic was so dismayed that he quite deliberately omits most of William of Poitiers' panegyrics on King William when drawing on his writings as a source, and prefers to substitute his own version of events.

The King's two governors simply held down the areas committed to them by force rather than guile. Some of their men, as Orderic states, 'governed their people well; others irresponsibly heaped heavy burdens on them' and so the English 'groaned under the Norman yoke', suffering the oppression of proud lords who ignored King William's injunctions. 'Petty men in charge of local castles oppressed the local inhabitants and heaped shameful burdens on them'. Bishop Odo and William fitzOsbern, as Orderic relates, 'swollen with pride would not deign to hear the reasonable pleas of the English or give them impartial judgements. When their men-at-arms were guilty of plunder or rape, they protected them by force and visited their wrath all the more violently upon those who complained of the cruel wrongs they suffered'. So the Normans became over-wealthy on the spoils garnered by others, arrogantly abused their authority and 'mercilessly slaughtered the native people like the Scourge of God'. This led the English to plot ceaselessly to find ways of shaking off this unaccustomed and intolerable yoke.[11]

Part of the problem, as far as the English were concerned, was that even at this early date, despite the tendency of many magnates to retain large numbers of knights (and the attendant men-at-arms) in their households, for their own protection, some lords began parcelling out their estates, scattered as many of them were into anything up to seven shires, into fiefs with which to endow those who had served them well. These were to be held by 'knight service', that is military service as and when the lord, or his lord, the King, required it. Lesser men of lower social status might receive fiefs held by 'sergeanty', a tenure suitable for those who were not eligible to become knights.

An example of the process is the action of Abbot Aethelhelm of Abingdon. He gave lands as manors to be held of the Church of Abingdon and 'in each case declared what would be the obligations involved in its tenure', using for the purpose 'the estates which had been held by men called thegns who had been killed in the battle of Hastings'.[12]

During the King's absence the first stirrings of resistance began to manifest themselves in an area where Norman rule had not yet been fully established. Before leaving for Normandy, the King had appointed Copsige, a former associate of Earl Tostig, to take control of furthest Northumbria (William clearly had little confidence in Earl Morcar). Copsige had readily collaborated and is said to have been 'entirely favourable to the King and supported his cause'. This appointment had convinced the Northumbrians that they could not expect any better treatment from King William than they had received from Earl Tostig. They believed, rightly, that Copsige had been sent to collect the geld ordered at the Christmas Court which Copsige had most likely claimed he knew how to collect. He had, perhaps, offered to 'farm' the tax, that is to guarantee the collection of the amount required, intending in fact to collect as much more as he could which he would keep for himself. The geld demanded was at least two shillings on the hide, possibly even more. But Copsige had no direct Norman support in his post, he was expected to be able to rely on his own contacts in the area. His supporters in the north tried to win him over 'to desert the foreigners', but when that failed they 'stirred up the people of the province against him'. Rashly, he immediately dispossessed Osulf of Bamburgh (against whom Copsige seems to have had his own vendetta, blaming him as one of those responsible for driving out Earl Tostig), and Osulf, naturally, gathered together a band of supporters (regarded by the Normans as mere outlaws). Five weeks after King William had made the appointment, Copsige, while feasting at Newburn, on the Tyne, was besieged in his own house by Osulf and his band. Copsige managed to escape and sought refuge in a church but Osulf set fire to it. Copsige was beheaded and his companions were cut down and killed as they vainly tried to escape from the flames, 11 March 1067.[13]

Naturally, this had no effect on Norman control of southern England. There it was the misgovernment of the King's governors which provoked stirrings of revolt, first in Herefordshire, then in Kent, areas, perhaps, where the oppression was at its worst.

Herefordshire saw a reaction from the Welsh, whose rulers Bleddyn and Rhiwallon had, in 1066, accepted King Harold's overlordship. The most powerful thegn in the area, Eadric, surnamed 'the Wild', had never fully submitted to the Normans (Orderic thought he had, but his chronology is faulty), and was probably only paying lip service to Norman dominance. Eadric was provoked into action because the Norman lords in the area, survivors from the reign of King Edward, Richard fitzScrob and Osbern fitzRichard, had been making inroads into his territories. The thegn therefore, following the example of Earl Aelfgar of Mercia in the 1050s, allied himself with the Welsh and, round about 15 August, advanced into

England against the Normans at the head of his own men and a Welsh army. They penetrated as far as the River Lugg near Leominster (a familiar pattern for Welsh incursions into England, at a point where Offa's Dyke runs out) and then besieged the garrison of Hereford Castle. Honour satisfied, Eadric then withdrew, having made his point. But, significantly, he had not been able to overwhelm the castles themselves. Nonetheless, the Norman knights had retreated to their castles until the storm had passed, unable to cope with the lightly armed mounted men from the Welsh hills. Heavy cavalry, as used by the Normans, was not entirely suited to more mountainous areas and so no attempt was made to pursue Eadric and his men back into the hills.

Kent was a different matter altogether. There the insurgents sought the cooperation and aid of Count Eustace of Boulogne (perhaps on the grounds that the devil you know is better than the one you don't). They organized an attack on Dover Castle and its surrounding burh. The Count was himself at odds with King William, because, in his own opinion at least, he had not been rewarded as fully as he had expected to be and because he was disappointed not to have been given charge of Dover, (as that would have given him control of both ends of a Channel crossing route).

It was arranged that he should bring a fleet to Dover, full of armed men, and make himself master of the Castle. The insurgency took advantage of the fact that both Bishop Odo and Hugh de Montfort (the greatest lay Norman lord in the shire) were absent from Kent, dealing with some problem north of the Thames. Eustace made a successful landing and was duly joined by the Kentishmen. They probably hoped that their action would attract spontaneous support and reinforcements from elsewhere in England, if they could only make the siege last more than a few days. But the garrison put up stiffer resistance than had been expected and even the citizens of Dover itself joined in against the attackers (there was no love lost between them and Count Eustace).[14]

The Count's nerve failed him and he retreated towards his ships. The garrison counter-attacked and Eustace jumped to the conclusion that Bishop Odo or de Montfort had returned unexpectedly. He and his men fled at the very mention of Odo's name, with heavy losses, many men falling from the cliffs. Eustace escaped, rather ignominiously, by ship and a 'nepos' (either an actual nephew, son or other male relative) of his was captured. Bishop Odo and Hugh de Montfort returned almost simultaneously and completed the mopping up of the rebellion.

In the background, behind all these events, the English exiles, especially those who had fled to Flanders or Denmark, were seeking help from overseas, either from the Danish King, Swein Estrithson, or from the German

Emperor. Certainly the late King Edward's former Steersman, Eadric, went to Denmark, as did other prominent Englishmen, seeking Danish assistance for the recovery of their lands. But King Swein preferred to watch the development of events, offering only fair words, and so lost his chance to make a decisive intervention.

Then, unfortunately for the Northumbrians, Osulf, the slayer of Copsige, by now calling himself Earl, was himself slain by a robber.

Everything so far had been successfully handled for the King by his representatives, Bishop Odo of Bayeux and William fitzOsbern. But there were ominous stirrings in the West Country where disaffected burgesses, mainly at Exeter, were preparing widespread resistance and there were attempts to form a league of West Country towns to oppose the extension of Norman power.

It was now that King William finally chose to return from Normandy on St Nicholas' Day, 6 December, 1067. He arrived at Winchelsea from Dieppe on the very day that Canterbury Christ Church burnt down. (Whether that had been an accident, such fires were frequent in a period when so many church buildings were made mainly of wood and candles and lamps were the only source of illumination, or whether it was a 'happy accident', allowing the construction of the Romanesque cathedral, remains uncertain.) Upon his return, King William was, it was said, 'at great pains to appease everyone' and he was especially gracious in his conduct at Court towards the English collaborators.

The King proceeded to hold a mid-winter Council at which various rebels were put on trial, even, in his absence, Count Eustace. (He was able to win his way back into King William's favour by the end of 1068, partly by means of 'beneficia', that is 'gifts' intended to appease the King's wrath). It was possibly during this Council that King William gave the bishopric of Dorchester to Remigius of Fécamp who was then consecrated bishop by Archbishop Stigand, despite the doubts about the validity of his position as archbishop, probable indication that King William was not yet ready to dispense with Stigand's services. Stigand still possessed Episcopal powers and could validly perform such a consecration, what he lacked was jurisdiction, the canonical right to exercise those powers. Stigand had been deprived of canonical jurisdiction by every Pope since 1052, other than Benedict X who had been rejected by the Cardinals as an anti-pope.

Now, the deaths of Copsige and Osulf had left the extreme north, that part of Northumbria called Bernicia, without any kind of governor. The position of Earl was vacant so it was now filled by Cospatric son of Maldred, of the House of Bamburgh, a descendant through Earl Uhtred of Earl Waltheof I.

Cospatric simply bought the earldom from King William at the Christmas Court, no doubt arguing also that he could ensure the collection of the geld. In later years he was to be a frequent visitor to King William's Court until he became involved in rebellion. The Earl was to end up in comfortable exile at the court of King Malcolm, as Earl of Dunbar.

English rebels were still desperately negotiating with King Swein, hoping to persuade him to invade, knowing instinctively that the Normans were unlikely to be driven out solely by means of an English insurrection, unless they had outside help. Thus, in 1068, Abbot Aethelsige of St Augustine's, Canterbury, would take gifts to Denmark and remain there for two years before returning to England, trying out his powers of persuasion on the Danish King. Other negotiators also tried to interest the powerful Archbishop Adalbert of Bremen, hoping he would bring his influence to bear on King Swein. But the Danish King made no attempt to intervene until 1070, by which time it was too late to be effective, and then did so only in order to profit from a Danish incursion into England. As for Abbot Aethelsige, he found that he had lost the support of his monks as well as that of King William and was outlawed in 1070, fleeing once more to Denmark. His monks resented the loss of Abbey lands to the Normans and blamed their Abbot for the loss. Any attempt by the Abbot to resist the alienation of lands would have irritated King William and contributed to his outlawry. He did, rather strangely, win his way back into the King's favour, in 1080, and was allowed back on condition that he retired to Ramsey Abbey rather than St Augustine's.[15]

Meanwhile, in the South West, particularly Devon and Cornwall, no official submissions had yet been made. The area had been a stronghold of the Godwinson family, though few men from there had fought at Hastings, possibly because the battle was fought and lost long before they could respond to King Harold's summons. Earl Godwine's widow, Countess Gytha, was at Exeter, which was at that time a city almost on a par with London, Winchester and York.[16]

The citizens had spent most of 1067 preparing resistance. They had strengthened the Walls and levied soldiers from neighbouring areas. Even foreign traders were contacted for their support and a sort of federation of western burhs began to emerge, as the Exeter men urged others to 'combine with them and fight with all their strength against the foreign king', although, in the end, it came to nothing. When King William arrived in the area, early in 1068, thegns of the shire of Dorset had submitted without protest, an example soon followed by towns further west. But Exeter had refused any submission, sending word to the King that the city would render the same dues and services as it had given in King Edward's time but refusing to admit the Norman King within its walls. The King decided that this could not be tolerated and summoned his forces to impose Norman rule on Exeter. The King set out to enforce his authority and everywhere he went, every city and all places where he had placed garrisons, were expected to obey his will. But he was aware that the marches, the border areas of his Kingdom, were still barbarous, from a Norman perspective.

8

The First Stirrings of Revolt:
February to December 1068

Late in 1067, on 6 December, King William had returned to England. He travelled from the mouth of the River Dieppe near Arques, propelled by a southerly wind, leaving during the first watch of a bitter night. He had a rough crossing but successfully reached Winchelsea the next morning, largely in order to deal with the situation resulting from the oppressive behaviour and misgovernment of his regents, William fitzOsbern and Bishop Odo of Bayeux. Orderic Vitalis and William of Jumièges reported that the King had heard 'evil news' which 'hinted that the Normans were to be massacred by the hostile English' who would be supported by the Danes and other barbarous people. There was to be, allegedly, a surprise attack during Lent (in 1068) while the Normans were doing penance in Church. There had certainly been the spontaneous decision by a number of leading citizens of Exeter to defy the Norman king.[1]

At Exeter the citizens were by no means unanimous in their opposition to Norman rule. Two parties had formed, one of those who preferred submission over defiance and the other, perhaps encouraged by the household and followers of Countess Gytha, widow of Earl Godwine, seeking to resist, possibly thinking that it was now too late to back down in that resistance. In December 1067 the party of resistance threw down the gauntlet, closed the gates of the city and prepared to defy the King. They refused point blank to swear fealty to King William, (although other towns further east had done so) and would promise only to render the same dues as they had rendered to King Edward, determined to maintain their ancient rights. Their resistance could well have been provoked by the demand for a heavy geld early in 1067. Domesday Book records that one of the privileges of Exeter under King Edward had been that they did not pay geld 'except when London, York and Winchester paid geld and that was half a mark of silver for the use of the thegns'.

The King arrived in the vicinity of Exeter early in 1068, having celebrated Christmas in London where he had been 'gracious to English bishops and lay lords... at great pains to appease everyone'. He had readily granted favours that were asked for and Orderic acidly remarks that such favours 'often bring back to the fold persons whose loyalty is doubtful'. As for the Exeter men, they said; 'We will neither swear fealty nor admit (the king) within our walls, but we will pay tribute to him according to ancient custom'. King William, filled with rage, replied that he was not accustomed to accept subjects on such terms and took steps to prepare his assault.[2]

That, however, had been only one part of the King's manoeuvres. While he had been in Normandy, a Penitential Ordinance had been issued, at an Easter Court, laying down penances for Norman soldiers who had killed or injured men during the invasion. Anyone who knew he had killed at Hastings had to do one year's penance for each victim. If he did not know how many he had killed, then a man had to do penance one day a week for life or he could commute this by building a church. That probably explains the proliferation of 'estate' churches built during King William's reign. The Ordinance had divided the campaign into three phases. The first took in the period from the initial landing to the end of the battle at Hastings, the second covered the time from then until the Coronation and the third applied to the period after William became king.

The first two were defined as periods of public war and the penalties applied were correspondingly reduced as killing or wounding opponents in public war was a less serious sin. The third period, after the coronation, was not one of public war and so the penalties were more severe unless, and this is striking, unless the victims were caught resisting the King, when the inference was that these were rebels against lawful royal authority, just as those who had fought against William before the coronation, at Hastings, had been rebels opposing King Edward's lawful heir! William of Poitiers actually says that William had 'laid low the people opposed to him which, rebelling against him, its king, deserved death'. The effect of this was to make it plain that only those who survived to submit and redeem their lands were legitimate citizens and all those who resisted were rebels who accordingly forfeited all their property and whose heirs also lost everything. The degree of casuistry in this line of argument is quite staggering. The message was clear, collaborate or lose everything. Yet the Norman had hastened to have himself crowned because 'when he had begun to reign, he would find it easier to put down anyone who dared to rebel against him' and that also implies the claim that he had been dealing with a rebellion even when he had not yet been crowned. No wonder some at Exeter wanted to offer submission.[3]

William set out from London early in January, 1068, and the towns through which he passed, on what was effectively a royal progress towards the South West of England, readily submitted. His march affected Dorchester and Bridport, which were ruined. Both towns could well have been members of the Exeter League. Abbot Godric of Winchcombe saw his monastery plundered while he himself was imprisoned at Gloucester and deprived of his abbacy. The Abbey was placed under the supervision of Abbot Aethelwig of Evesham for the next three years until a Norman abbot could be appointed.

Yet King William still warned his Normans everywhere 'never to relax for a minute' because the men living in the border areas of England had only obeyed even King Edward 'when it suited their ends'. His plan was to march on Exeter and besiege it. Eleventh-century warfare in North West Europe usually took the form of a series of sieges and the Normans were well versed in such warfare with the use of siege engines such as towers and ballistae. One such engine in use was the 'tormentum', a form of catapult.

Once at Exeter, the King rode nearer with an escort of 500 knights to survey the ground and examine the fortifications in order to learn what measures the enemy had taken to prepare for his attack. Then William's men, eager to impress their lord, launched a series of over-hasty assaults which resulted in heavy casualties. They also suffered from the weather in a harsher than usual winter. The King then launched a relentless assault in order to drive the citizens from the ramparts and undermine the walls. Yet the defenders remained optimistic and at one point during the siege one of the defending soldiers 'mooned' at the Norman attackers, dropping his trousers and baring his buttocks.

But all was not well within the town. A peace-seeking party had developed among the property-owning thegns, who feared confiscation of their houses and their lands outside the town. So this more pliant party wanted to sue for peace and actually surrendered hostages demanded by the Norman. The Bastard now ordered one of them to be blinded and hanged another within sight of the walls. This example of Norman ferocity served only to stiffen the resistance of the insurgents. King William made his usual dispositions, surrounding the city, and a siege of eighteen days followed.

However, after almost three weeks those in favour of submission prevailed over those who wished to resist. Terms for a surrender were sought and the gates were thrown open to the King. Rather surprisingly, and possibly indicative of a desire on William's part still to win over as many of the English as he could, the King decided to put on a display of magnanimity. He did this despite receiving reports of how the citizens had ill-treated and insulted some of his knights who had been driven by a storm to take refuge in the harbour. His motive might have been that clemency would encourage other towns further west to submit. So, the burgesses were permitted to render exactly the same dues and services as they had previously done and there were no further punishments.[4]

Direct evidence is lacking, but, judging from King William's tactics on other occasions, it could be that he had let it be known that he would accept the traditional dues and that there would be no reprisals if surrender was prompt. But he did impose direct Norman rule. A castle, known as Rougemont (of which the Gateway still stands), was built and forty-eight houses, as Domesday Book records, were destroyed 'since the king came to England' to make way for it. The castle occupied the northern angle of the Roman city walls. It was placed under Baldwin de Meules, (brother of Richard fitzGilbert and a son of Gilbert, Count of Brionne,) who received one third of the annual render of eighteen pounds. For a time Baldwin was Sheriff of Devon and ruled the whole Cornish peninsula which, up to that moment, had never even seen a Norman soldier. King William's magnanimity paid off because the men of Exeter even fought to defend the city and the castle against their own fellow countrymen when it was attacked by men supporting the Sons of Harold later in the year. The whole of Devon submitted without a struggle and a march through Cornwall, which also gave no resistance, satisfied William's pride. The towns of Gloucester and Bristol also submitted at this time. Countess Gytha and the 'wives of other good men' escaped (perhaps she was allowed to do so in order to remove an awkward prisoner) and took refuge with her close household on the Isle of Flatholme in the Bristol Channel. Her flight seems to bear out the idea of her complicity in fomenting opposition. But fear spread throughout England and, at about this time, Abbot Ecgfrith of St Albans took refuge at Ely. The Liber Eliensis seems to suggest that Archbishop Stigand was also at Ely at this time and deposited some of his treasure there. It also looks as though Oxford had fallen into Norman hands after a brief resistance at much the same time.

King William had now taken effective control of the Western region as the subsequent failure at other attempts at rebellion in the south west demonstrates. The attempt to form a league of towns to resist the King, together with the involvement of Countess Gytha and the subsequent raids by Harold's sons, could suggest that all this might have been intended as a part of a more general uprising, but if so, then Exeter had acted alone and too soon. The burgesses might have been expecting outside support, especially as the Sons of Harold, (Godwine, Edmund and Magnus, together with Tostig the son of Swein Godwinson) arrived in the summer of 1068 with a fleet and armed men provided by their father's former ally, King Diarmaid Mac Mael n'Ambo, of Dublin and Leinster.

But for the moment, King William was satisfied that he had repressed the stirrings of revolt and proceeded to hold his Easter Court at Winchester on 23 March (which is as early as Easter can be) where he decided to bring his wife, Matilda, to England so that she could be crowned Queen. Accordingly, Matilda arrived and was duly crowned and anointed as Queen at Westminster at Whitsun on 11 May. King William also held a solemn crown-wearing to underline his supremacy. Such ritual demonstrations of the power and prestige of his monarchy were held, 'as often as he was in England' (which was not that often) and, allegedly, by turns at each of the three festivals, Christmas, Easter and Pentecost, at Gloucester, Winchester and Westminster. This could well have been the original intention, but in fact there is little evidence that William did so at all regularly and, on at least one occasion, he held his crown wearing at York.

These were, however, spectacular affairs, with the King robed in splendour, enthroned with all royal regalia, surrounded by Archbishops, Bishops and Abbots and his great Officers of State (as twelfth-century writers saw them). It was on one of these occasions, possibly shortly after Lanfranc had become Archbishop of Canterbury, that a 'silly cleric', awestruck and overcome, cried out 'Behold, I see God! Behold, I see God!', only for the Archbishop to rebuke him publicly and order him to be flogged, presumably for blasphemy. King William's reaction is not recorded though he permitted the flogging.[5]

Despite the splendour of King William's celebration of his wife's coronation, his hubris brought with it an attendant nemesis. He had assumed that it was now safe to bring Matilda to England and have her crowned. The ceremony had been attended by many prominent Englishmen, yet now it was almost immediately followed by a series of rebellions which bade fair to disrupt the King's control over his kingdom had he not responded decisively. In the end they brought about only the loss of all political authority and influence for the remnants of the English nobility.

Shortly after the queen's coronation the Normans became aware of rising discontent in Mercia and Northumbria. The Worcester Chronicle reports that 'then the King was informed that the men of the North were gathered together and meant to make a stand against him if he came'. Resistance had begun to coalesce around Earl Edwin (who seems to have absented himself from the Queen's coronation). Earl Edwin now felt himself threatened by the building of castles within his Earldom, especially along the Welsh border where a chain of castles had been or was being constructed by William fitzOsbern and others. He could have felt slighted by the authority gradually being acquired by the collaborator, Abbot Aethelwig of Evesham. King William made more and more use of this able and intelligent cleric, granting him 'baillia et justicia' (power of administration and jurisdiction) over seven shires, three of which lay within the boundaries of Mercia. Orderic Vitalis says that after his formal submission at Barking, Earl Edwin had been given authority over much of northern England and that he had been promised the hand of one of King William's daughters in marriage, yet others had been given power in Mercia and there was no sign of any marriage. Orderic says that this was because the King had listened to 'dishonest counsels' from 'envious and greedy followers' and so had not kept his promises and in fact had 'withheld the maiden', his daughter and so prevented the marriage. The Mercian Earl was also under increasing pressure from the appointment of Roger of Montgomery to the Earldom of Shrewsbury. Roger is named 'Comes', that is 'Earl' in a writ issued at Whitsun 1068. In contrast Earl Waltheof and Earl Edwin are only named as 'Duces', implying a distinction between Norman and English 'Earls'. Montgomery's castle at Shrewsbury was certainly built by 1068. So the Mercian Earl's patience had run out.[6]

Accordingly, Earl Edwin now allied himself with the Welsh prince Bleddyn of Gwynedd (just as his father, Earl Aelfgar, had allied with Grufydd ap Lewellyn in King Edward's reign). Prince Bleddyn was also the ally of the powerful Shropshire thegn, Eadric the Wild, who also approved of further resistance. The Earl therefore gathered his forces and contemplated open rebellion.

But the real centre of disaffection lay in Northumbria. That province and its nobility had not yet fully submitted to the Conqueror. They had, as yet, seen no Norman troops and thought, like the burgesses of Exeter, that they could bargain with William the Bastard in the same manner as they had struck a bargain with King Edward in 1065. But the Conqueror's response was very different. He had no Earl Harold at his side to calm his wrath and advise conciliation. He therefore gathered his forces once more and set out northwards from Winchester into Mercia, making a military rather than a royal progress, building castles as he marched north.

First he built the motte and bailey at Warwick, on the bluff overlooking the Avon and within the walls of the borough. The motte, known locally as 'Aethelfleda's Mound (since she, sister of King Edward the Elder, had built the burh at Warwick), still stands within the bailey of Warwick Castle. Henry of Beaumont was left there, with a garrison, as castellan, and the King went on towards Nottingham. His march took him via Leicester (where a second castle might have been begun, though the chronicle does not mention it) and once at Nottingham the King built a castle there as well.

This unexpectedly swift and determined advance shocked the Mercians into submission and Earl Edwin, with his brother Earl Morcar, hastily disbanded their forces and faded away into the countryside. The building of a castle at Warwick had been enough to intimidate the Mercians.

At Nottingham the King left another Norman castellan, William Peverel and it is possible that it was at this time that Hugh de Grantmesnil took control of Leicestershire. King William then advanced to York where he entered the city unopposed as all signs of rebellion had melted away before him. Led by a prominent Yorkshire thegn, Archil, the leading thegns made peace and submitted, Archil's son being surrendered as a hostage. The King built his first castle at York, on the site of what is now Clifford's Tower, and left Richard fitzRichard in charge as castellan with a garrison of 500 knights (a sign that the threat had been more serious than the sources admit) and appointing William Malet as Sheriff of Yorkshire. King William made gifts to the Abbey Church of St John of Beverley, on his way south, possibly in thanksgiving for his swift success.

According to Geoffrey Gaimar, (who had access to Lincolnshire sources of information) the King sent Archbishop Ealdred to York with authority to offer men safe-conduct and the promise of confirmation of their inherited property if they would come over to the King and submit, but what the Bastard actually did when they submitted was to imprison them and give away their land. The King had demanded hostages, including Cospatric the son of Arnkell. Forfeiture and imprisonment was still the punishment for rebellion. Nor were the Normans too nice about the way in which these confiscations were carried out.

It was easy enough to ascertain the holdings of wealthy thegns by consulting the shire courts and sheriffs or through special commissioners who were appointed to require the courts to identify such lands. No doubt collaborating bishops, abbots or stallers were ready to give evidence. But Domesday Book reveals that due process was not always followed. William Malet, who acquired land in Holderness, was reported by the jurors of the shire court (in 1086) to have acted illegally. They said that 'they saw him having and holding (certain estates) but they have not seen the King's writ or seal for them' and at Northorpe in Yorkshire, a certain Richard de Neville held land from Abbot Turold of Peterborough (appointed in 1069) 'but he did not have a livery officer for it'.[7]

The threat to Mercia had also been far more serious than the sources reveal since they were more concerned to report what happened in Yorkshire. The Earls had not dared to offer battle (remembering perhaps how they had suffered at the hands of King Harald Hardrada) and their men too were unwilling 'to face the doubtful issue of battle'. So they wisely preferred peace to war, seeking the King's grace and favour again later in the year and apparently receiving it although King William seems to have required their permanent attendance at court. William of Malmesbury, however, reports that some time later the Earls had 'disturbed the woods with secret robberies' rather than meet the King in open battle.

Returning south the King built a chain of castles at Lincoln, Cambridge and Huntingdon, something which must have both enraged and intimidated the Fenmen. Lincoln castle was probably given to Turold of Lincoln who is recorded as sheriff later in the 1070s. William also demanded hostages from 'all of Lindsey' (an area of North Lincolnshire close to the River Humber). Such castle building always had a salutary effect on King William's opponents, from the Norman standpoint at least. The castles provided bases for conrois of knights, supported by men-at-arms and archers, and dominated the countryside for miles around. It is likely that the building of a castle at Lincoln led to the appointment of Ivo Taillebois as sheriff of Lincolnshire as a replacement for Maerleswein. Little resistance had been offered although the borough of Torksey was, at some time, laid waste, reducing the number of burgesses there from 212 to 102 and destroying 111 houses, which does look like punishment inflicted, in 1068. At Cambridge the castle occupied the site of twenty-five houses standing in their own grounds, causing the citizens to move down the hill and across the river to create a new town well away from the Norman garrison.

At York the Norman garrison went further than elsewhere in ensuring their safety. The Coppergate area of the City was flooded, by damming the river Foss, so creating a moat for the castle. But, despite the apparent success of the campaign, the Normans had not in fact destroyed their enemy's military strength. The Northumbrians had merely carried out their traditional strategy, melting away before the foe into the northern wilderness from which they could launch guerrilla attacks and ambushes. Such tactics had not yet proved unworkable and King William had therefore achieved only a partial success.

Orderic Vitalis, in his account of these events, argues that the whole situation had been far more menacing than the succinct summaries provided by the Anglo-Saxon Chroniclers would suggest. He calls it a 'fierce insurrection' caused by King William's failure to keep his word to the English, to provide good government and maintain the law of King Edward. He further insists that large numbers of leading men in England and in Wales had met together to complain to each other about Norman injustice and tyranny and to demand what should be done about it. He says that there was a general outcry among the English against Norman rule, which he calls 'the Norman yoke'. It was decided to send out appeals to 'all corners of Albion' (as Orderic rather floridly puts it), that is, to the whole Island of Britain, inciting men to act, openly or in secret, against the enemy and prayers were said in Churches for the success of the rising. Men were being urged to 'recover their former liberty and bind themselves by weighty oaths against the Normans'. Even William of Jumièges talks of the existence of a general conspiracy, though he, as usual, gives no date for it. Appeals were also made to urge King Swein Estrithson of Denmark to 'claim the throne of his ancestors' (the Danish Kings Cnut, Harold Harefoot and Harthacnut).[8]

But the action, when it came, proved to be premature. The Chronicle makes out that the rising of 1068 was a mainly Northumbrian affair, playing down the role of Earl Edwin (the Worcester Chronicle is a Mercian work) and implies that his actions only happened to coincide with those of the Northumbrians. It is likely the Earl Cospatric, then ruling Northumbria, had been partly to blame since he neither made any real attempt to govern his new earldom nor to discourage disaffection. Nor did he make any attempt to build a real coalition against the Normans. In fact, the root of the trouble in the North could have been a reaction to the demand for a more formal act of submission, possibly presented to them at York by Archbishop Ealdred, as Geoffrey Gaimar claims, and Orderic records that the citizens of York showed no respect for the Archbishop when he 'tried to appease them'. But Archbishop Ealdred and some other bishops did prefer collaboration with the Normans, they acted 'in the King's interests' in conjunction with leading citizens in the towns and native lords 'of wealth and good name' and they, together with many of the common people, were ready to act unequivocally on the Norman side against their fellow countrymen, as the Staller Eadnoth did in Somerset.

It is likely that Edgar, the Aetheling, was, in some sense, the figurehead of the rising, as he was to be again in 1069, supported by the exiled Sheriff of Lincolnshire, Maerleswein, and Earl Cospatric who had participated on a whim, acting impulsively without forethought as to the consequences. Just as Cospatric ought to have taken decisive action he allowed himself to be distracted by news that King Malcolm's men were harrying in Bernicia, apparently in revenge for an alleged attack by Earl Cospatric's men on Cumberland. The exact sequence of these events remains obscure but the effects are plain enough. King Malcolm seems to have intended to attack down the western side of the Pennines but had lost control of his wild Scots who began harrying Edenvale.

Meanwhile, Sheriff Maerleswein and the Yorkshire thegns were fortifying sites on the Humber and in the marshes of the West Riding (into which they were to retreat when the rising collapsed). Their aim had been to hold the

Humber-Aire line against the Normans and wait for the Mercians to join them before taking real action. They probably also hoped that the Danes would arrive with reinforcements. It would appear that word of all these preparations had reached the ears of King William and allowed him to take pre-emptive action.

In consequence of this failure, the Northumbrian reaction had taken three forms. Some, naturally, had chosen to submit, others fled to exile in Scotland, the rest simply faded away into wood and marsh to become what Orderic called 'silvatici', wild men of the woods and so guerrilla fighters. Those who took to the wilderness then adopted the tactics of striking the enemy when he least expected it and scattering into hiding when he reacted with force. This kept the Normans in Yorkshire in a permanent state of alarm, causing them to waste resources on their own protection and unable to relax their guard. The Normans chose to regard such tactics as treacherous behaviour but they were the perfect way to wage war in an area of rough terrain and small population. As for the Northumbrians, they could only wait and hope for the arrival of a relieving force large enough to contend with the enemy on even terms. That force was hoped for from the Danes, but, as events were to reveal, the Danes themselves had other ideas.[9]

Earl Cospatric had been caught out by the speed and ferocity of King William's response and had promptly returned to Scotland, where he made his peace with King Malcolm and was granted asylum. The speed with which the Earl fled probably contributed to the collapse of the resistance. Among those who returned, temporarily, to King William's favour, was Bishop Aethelwine of Durham. King William now sent him to Scotland to offer terms to King Malcolm which would end, at least for a time, his support for the disaffected English. King Malcolm listened to the proposed terms and accepted them, possibly because he was now pre-occupied with his marriage to the Aetheling's sister Margaret. King Malcolm sent the Bishop back to King William accompanied by ambassadors who swore fealty and obedience to King William in King Malcolm's name, or so Orderic claims. The terms cannot have been to King William's entire satisfaction nor can they have been a genuine acknowledgement by King Malcolm of King William as his feudal overlord for the Kingdom of Scotland. It is more probable that they acknowledged some sort of right for King William over debatable areas like Cumbria or parts of Lothian. Bishop Aethelwine had done himself little permanent good in King William's eyes.

However, according to Orderic, the King now thought that he had 'completely rid the kingdom of all his enemies', and then proceeded to disband the mercenary part of his army, not because of any dissension in their ranks but probably because it was the end of their term of service. The barons, however, continued to be perturbed by continual small scale risings, although they feared being branded as cowards and deserters if they chose to leave England. A few did in fact do so, claiming that their wives were missing them and demanding their return. One who did so was Humphrey de Tilleul and another, though he quickly returned, was Hugh de Grantmesnil. No forfeitures are recorded, and it may be that most remained in Normandy only for a short time.

Orderic reports the continuous suffering of the English from fire, rapine and daily slaughter 'wreaking destruction and disaster on the wretched people'. The land, he claimed, was wasted wherever the King and his army passed. It was now said that 'fiends' stalked the land. One effect of the treatment meted out at Exeter had been to reinforce the change in English attitudes towards the Conqueror. They became distrustful and defiant and that in its turn made the King more suspicious about the trustworthiness of Englishmen. All that the English had so far achieved was to set the stage for the events of 1069, though King William could not have known that.[10]

A flicker of further revolt troubled the Kingdom that summer with the arrival of the Sons of Harold (that is Godwine, Edmund and Magnus together with Tostig the son of Earl Swein) from Ireland with a fleet of fifty-two ships and a goodly number of armed men. They landed at Avonmouth, taking the local forces unawares, harried the area and attacked Bristol, intending to capture the town. But the townsmen there resisted bravely and forced the attackers to return to their ships with their plunder. From there they descended on Somerset, at Porlock, where they landed and moved inland. There they were met by the Staller Eadnoth who gave battle at Bleadon. He was slain, along with 'many good men' on either side, and the Sons were driven off, forced to return to Ireland. They were to come back again in the following year and it must have seemed as though their attacks were going to become an annual affair. They are known as 'The Sons of Harold' which suggests that that was the name taken by an organised group, of which Harold's sons were the leaders.

With this first defeat of the Sons of Harold, relative calm returned and the King continued to hold his nerve until December. King William then held a crown-wearing at Christmas, probably at Gloucester. The West Country had certainly been subdued and the King was able to issue writs or charters confirming men in their possessions. One such was Bishop Giso of Wells who had cooperated with the Normans from the beginning. He was given back the manor of Barnwell in Somerset which had, he alleged, been taken from him by King Harold. The Charter is noteworthy in that Harold is called

'King', a practice which disappeared after 1068. It names an English thegn, Tovi, as sheriff of Somerset, a wealthy thegn called Dunna and Wulfweard White who had been an official in the Household of Queen Edith and was now serving Queen Matilda. Others still thought worthy of inclusion were Eadnoth the Staller's son, Harding (a merchant at Bristol), Azur son of Thoth of Combe St Nicholas and the wealthy thegn Beortsige, all men who had submitted in late 1066 or early 1067. They appear alongside Normans such as William de Courcelles, Serlo de Bucy and Roger of Arundel.

At this point William could still be said to be trying to create a genuinely Anglo-Norman realm. But attitudes were hardening as the balance tipped further towards Norman interests and all chance of creating such a society began to ebb away. Edgar the Aetheling, despite the assertions of William of Poitiers that he had been showered with honours and lands, had defected to Scotland, probably early in 1068. According to the Worcester Chronicler he went to Scotland 'that summer' which, at that time, meant any time after the first of May. He took the whole of his family with him, including his mother Agatha (which looks like a fairly clear decision to remove them from Norman control) and they were welcomed by King Malcolm who, it seems, immediately began wooing the Aetheling's sister Margaret to whom he was married by 1070. There is no indication that any of them attended Matilda's coronation. The Aetheling had by now realised that there was very little rapport between himself and King William and resented the fact that he had been given no post of importance within the regime of the sort he thought he was entitled to, though there had been no open breach.[11]

Apparently unconcerned about the activities of various disaffected English nobles, King William decided that it was now time to appoint a Norman as governor of Northumbria proper, between the river Tees and Bamburgh, that is St Cuthbert's Land, leaving Yorkshire to William Malet and Richard fitzRichard. So the King's choice fell on a certain Robert de Commines who was made Earl of Bamburgh in place of Cospatric. He arrived at Durham in late December 1068 with an escort of 500 knights (which looks like the standard entourage of a castellan), where, despite warnings and protests, he occupied the Bishop's House. He proved to be a man of the same stamp as fitzOsbern or Bishop Odo, haughty, arrogant and rapacious. His actions ensured that the reaction of the Northumbrians, when it came, would be savage. He proceeded to treat his new province as in need of conquest, ravaging the countryside and treating the inhabitants of Durham 'as if they had been enemies', looting their homes and allowing his men a free hand to plunder unchecked. In effect he paid the wages of his men by 'licensing their ravages and murders'. Bishop Aethelwine warned de Commines that he could expect trouble but was ignored. The Norman really should have known better than to take risks in St Cuthbert's Land, that 'whirling chaos surrounding the emerging power of Malcolm of Scotland'. It was still seen as eminently possible that a realm might be created for the Aetheling Edgar, supported by the Danes and King Malcolm, and crowned by an Archbishop at York.[12]

The Norman position in England, as a result of the events of 1067 and 1068, was a formidable one. They now controlled all of England from the South Coast to Yorkshire and Chester and from the South West of England and the Welsh Border to East Anglia and Lincolnshire. In Devon and Cornwall, for example, the spoils of conquest had been given principally to Robert, Count of Mortain, the Conqueror's other half-brother, as Earl of Cornwall, and Montacute, the site of the staller Tofig the Proud's discovery of the miraculous Holy Cross (which he had moved to his renovated and endowed church at Waltham in Essex), became the location of Earl Robert's castle.

Further north, in Leicestershire, Hugh de Grantmesnil had now stepped into the holdings of an unidentified great man. He is not identified in the Leicestershire Domesday (although elsewhere in other shires the 'antecessor' or previous holder in King Edward's time is frequently named or can be identified). He was clearly someone who was so obvious that it was taken for granted by the Domesday Commissioners that everyone knew of him, so they found it unnecessary to name him. It had to have been someone who had dominated Leicestershire and that suggests that it was the great Earl himself, Leofric, whose lands had come down through his son, Earl Aelfgar, to Earl Edwin. The latter had been involved in the rising of 1068 and it is all too probable that he had now been punished by the forfeiture of much of his land, reducing both his power and importance. King William had struck north through Mercia from Warwickshire to Nottinghamshire and the natural route is along the Fosseway via Leicester. The decision of the brother Earls in 1069 to desert the King again might well indicate resentment at such a loss of power, especially as Earl Morcar now had no authority in Northumbria.

King William had been aware that trouble was brewing during 1068 and had seized control of several towns, one of which, Oxford, appears to have been taken by storm although the chronicles do not mention it. It had always been regarded as a Mercian town. In Warwickshire, Coventry, another of Earl Leofric's former holdings, had submitted as King William passed through, and Thurkill of Arden, son of sheriff Aelfwine, had hastened to submit. Most of the rebels had withdrawn north of Durham, retreating in the face of King William's advance.

If local tradition in Leicestershire is to be accepted (as in the foundation legend of Leicester Abbey), the burh there was destroyed by Count Robert of Mortain, in which case 1068 is the most likely date for such an event.

The King's writ now ran as far north as York where the castle occupied one of the six 'scyra' or wards of the city.

One event occurred in 1068 which must have given the King much pleasure and that was the birth of his fourth and youngest son, Henry, in September. The story of his birth claims that he was born at Selby in North Yorkshire which, on the face of it, seems unlikely as the Queen was resident in Winchester, where her coronation had been held, and had no reason to travel to such a remote location when pregnant. The tale is connected to the foundation of Selby Abbey and is therefore part of its foundation myth. It possibly derives from the fact that King William issued a confirmation charter in the abbey's favour, confirming its right to the lands given it by, among others, Gilbert Tison (who had acquired the lands of the Yorkshire thegn Gamal Barn) and the English collaborator, Edward of Salisbury, known as Edward the Rich. The Abbey History attributes its foundation to Hugh fitzBaldric, the Sheriff in about 1070.

It is customary for historians to dismiss the English efforts at rebellion as uncoordinated and disjointed. They point out that there is little evidence that the various participants made any attempt to work together, that the risings remained sporadic and that the English never managed to combine against their foe. There is much justice in this argument but it does tend to ignore the difficulties faced by any movement which has no outside help to throw off the yoke of a foreign invader. Successful wars of liberation have almost always been fought with outside help. It also tends to underestimate the importance of the evidence offered by Orderic Vitalis. He does insist that efforts were made to coordinate the risings and he also insists that efforts were made to obtain outside help, from Denmark and from Scotland. That neither Malcolm, King of Scotland, nor Swein Estrithson, King of Denmark, was prepared to meet William of Normandy in battle can hardly be blamed on the English.

What they could do they certainly did do and one of the most striking aspects of English resistance to the Normans was the activity of those Orderic says the Normans called 'silvatici'. Usually rendered as wild men and defined as men who took refuge in the forests and the fens, these men caused the Normans far more trouble than is usually appreciated. Orderic reports that these were men who chose to live in tents, rather than houses, despising those who skulked at home as soft and flabby. It looks as though the root of the word 'silvatici' is the Latin 'silva' a wood. More probably it derives from 'silvescere', to run wild. So 'homines silvestris' are men of the woods running wild and some identify them with some of the images known as 'Green men'. William of Malmesbury adds that these men resorted to brigandage (that is, guerrilla tactics) never fighting openly or at close quarters. He says that these 'wild men' were often captured or surrendered and that sympathy for their good looks or high birth secured release without penalty. One can see how passages like this led to the belief that Hereward, like Earls Edwin and Morcar, might have been temporarily reconciled to the King. The writer adds that the Earls themselves were both 'cut down by the treachery of their own men' (though in fact this applied only to Earl Edwin) and that William himself was moved to tears by this as he would have married them to one of his own kinswomen (not daughters) 'had they been content to remain at peace'.[13]

The activities of these men, the silvatici, emerged during 1067 and were a constant theme over the next four years at least, though they never entirely disappeared. They can be compared to the later outlaws who lived in the greenwood and gave rise to the stories of Robin Hood (men like the Cumbrian outlaw William of Cloudsley). They wore the 'Lincoln Green' and hid in forests like Sherwood, preying on passing Norman travellers. The eleventh century silvatici were remembered as 'wild men' and figure in outdoor shows and plays. Their tents could well have been like the 'benders' devised by modern eco-protesters, made of branches covered with cloth or hides and well camouflaged. Some were remembered, too, in medieval churches in carvings and paintings, and became confused with more mythological figures. These were the well known carvings and paintings of the 'Green man'. That figure also appeared in rural shows dressed in greenery to represent the wild men of the woods.[14] The figure of the 'wildman', also called a 'woodwose' is found carved in lay settings also. There is one preserved on a beam at the Bull Hotel in Long Melford. It is the complete figure of a man dressed in skins and is certainly not mythological.

There were examples of such figures in at least eight Norfolk churches alone but they can be found in churches built throughout the medieval period. At St Peter and St Paul, Salle, in Norfolk, there is a painting of a bearded man's face peering through green branches and leaves. It is quite different from other images of faces with branches and leaves growing out of the man's features and there is nothing pagan or mythological about it. This image, and other similar images, are surely recalling the real wild men, the silvatici. Also, at Cawston St Agnes, a boss on the spandrel of the west doorway shows the head of a longhaired bearded man (usually taken to be a 'green man' but lacking the characteristic foliage growing out of the face).

At Little Paxton in Cambridgeshire, the tympanum of the arch over the doorway shows a male figure wearing a long and belted kilted skirt and holding a sharply pointed cross-handled staff or spear. It has been identified as the figure of a 'homo silvestris' or wild man. Such figures are often shown in combat with a centaur or Sagittarius; a poetical image for a warrior on horseback, that is a knight.

So, the rebels who hid in woods, among the hills or in the fens were denizens of the forests, just like the French resistance during the Second World war who hid in the French scrub land and bush of the Massif Central and were known as 'maquis'. These were men who were said to 'prendre le maquis'.[15]

The names of some of those who became silvatici can be discovered in Domesday Book and elsewhere. The most famous example is the Shropshire thegn, Eadric the Wild. One entry concerning him has the word 'salvage' (i.e. sauvage or savage) interlined above his name in the text. There were two others identified by the word 'wild'; Wulfric Wild of Newton in the South Riding of Lincolnshire and Wulfwig Wild with land in Kent at Atterton, Shelving and Perry. Others are labelled as 'outlaws', such as Skalpi the thegn of King Harold who 'went away to York in outlawry' and died there or Aelfric, a freeman holding land under Archbishop Stigand, who was similarly outlawed.[16] Even the Earls, Edwin and Morcar, are reported to have 'wandered at large in woods and fields' for at least six months before ending up at Ely in the Fens. The Abingdon Chronicle reports that men 'hid in woods and some in islands, plundering and attacking those who came their way; others called in the Danes and men of differing ranks took part.' The Evesham Chronicle adds further information and says, after the harrying in the North, that it had been done 'on account of the outlaws (in the Latin, 'exules') and the robbers who hid in woods and did damage to many people' as they were seeking 'to wage a war of vengeance'. But, what the silvatici could not do, without armed help from overseas, was drive the Normans out.

The North in Flames:
Christmas 1068 to Winter 1069/70

Earl Cospatric, (son of Maldred, Abbot of Dunkeld,) scion of the House of Bamburgh, was appallingly well suited to the chaos now developing in Northumbria, as Kapelle has remarked, because of his close connections with both Scotland and Northumbria.[1] His appointment to govern the north had been King William's last attempt to rule there through an Englishman, in the hope of reconciling the Northumbrians to Norman rule. But the Northumbrians had, as might have been expected, rebelled and rejected the Norman King's authority. As none of the hoped for assistance from Denmark had materialised, the intimidated Northumbrians had simply melted away before the Norman advance, back into the hills and forests, resorting once more to their traditional guerrilla warfare. Their fundamental military power remained intact.

Only diplomacy could now help King William, or so he seems to have thought. Bishop Aethelwine of Durham, reconciled to the king once more, was sent to negotiate with King Malcolm in the hope that, if he could not be persuaded to expel the English exiles, he might at least be persuaded not to give them any assistance against the Normans. The Bishop duly returned, accompanied by Scottish ambassadors who readily swore to accept King William's terms. Having achieved as much as he could, thinking that the North had been pacified, King William had returned to Gloucester to celebrate Christmas, 1068.[2]

At a Council held that winter, the King decided, at last, to impose a Norman Earl on Northumbria, and his choice fell on a certain Robert de Commines, most likely a soldier of fortune.

Before returning south, the King had taken the precaution of building a castle at York, with a Norman castellan, Richard fitzRichard, and a Norman sheriff, William Malet. They proved to be just as rapacious as Earl Tostig had been and proceeded to levy the second geld which the King had demanded in 1068 and which Earl Cospatric had signally failed to collect. This would have been seen by the Northumbrians as 'gafol', that is tribute rather than taxation, and they refused to pay it. Thegns who failed to pay were imprisoned and their estates forfeited. William Malet, in particular profited from such forfeitures as he had acquired many manors well before 1069. By autumn of 1068 a vast treasure had been amassed and was stored in the castle at York.

The King was encouraged by this to extend direct Norman rule into Northumbria proper, Northumberland. Robert de Commines was therefore sent north and headed directly for Durham in January 1069. He had a force of knights and men-at-arms estimated variously as either 500 or 900 (depending on whether the report included the men-at-arms as well as the knights.) He was greeted by Bishop Aethelwine who tried to warn him about what to expect and to stay out of Durham, since occupation of the city would be regarded as provocative. The Norman disregarded the advice, ejected the Bishop from his lodgings in Durham, and took up residence himself. He then proceeded to treat Durham like a city conquered by force, as though he had taken it by storm. His men were allowed to run riot, massacring many of the population, a war crime by any standard.

Naturally, the Northumbrians counter-attacked, slaying the Normans. The Bishop's house was set on fire and the Earl and his companions were trapped and killed, probably while trying to escape. The rebels, exhilarated by their success, gathered in force and agreed to take up arms against the Normans in York. There is evidence of some degree of planning for further action. William of Jumièges reports that the English built themselves a castle (castellum) there 'with a most powerful rampart', which indicates that they strengthened the walls of Durham in anticipation of a Norman counter-attack. He further claims that after making 'various attacks' (where is not specified) they returned to Durham to await the arrival of King Swein Estrithson of Denmark, 'to whom they sent messengers requesting aid. They also sent to enlist the people of York to their cause. So they furnished themselves with abundant supplies of money and arms and prepared themselves for strong resistance, choosing as their king a certain boy, nobly descended from the stock of Edward', that is, Edgar the Aetheling.[3]

They descended on the city, besieging and capturing the castle bailey, killing Richard fitzRichard the castellan. Apparently the garrison made a rash sally in an effort to drive off the attackers, they 'engaged them ill-advisedly within the city walls but were unable to resist such huge numbers and were all slain or taken prisoner'. The citizens of York joined the rebellion and the leaders of the Northern Army, under the great thegn Arkill, sent word to Edgar the Aetheling, inviting him to become head of their movement and come to York. In 1065 the Northumbrians had chosen their own Earl,

Morcar, to replace Earl Tostig, they now chose their own King in the hope that he would replace King William. But Archbishop Ealdred died before he could be prevailed upon to anoint and crown Edgar. That could explain King William's decision to hold a crown-wearing at York, to demonstrate that there was only one indisputable King of England.

The Earls Edwin and Morcar appear to have decided to keep out of the rising this time and could have been already under some sort of house-arrest at Court. But the attitude of their men, the Mercians and Yorkshiremen, was a different matter, and, as King William's later actions reveal, rebel movements developed in Cheshire and Staffordshire, Eadric the Wild became involved and the Welsh Prince Bleddyn led his men into England against the Normans.

William Malet desperately sent for help lest he be driven to surrender and King William responded promptly. He raced north, bursting in upon his enemies by 20 September. He 'came upon them by surprise from the south with an overwhelming army and routed them and killed those who could not escape, which was many hundreds of men'. He relieved the castle, drove off the rebels and built a second castle, on the right bank of the river, the Baile Tower, constructing it in eight days. He sent out a large contingent of knights and men-at-arms, hoping to disperse the rebels, who had by this time withdrawn into the hills. His men advanced as far as Northallerton but then their nerve failed them. According to Northern legend, St Cuthbert acted to defend his land against them. Apparently, a 'great darkness' fell on the Normans, most likely a tremendous fog, which completely disorientated them, and, terrified, they retreated to the safety of York.[4]

During the relief of the castle, William fitzOsbern is reported to have played a significant part. Some of the English had penetrated the bailey, confining the rest of the garrison to the 'donjon' but fitzOsbern, arriving with a strong force, caught the English in the open and killed many of them. The garrison, seeing what was happening, arose, made a sally and completed the rout of the English.

King William was unmoved by the return of his expeditionary force, he had only intended the move as a demonstration in force. He had no intention as yet of dealing with Durham. Having reasserted Norman control over York he returned south, intending to hold his Easter Court at Winchester. It was now March 1069. The King had left a much sterner representative to hold York, the redoubtable William fitzOsbern. His importance was recognized, according to a phrase in a Charter issued at Holy Trinity, Rouen, (granting land at Winchester at his request). He was now regarded as 'chief of the palace', that is, like Robert fitzWymarc before him, steward of the royal palace.

King William held a Council, as usual, at Easter at Winchester. During this Council a curious incident occurred which illustrates William's character. The King had occasion to make a grant of land to a local abbot. During the ceremony he made as if to stab the abbot in the hand, to signify the permanent nature of the grant. The King laughed the gesture off, saying that he but jested, but it had required strong nerves on both sides! William was prone to disguise such displays of power under the cloak of such playfulness.

Understandably, Edgar the Aetheling and his closest supporters had at about this time, returned rather promptly, to Scotland. But his return had only been the opening move in what proved to be a much more dangerous rebellion than that of 1068. Despite his apparent success, King William took the precaution of sending Queen Matilda back to Normandy for safety.

In the summer, around 24 June, the Sons of Harold made a second attempt at an invasion, and were reported to have either sixty-four or sixty-six ships, possibly meaning some 2000 men. They entered the River Taw and began ravaging and plundering Devon, attacking Exeter, only to be repelled by Castle Rougemont and its garrison, aided by the citizens of Exeter itself. They were then driven off by a force led by Count Brian of Brittany and William Gualdi. But reports suggest that they were only beaten off after the loss of 1700 men 'some of them great men and, had night not put an end to the battle, all would have been cut down by death's razor'. The attack had proved to be a disaster for the Sons of Harold, they left the area in only two ships and never made another attempt. English efforts to throw off the 'Norman Yoke' were suffering badly from lack of a strong guiding hand to coordinate them. The Exeter Book (which contains some of the returns for Devon from which its entry in Domesday Book was composed) records some evidence of the incursion and states that nine manors belonging to Judhael of Totnes were devastated 'by the Irish'.

It was about now that the Danes finally arrived, some time between 15 August (The Assumption of Our Lady) and 8 September (her Nativity) and, as on other occasions, King William heard the news while out hunting, this time in the Forest of Dean. The Danes were under the command of Jarl Asbiorn, brother of King Swein, and Jarl Thurkil accompanied by three sons of King Swein, Harold, Cnut and Beorn (also called Leriz). They had with them a Danish Bishop called Christian of Aarhus. The Danish fleet, of at least 240 ships, raided South-East England, starting at Dover and going on to Sandwich, and then around to East Anglia hitting Ipswich and Norwich. At each of these places they were repelled, at Norwich by Ralph de Gael who 'fell on them and drove many of them to death by drowning'. (The Danes possibly found it too difficult to overcome the castles and their garrisons). At least fifty Danes were slain at Ipswich alone.

Orderic Vitalis, rather strangely, claims that King Swein had been motivated in doing this 'by the death and disaster which had overtaken his men in Harold's war'. But there is no real evidence that there were Danes at Hastings, despite the fact that William of Poitiers thought there were Danes in Harold's army. Possibly the Norman writers were confused by the Danish names of so many of the thegns from the Danelaw into thinking they were actually from Denmark or, which is not impossible, King Harold, who had Housecarls in his service, had some men who were mercenaries from Denmark. More cogently, Orderic adds that King Swein's action arose from 'his desire for the kingdom to which, as 'nepos' (meaning kinsman) of King Edward and son of Harthacnut (sic!), he had a claim by inheritance'. King Swein was related to both Harthacnut and Edward, as son of Cnut the Great's sister Estrith. Edward and Harthacnut were half-brothers (both sons of Queen Emma). Edward and Swein were thus, by the conventions of the time, cousins. (Harthacnut was full cousin to King Swein, so the Danish King and Edward were kinsmen). Swein and Harthacnut were supposed to have agreed between them that whichever lived longest would inherit the other's throne, or so the source for all this, Adam of Bremen, claimed. Swein also claimed to have made a similar agreement with King Edward.[5]

There seems to have been a curious convention by which, whenever a peace treaty was made, an arrangement of this kind was included, providing a rather tenuous claim to the inheritance of a rival's throne. Such claims always depended, as did William of Normandy's claim to the English throne, on the claimant's ability to enforce it.

During the month of September, the Danes took up station on the Humber and the English began to rally to them. Florence of Worcester's account of events implies that more ships arrived while the Danes were on the Humber and that could have been a fleet from Scotland bringing Edgar the Aetheling and his men to join the Danes. A skirmish was reported at Lincoln where English rebels were repelled by the garrison of the castle which fell on them unawares and took many Englishmen prisoner. This was a foraging raid by the Aetheling but, fortunately for the English, he escaped injury or capture.

Orderic furnishes the names of other leaders on the English side as among the supporters of Edgar the Aetheling at this time. He lists Earl Waltheof, a thegn named as Siward (possibly the wealthy northern thegn Siward Barn) and a thegn he names as 'Adelinus' (unidentifiable, could be an Aethelwine, and so possibly the Bishop). Other sources reveal that at the same time Earl Cospatric had brought in his Northumbrians and had been joined by Sheriff

Maerleswein and some of the Yorkshire leaders such as Archil, Siward son of Aethelgar, Karli and his four sons (Cnut, Summarlithr, Thorbrand and Gamal) and the equally unidentifiable 'Elnochus' (possibly an Alnoth, like Eadric the Wild's son). Also among the rebels were a number of nobles from East Anglia as is evidenced by the reports of East Anglian exiles after the rising was defeated. These included Aelfwold, the Abbot of St Benet's at Holme, Eadric, who had been King Edward's Steersman, the thegn Ringulf of Oby and Abbot Aethelsige of St Augustine's who had taken refuge at Ramsey. They all eventually went into exile in Denmark. It is not unlikely that another participant could have been the Lincolnshire thegn Hereward since his legend reports tales of his involvement in fighting in Northumbria and an encounter with Gilbert of Ghent (who was one of the barons holding York), though it erroneously dates this to 1063.[6]

That the thegn Karli could be found in the company of Cospatric was, in itself, an indication of just how hostile the Northumbrians were to the rule of King William. Karli had killed Ealdred, uncle of Cospatric, and Thorbrand the Hold (who gave his name to Holderness) had killed Earl Uhtred, Cospatric's grandfather, yet they were prepared to sink their differences and make common cause against the Normans. So Northern factions coalesced against King William, the House of Bamburgh, the descendants of Thorbrand the Hold (a title originally signifying command of a Viking army) and the supporters of St Cuthbert's men (the rich landed community of clergy who preserved the body of St Cuthbert). They resented Norman occupation of lands that had formerly been theirs, such as Karli's estate of Hunmanby, held by Gilbert of Ghent.

King William was now fully aware of all these manoeuvres and of Earl Waltheof's defection. William Malet, at York, reported that he was confident that he could hold out there 'for a year if need be', or so he unwisely boasted. The King would have heard how all the English leaders had descended on York to join the Danes, 'and all the people of the land, riding and marching, forming an immense host, greatly rejoicing; and thus all resolutely went to York and broke down and demolished the castle'.[7]

It was now 19 September, and the Normans in the castle at York took pre-emptive precautions against a repeat of the attack in 1068. They set fire to the houses surrounding the castles, so creating a 'dead zone' of open space around the castle, (probably the one that stood where Clifford's Tower now stands). But the fire quickly got out of control and destroyed much of the rest of the city, including York Minster. The Danes arrived in York on 21 September though they made no attempt to remain there. There was now no plunder to be had and they had no means of laying siege to a castle, but fire drove the garrison out and, it was said, some 3,000 Normans (probably an exaggeration) were slain. Earl Waltheof alone was credited with slaying one hundred. The corpses were left for wolves to devour.

There is evidence that the desire to revolt was becoming widespread. The Abingdon Chronicle reports that 'men of all classes took part' and that 'many plots were hatched in the Kingdom of England by those who resented the unaccustomed yoke of foreign rule'. As other evidence indicates, and Abingdon confirms, men took refuge in woods and on islands 'living like outlaws and plundering and attacking those who came their way'. That was the sort of resistance associated with Hereward.

The Chronicle confirms reports that other men sought to persuade the Danes to come to England and that when the Danes answered the call, they in their turn plundered the land and laid it waste by fire, taking away many people into captivity. Much of this sounds like an echo of events in the Fens from 1069 onwards. The Chronicler admits that the English were not strong enough to wage a pitched battle against King William, nor could they subdue the Kingdom. The source of Abingdon's information is known. The Chronicle reports that Bishop Aethelwine of Durham had taken part in the resistance and that, after he was taken prisoner (in 1071) he was brought to Abingdon 'and ended his days there in captivity'.

Meanwhile there were risings being attempted elsewhere, especially in the West of England. The whole South Western peninsula rose against the Normans and there were more risings further north in Cheshire and Staffordshire. So serious was the situation in the North West that King William himself was eventually forced to break off from his Northumbrian campaign to deal with it. Even the Welsh, under Prince Bleddyn, became involved, allying themselves with Eadric the Wild and some of the Mercians. Eadric led the Welsh and men from Shropshire and Cheshire in ravaging the area and threatening the castle at Shrewsbury. He was unable to capture the castle as he was ill-equipped to mount a siege, and so he by-passed it, burning Shrewsbury itself and ravaging into Staffordshire.

Unfortunately for the English, these various risings were still terribly uncoordinated with no master hand at work behind them; they were only ever loosely arranged to occur at similar times but were never linked up in a comprehensive all-out war against the Norman King. Communications between the different rebel groups would have been extremely difficult. There are few details available about these localised risings. In the South West they were easily put down by Norman forces led by Bishop Geoffrey of Coutances and Count Brian of Brittany and, of course, William fitzOsbern. Winchester tradition insists that William fitzOsbern ordered the right hands and noses of the captives (taken by the Bishop and the Count) to be cut off. The Normans had advanced from London, Winchester and Salisbury and pacified the area by killing, capturing and mutilating the rebels. At Exeter the citizens took the Norman side, and the garrison of the castle broke out to drive off the besiegers who were then caught by the Normans with great slaughter.

Bishop Geoffrey of Coutances advanced to the relief of Montacute Castle (in Somerset near Yeovil) and he too mutilated those he captured. This action was to bring about an extension of Norman settlement, permitting a move north into Mercia and from there into the lands beyond the Ribble and the Mersey. Either then or earlier Bishop Geoffrey of Coutances became Portreeve of Bristol (who presided over the borough court) as he is recorded as receiving the third penny of Bristol (of the profits of justice while the King received the other two-thirds) in 1086.

King William himself was most concerned about the Northumbrian rising, which was potentially the most dangerous since it had been reinforced by a Danish raiding army and was backed up by the Scots. So his first move was to launch an attack against the Danes themselves in Lindsey, North Lincolnshire, in order to drive them back into Holderness. He is said to have 'sought them out in almost inaccessible marshes' (those around Axeholme) and wiped out their hiding places', putting them to the sword. That move drove a wedge between the Danes and the Northumbrians and allowed King William time to show himself in Staffordshire, where his advance in force repelled Eadric the Wild, and then return to Nottingham. Orderic insists that there was fierce fighting but gives no further details. Dealing with the Danes and Staffordshire proved costly. Despite the scorched earth around the castles at York, the Northumbrians were able to storm them, slaughtering the garrison and taking William Malet and his family prisoner. He probably expected to meet the same fate as Richard fitzRichard but was spared.[8]

The Fleming, Gilbert of Ghent, was also taken prisoner. He is said to have possessed Holderness 'until the Danes captured him'. There had been a desperate struggle on the part of the garrison, but the castle was taken, possibly fired, and the defenders resorted to a last sally in an effort to drive off their attackers but, as the skald Thorkell Skallason, the Icelander, sang, relating the exploits of his lord, Earl Waltheof took a prominent part in dealing with the breakout, and 'he single-handedly killed many Normans in the battle of York, cutting off their heads one by one as they entered the gate'. The Norse sagas thought Waltheof fought at Hastings, but that is unlikely. What is related of him is a memory of his activities in 1069. He is said to have encountered a force of one hundred Normans seeking to escape into an oak-wood and he and his men set fire to the wood (especially the brushwood) so that many of the Normans perished in the fire. Thorkell Skallason in his poem on Waltheof said; 'Waltheof burned a hundred of William's Norman warriors; As the fiery flames raged, What a burning there was that night!' The Earl's alleged participation in the battle of Fulford is probably also an echo of his exploits at York, though some of his commended men could have been part of the force which fought there.

The rebels then retreated from the devastated city and hid in the marshes of Lindsey, hoping to link up with the Danes. But they had retreated from York (which had been rendered uninhabitable by fire) to the Isle of Axeholme, seeking the protection of the marshes surrounding it. Before King William arrived, some of the Danes retreated to their ships, others had dispersed themselves all over Lindsey where they were welcomed and feasted in the villages, but now they had been driven back.

Nonetheless, for a time the whole Norman enterprise hung in the balance. Resistance threatened to become more coherent as news of the risings spread causing fresh revolts in many places. But the centre remained in the north, in St Cuthbert's land (the area dominated by the estates of the St Cuthbert Community which lay around Durham and Chester-le-Street on the North East Coast) where King Malcolm was exerting his influence, occasionally throwing his weight behind King William's enemies. His marriage to Edgar the Aetheling's sister Margaret seemed likely to commit him more firmly to Edgar's cause and there was a distinct possibility of the emergence of a separate northern Kingdom under Edgar, supported by King Malcolm and King Swein. The death of Archbishop Ealdred was reported on 11 September, and that opened up the possibility of an independent Metropolitan Archbishop chosen by the Northumbrians rather than one imposed by the Normans. Archbishop Ealdred had last been heard of at York for one of the great feasts, either Easter or Pentecost and had been involved, it was said, in a dispute with William Malet. The Archbishop claimed that he had been robbed by some of the Sheriff's men, who had seized a consignment of wheat and other food intended for the use of the Archbishop, and in consequence threatened Malet with excommunication, demanding the return of his stolen property. But the Norman was scornful of the Archbishop's threats, probably because he was an English cleric, and ignored him. Archbishop Ealdred therefore went to London seeking out the King in order to secure compensation. The Archbishop's later legend relates that he was equally unsuccessful in obtaining satisfaction from the King, despite pointing out that it had been he who had anointed King William and crowned him. When they met, the Archbishop refused to give the King the Kiss of Peace and was said to have cursed the King on account of his misdeeds and to have accused him of persecuting the English Church. He reminded the King that God had permitted him, William, to punish the English for their sins, with much bloodshed. In words attributed to him, Archbishop Ealdred is reported to have said:

'I give thee my curse, as thou art a persecutor of God's Church and an oppressor of Her Ministers, breaking the oaths you swore to me at St Peter's Altar. As I once blessed you wrongfully so now I curse you rightfully'.

The legend goes on to claim that an abashed and alarmed King fell at the Archbishop's feet, begging forgiveness and asking what he had done to deserve the Archbishop's wrath. The King's men then threatened harm to the Archbishop but he defied them, saying:

Let him (the King) lie there, he lies not at my feet but at the feet of St Peter, as he has done wrong to St Peter's Vicar.

He then raised the King to his feet, relenting and lifting his curse. He was, of course, sent back to York with a writ ordering William Malet to restore his property.[9]

From what is known of King William's character, the tale is unlikely to be true as it stands but it may be taken as illustrating the change in English attitudes towards the King and to reflect that there had been disputes between King William and Archbishop Ealdred, who no doubt resented the influence Archbishop Lanfranc had over William. There must have been something known about a change in Archbishop Ealdred's attitude towards the King that gave rise to these stories. More reliably, William of Malmesbury reports complaints on the part of Archbishop Ealdred about the high level of taxation and that might be what gave rise to the legend. He remarks that the Archbishop honoured the King just as long as he ruled with moderation, but that, when he levied heavy tribute on the provinces, Archbishop Ealdred reminded him of the law of his predecessor, King Edward. It is possible that the Archbishop was known to have prayed publicly that the King might change his ways. Orderic Vitalis reports that prayers were said in Churches in 1069 for the success of the rebellion. That might be the basis behind the other stories. In any event, the Archbishop died before the King's response to his complaints was known, and perhaps before the curse, if there was one, had been lifted. Some attributed the Archbishop's death to grief caused by his quarrel with King William.[10]

In the North, King William had advanced against Axeholme, pushing the Danes further back into Holderness. He had left Count Robert of Mortain and Count William of Eu to keep a watch on the Danes and to prevent any outbreak while he himself went west to deal with the Staffordshire rising, and from where he had now hurried back to Nottingham where he heard that the Danes were planning to re-occupy York, hoping to spend Christmas there. So the King gathered his forces and turned north to go through the Aire gap into Yorkshire. There he was delayed at the Aire for three weeks, partly by the weather and partly by the search to find an unwatched ford where he could cross the river. A ford was found, by Lisois de Moutiers leading a party of sixty knights and the King beat off all attackers and established a bridgehead not far from where Pontefract Castle was later built.

Shortly after this the King arrived at York for the third time. As he advanced he devastated the land, following the Roman Road through woods, hills and valleys and even marshes, sparing nothing and no one he found in his path. He found York a burnt city surrounded by a desolate countryside. The knight Toustain led a squadron of men to Beverley but was killed when his horse fell on him as he attempted to ride into the Minster. He was found with his arms twisted behind his back in 'a most monstrous way'. As King William is reported to have confirmed the Minster of St John of Beverley in all its possessions the story, in this embroidered form, could have arisen as an explanation as to why the King did so.

The castles were rapidly restored and strengthened and the king decided to spend Christmas at York, sending to Winchester for the royal regalia so that he could hold a crown-wearing to set his seal firmly on the area. He also demanded and received hostages, including Thorgautr, Bishop of St Andrews, who was kept hostage 'for all of Lindsey' in the castle that King William had built at Lincoln in 1068. The Bishop eventually won his freedom by bribery and fled to Norway by stowing away on a ship. It is likely that it was at this time that Count Alan, the Breton, was given the castlery (like those around the castles in Sussex) and extensive lands which formed 'Richmondshire'. Ilbert de Lacey was endowed with lands around Pontefract. Other lordships were created for the defence of York, especially for William de Percy and for Hugh fitzBaldric, (the latter became sheriff of Yorkshire). After celebrating Christmas, King William set in train the systematic harrying of the north.

The Danish army had certainly been large enough to challenge the Normans in open battle but it never did so nor does it seem that there was ever any intention on the part of the Danes to do so. Their sole objective was to take advantage of the situation in order to gather as much plunder as possible. They moved far too slowly on campaign, leaving themselves open to harrying by mounted Norman forces. Unlike the Danes who attacked England in the ninth century and later, there was no effort made by these men to seize horses and become mobile. When they moved it was by sea, with even Edgar the Aetheling seeming to have arrived in the area by ship with a fleet provided by King Malcolm.

It seems to have been part of the plan to harry the Normans by means of sea-borne raids which might have looked feasible at first when York fell and its garrison was wiped out. If that was the idea, then the Danes and their English allies ought to have attacked in southern England and fought a pitched battle, just as William had done in 1066. But the taking of York satisfied the Northumbrians under Cospatric and Maerleswein, who seem to have been seeking revenge rather than actually to drive out the Normans and conquer the whole country, perhaps hoping to set up a separate kingdom based on York, as had been done in the tenth century. With the onset of winter the northern rebels retired from the field, thinking King William would not campaign in the bitter cold. They could have been waiting for King Swein Estrithson to arrive in person as he was to do in the Spring of 1070, only to find that his expeditionary force was now in a bad way, suffering from an excessively cold winter.

York had proved of no use as a base, because of the fire, whereas, if it had been taken intact, the Danes could have remained there that winter in comparative comfort. They certainly had need of a place where they could survive the coming winter. King William, however, gave them no chance to find one. They had taken refuge on Axeholme and attempted to fortify it, as it was, at that time, a genuine island. But that had been frustrated by King William's arrival in Lindsey before the defences were complete. An attempt by the Danes to return from Holderness while the King was in Staffordshire was prevented by the Norman force left to contain them. It was perhaps this that led King William to conclude that they had no intention of waging all out war. The crossing of the Aire then forced the Danes to retreat to their ships and Jarl Asbiorn had to concede defeat. He was allowed to forage for supplies as best he could, by ravaging, and was forced to agree to leave England the following Spring. He did however, acquire a large quantity of treasure and kept some of the chief men of York as hostages. During the winter food was in very short supply and many of the Danes died of starvation.

That allowed King William to concentrate on the Northumbrians. They had expected him to do as he had done previously and, having rebuilt his castles, return south for Christmas. But he did nothing of the sort. He set detachments of men to hold down the Danes and rebuilt the castles but he did not leave. He spent Christmas in York and then, early in 1070 initiated his final solution.

But first he had to settle the matter of the Danish fleet and he did so in time honoured fashion by resorting to bribery. In effect he paid Danegeld! It could be that this was forced upon him because he had no war fleet with which to compel the Danish fleet to leave, and its presence remained a menace. Jarl Asbiorn and his men 'lay all that winter between the Ouse and the Trent'. The bribes could also have been intended as ransom for William Malet and his family and Gilbert of Ghent.

It is possible that it was at the crown-wearing and Council held at York that Christmas that King William followed the example of King Edward who had confirmed the 'Laws of Cnut' to persuade the Northumbrians to cease ravaging in 1065. So now, if the reference in the twelfth century lawbook, which goes under the title of 'Leges Edwardi Confessoris', be accepted, King William confirmed 'in the fourth year of his reign' the 'Laws of King Edward'.

Various leading Englishmen reacted differently to the situation arising from King William's reoccupation of York and the failure of the Danes to act. Bishop Aethelwine of Durham was too fearful to attempt another reconciliation with King William, and with the Community of St Cuthbert took refuge as far north as Lindisfarne that winter, 'fearing lest the king's sword should include equally the innocent and the guilty in indiscriminate slaughter'. They took with them all their portable wealth (as they had done for so many years previously) and the body of Saint Cuthbert. There was no immediate reconciliation either for Edgar the Aetheling although he was eventually allowed to return to William's favour in 1074 (when he again was granted unspecified honours which he was to find inadequate). Earls Waltheof and Cospatric were allowed to retain their earldoms and renew their submission (though now earls only in name, one suspects, like Edwin and Morcar). Cospatric was discreet enough to make his submission by proxy rather than in person. They surrendered when King William led a force as far north as the Tees. Neither remained loyal for long. William was willing to allow this because the practical limit of his authority was still York.

Even Eadric the Wild was allowed to seek the King's peace although not until after the reprisals of 1070. Earls Edwin and Morcar seem to have been allowed to retire to Chester, after their men were driven out of Stafford. The northern Mercians had got involved in rebellion out of resentment at having a Fleming, Gerbod, brother of Frederick Oosterzele-Scheldewindeke (and so a brother-in-law of William of Warenne) as Earl of Chester. Gerbod was so disturbed by the disruption caused by the rebellion that he chose to return to Flanders in 1070 and was replaced by Hugh d'Avranches, castellan of Tutbury.

King William was now determined to find a way of countering the Northumbrian tactic of attack and retreat. The Northumbrians had already, after retreating in 1068, hidden out in the hills until the Danes had arrived in September 1069, as they fully expected them to launch an all out war against the Normans. King William had not left York and the Danes had been unwilling or unable to press home an attack. It was still possible, in William's eyes, that the North would rise against him again and he was determined that it should not.

The Harrying of the North:
February to December 1070

Niccolo Machiavelli wrote, in 'The Prince', that 'in order to maintain the State, a prince will often be compelled to work against what is merciful, loyal, humane, upright and scrupulous'. Of no action of William the Bastard is this more true than of the way in which he now 'pacified' Northumbria. Even the Norman chroniclers were scandalized when he and his lieutenants spent almost a year ravaging the north of England, turning almost 1000 square miles into a wilderness. He is described as succumbing to the vice of cruelty, making no attempt to restrain his men, allowing them to cut down many in vengeance, harry the land and turn homes to ashes. Crops, herds, chattels and food of every kind were brought together and burned. So he stripped the area north of the Humber of all means of sustenance. Orderic puts the death toll at 100,000. Even William of Poitiers seems to have been unable to bring himself to chronicle the events of 1070 and brought his 'Gesta Guillelmi' to a premature conclusion.[1]

Late in January 1070 or more likely during February, the King, contrary to all the expectations of the Danes and the Northumbrians, launched a midwinter campaign of devastating ferocity and barbarism, which extended as far north as the Tyne. The Earls, Waltheof and Cospatric, submitted once more. Waltheof was actually bound closer to the King by being married to Judith, daughter of King William's sister Adelaide, wife of Enguerrand of Ponthieu. Earl Cospatric had retreated to Lindisfarne via Bethlington and a place called 'Tughala', taking three days and three nights to do so including one at St Paul's at 'Girvum', that is Jarrow. Then he went to Bamburgh, and there submitted to King William by proxy, not daring to face the King in person.

The King himself set out on campaign to the far north, into St Cuthbert's land, penetrating as far as Jarrow and Wearmouth on the Tyne, destroying Jarrow Church by fire. He remained by the river for some fifteen days until the two Earls had submitted. He had learned that his enemies had hidden in a narrow neck of land, sheltered by sea and marshes. This has been identified, as one suggestion has it, as Tod Point near Coatham on the southern shore of the mouth of the Tees. Others have suggested that it was further north again, at Bamburgh. No certain identification can be made as there are many possibilities. The enemy hiding place was attainable only along a narrow causeway some twenty feet wide. King William's approach so terrified the rebels that they fled despite the defensive strength of their position. In all the King spent fifteen days on the Tees. Elsewhere his forces were sent to hunt down every Englishman they could find. In the process he spread his camps widely, covering a one hundred mile area. Nowhere else in the country did he display such cruelty as in the North and made no effort to restrain his fury. So thorough was the ravaging that one effect was to exclude Durham and northern Northumbria from the Great Survey of 1086.

There was simply no need to survey the extreme north as, so far as is known, no Norman found it beneficial to settle there, and some parts of the area would have been uncultivated land. The King himself returned to York, probably via Helmsley although Orderic thought he passed through Hexham. He might well have pursued rebel Englishmen up the Tyne valley to Hexham before returning to Jarrow and then south. (Orderic names Hexham correctly by its Roman name of Hagustald.) Helmsley is thought by some historians to be more probable simply because it lies on the direct line of King William's march southwards, down the Roman road through the Pennines, and argue that a visit to Hexham would require a major diversion. But that would not be the case if the King had simply followed the Tyne eastwards and then decided to turn back.

That winter was a most severe one and the Norman march south proved arduous in the extreme. The men suffered badly from the cold and the blizzards. King William's return was between towering peaks through precipitous valleys deep in snow. He lost many horses and, for a time, the King himself was said to have lost contact with his men, having only six knights with him. But he eventually managed to reach York.[2]

The canons of St Cuthbert had again fled north away from Durham as the Normans approached, and the Bishop, Aethelwine, had taken refuge at Lindisfarne. The canons had been forced to leave behind the Great Crucifix, given to Durham by Earl Tostig and his wife Judith. It was too big and heavy to shift. When the Normans arrived, on Quadragessima Sunday 7 April, they pulled the Crucifix down and stripped it of its precious ornaments. King William heard of this and, apparently enraged, chose not to punish the men himself but to send messengers to Bishop Aethelwine, ordering him to excommunicate the offenders (just as his brother Aethelric had excommunicated Hereward and his men earlier). But nothing was heard from Aethelwine and perhaps he was too afraid to do as he was asked. That meant that he had disobeyed a royal command and it seems that he decided to gather up as much moveable treasure as he could and set out for Cologne. He took ship to do so but a storm wrecked it and he ended up in Scotland. He was to set out again in Spring 1071 and to meet up with Earl Morcar at Ely.

Back at York, King William learned that reports had come in suggesting that Chester was still a major centre of disaffection and he decided to mount an expedition to deal with it. It was now mid February, the coldest time of the year, but the King set out on a route which meant penetrating the wildest part of the Pennines, through a wintry wilderness. He could well have taken his men up the valley of the Wharfe and then across the moors in a south westerly march towards Chester, passing between Pendle Hill and Boulsworth Hill and down on to the Lancashire Plain. Some route similar to that was followed.

Conditions were so harsh that a section of his army, led by protesting Bretons, supported by the men of Anjou and Maine, actually reached the point of mutiny. They complained that 'we cannot obey a lord who commands us to do the impossible!' He was leading them 'along paths so narrow that two men could not walk abreast'. But King William's ferocious demeanour and force of character quelled the attempt. He rejected such men as cowards unfit to serve in his army and promised great rewards for their great labours if they persevered. He led them over steep mountainous country, through steep valleys and over streams and rivers, past deep abysses. They were reduced to eating horses which had perished in the bogs. Having crossed the Pennines, the King marched directly to Chester. No details of what followed are recorded, only the results. The City of Chester, at that time controlled by a number of 'judices civitatis' or civic judges (like the lawmen found in Danelaw towns), a type of magistrate, promptly took the course of discretion and submitted. Even so, the whole district around the city was ravaged, a typical example of what has rightly been called 'government by punitive expedition'. The ravaging was then extended, as King William gave his men free rein and unleashed them on the terrified inhabitants, into the rest of Cheshire, and into Shropshire, Staffordshire and Derbyshire.[3]

Many of the people were driven out of their homes and fled the area. Some went looking for food as far south as Evesham in Worcestershire, as the Evesham Chronicle records. The famine resulting from such ravaging was so severe that five or six people who had reached Evesham were dying daily. They were buried by Prior Aelfric. Those who reached Evesham were so enfeebled by starvation that they could scarcely manage to eat the food provided. Castles were built at Chester and Stafford. This time, no rebels emerged in the Spring to renew their attacks because King William had manufactured an artificial famine. King William had even ravaged the salt works at Nantwich despite the fact that salt was essential to people's diet and for preserving food during winter. The King certainly justified the judgement passed on him when he died:

> A stark man he was who thought nothing either of men's sufferings nor their hatred.

King William then returned directly to Salisbury. It was now March, and there he reviewed his troops, rewarding those who had remained loyal and served him well, allowing them to stand down from active service, and he gave them money and lands. But the mutineers were punished by having their period of service extended.

The King was still faced with the problem of the Danes. Jarl Asbiorn had remained on the Humber during the winter, carefully keeping his men beyond William's reach. The Danes were starving and had been reduced to eating rancid meat and putrid flesh. They were so exhausted that they were only too ready to agree to return to Denmark. Even so, the King had to resort, in effect, to bribery. He had reached agreement with the jarl, permitting the Danes to overwinter and live by ravaging, provided they did not attack any of the King's forces.[4]

Having made his dispositions for the defence of York and after returning from his punitive expedition to the Tyne, King William had ordered the harrying of Northumbria. His forces had been sent out to destroy all means of livelihood in order to drive all hostile forces out of the province and cow the peasantry into submission. Both the northern warriors and the Danes had withdrawn and the peasantry had been left unprotected. King William nonetheless had unleashed his men against them, aiming to bring peace to the north Roman style; 'Make a desert and call it peace'. All seed corn was destroyed, houses were burnt down, animals were slaughtered and crops were uprooted and burnt. It was an act of deliberate cruelty which was never to be forgotten. The whole area must have looked much like those farms where, in modern times, animals had to be slaughtered and burnt to eliminate foot and mouth disease. No spring crops could be planted and even ploughs and other tools were destroyed. Native society from Yorkshire to Teesside was severely disrupted, and even the Tyne valley was devastated. Later writers such as Roger of Hovedon, lamented how the harrying provided 'a horrid spectacle, to see on the high roads and public places and at the doors of houses, human bodies eaten by worms, for there remained no one to cover them with earth'. Many people were driven to eating cats and dogs and horses or even, so it was said, human flesh. Others became slaves in order to survive and there are tales of benevolent owners setting men free in later years. A Lady called Geatflaed was said to have freed several persons, including some of Earl Cospatric's followers. Durham became a refuge for the poor, weak and sickly, who then lay there dying of disease and hunger.[5]

The Norman settlement reached a new phase as Mercia was occupied and the lands beyond the Ribble and the Humber into Yorkshire and what is now Lancashire and as far north as Durham. Frontier castles were pushed northwards in order to dominate newly occupied territory. The Breton, Count Alan the Red, was established at Richmond and Drogo de la Beuvrière in Holderness. Sheriff Maerleswein's lands went to Ralf Paganel. The Flemish Earl of Chester, Gerbod, gave up his post and was replaced by Hugh d'Avranches some time before 22 February 1071. Hugh, assisted by Robert of Rhuddlan and Robert of Malpas was to inflict great slaughter on the Welsh. Gerbod had found the task too onerous and his decision might also have been affected by the assassination of his brother Frederic by Hereward the Outlaw and his men. Earl Gerbod had complained of being continually disturbed by the attacks of the Welsh and the English. He was glad to respond to a call to return to Flanders to administer his hereditary lordship as Advocate (Protector) of St Peter's, Ghent. When Drogo also decided to leave he was in due course replaced by Odo of Champagne.

As Normans were installed in new lordships, so Northumbrian thegns found themselves dispossessed. The great lord Arnkell was exiled, as was Alwine son of Northmann (who fled to Scotland). Arnkell's son, Cospatric, who had been one of the hostages in 1068, survived. He still held some land in 1086 and is one of the few English tenants-in-chief. But he held some of his land under Count Alan. The lands of Gamal son of Orm, Northmann and Gamal Barn all went to William de Percy. No one else of note survived in Northern England during the Conqueror's reign. It must have been during 1070-1071 that William fitzOsbern found time to take possession of Brecknock and defeat Cadwgan, Rhys and Maredudd the Welsh leaders, because in the fifth year of the reign, King William sent fitzOsbern to Normandy to act as regent there along with Queen Matilda. The Earl then involved himself in the affairs of Flanders and got himself killed at the battle of Cassel 20 or 21 February 1071.

Over all, Orderic Vitalis records the rewards granted by King William to his followers in a context which suggests that many of them only received their fiefs in 1070 or shortly afterwards. These grants included the distribution of many of the estates of the Godwines, that is those which were not retained as part of the royal demesne. Orderic puts his list well before mentioning the King's return to Normandy in the winter of 1071-72. That the fiefs were distributed after 1070 is indicated by the gifts to various abbeys. Bury St Edmund's received land at Brooke 'when he (William) first came to St Edmund's'. Battle Abbey, which was founded in 1070, received land belonging to King Harold's estate at Limpsfield. Another estate, at Bromfield, was owned by the Abbey and that land could well have been the site of the battle of Hastings itself. St Stephen's, Caen, received lands at Brincombe and Frampton, in Dorset, belonging to King Harold and his mother Countess Gytha.

Orderic supplies the names of several thegns involved in the rebellions of 1069-70 and they all have well-defined successors, as recorded in Domesday Book, clear proof, if it were needed, that King William handed out to his followers the estates of powerful but disobedient thegns. Their estates can be found scattered the length and breadth of the shire. Ralf Paganel's lands, those of Sheriff Maerleswein, are found spread over all three Ridings of Yorkshire, down into Lincolnshire and they include what he held in the West of England as well. They also show that Norman fiefs did not necessarily form compact blocs of territory. They resulted, instead, from transferring the lands of a particular rebel Englishman into Norman hands and were sometimes formed out of the lands of several separate individuals. Just as King William had 'inherited' his kingdom, so his Norman followers claimed to have 'inherited' the lands of their 'antecessors' who had held them in 1066. This also provided a motive for some Normans marrying the widows or daughters of their predecessors, to provide spurious evidence of 'inheritance'.

This period of the conqueror's reign, 1069-71, was a period of 'jarring territorial discontinuity', as it has been described, rather than a period of 'peaceful settlement'. King William certainly did not, as some of those who eulogise him claim, conduct himself as a Christian monarch in a Christian land. The pre-conquest pattern of landholding was 'savaged' along the Welsh border, by the establishment of marcher (or 'palatine') Earldoms (Shrewsbury, Chester and Hereford) and there were marcher fiefs established there and in Cornwall (Robert of Mortain the King's half-brother), Kent (Bishop Odo), Norfolk (Ralph de Gael), Sussex and South Lancashire.

King William had decided on his barbarous course of action because the rising of 1069 had imperilled his whole venture. Resistance had for a time threatened to become more coherent, supported as it was by King Swein of

Denmark and King Malcolm of Scotland. That King William successfully put down the rising and neutralised the threat represented by the Danes, owed as much to the unwillingness of the two Kings to engage in all out war, preferring only to benefit from the plunder to be got from ravaging, as to King William's military skill. King William had therefore set in train a programme of systematic destruction and returned to Winchester to celebrate Easter. The methods he had chosen to use were seen as exceptional and beyond excuse. Orderic Vitalis, writing when it was safe to voice concerns, wrote; 'I dare not commend him. He levelled both the bad and the good in one common ruin by a consuming famine... he was... guilty of wholesale massacre... and barbarous homicide'.

The northern annals included in the works attributed to Simeon of Durham record horrifying destruction. They tell of rotting and putrefying corpses, of pestilence and famine and of men and women rendered destitute. The effects can be seen in the records of Domesday Book, especially those for Yorkshire, where prosperity was destroyed for a generation or more. Entry after entry records estates as 'waste', meaning that previously cultivated land was now bare of crops or stock and rendered nothing. Even allowing for the effects of Viking and Scottish raids and the endemic fighting caused by feuds, and for lands where no information was available to the commissioners, the volume of wasted land in Yorkshire recorded for the period after 1066 and well before 1086, is staggering. Some missing information could be due to the casual manner in which Yorkshire was surveyed but is more likely due to the fact that the information readily available elsewhere was not to be found in Yorkshire because there was no one living who could provide it. The affected area extended as far north as Durham, as far west as Merseyside and as far south as Derby. [6]

The pattern of entries for Yorkshire in Domesday Book is unlike that in other circuits. The account gives in many places only the name of the vill or manor, its assessment for geld, the name of its new holder and, for some places and where known, the names of those who held land in 1066. These entries are really only a list of geld liabilities. But some inhabitants did survive since in 1086 it was still possible to record customs and they were to survive into the thirteenth century. Significantly, no lands had been given to sub-tenants north of the Ribble even by 1086.

As a consequence, Yorkshire was to be fully integrated into the administrative system which operated in the rest of England. The earldom of Northumbria was suppressed and the royal demesne was increased, while sheriffs were imposed on the North.

Critics of the view that the harrying was extreme, argue that it was not as severe as the ravages of the Vikings and the Danes. It is claimed that the

Chronicle is relatively restrained in its criticism (and so it is when compared to Orderic's account); so the Worcester Chronicle says only that the King wholly 'ravaged and laid waste the shire' and Peterborough that he 'ruined it completely'. This it is said is less damning than the account of the Danish raid of 1006, when the Danes 'cruelly left their mark on every shire of Wessex with their burning and harrying', though the 1070 entries are stronger than what was said of King Harthacnut who 'had all Worcestershire ravaged'.[7]

Too much should not be made of variations in the language used by different scribes in describing similar events. Chronicles were public documents, open to being read by visiting Abbots and Bishops, and writers would have needed to exercise discretion. As it was said of those who were critical of the actions of King Henry I, 'the feet of those who bark shall be cut off'.

Florence of Worcester, writing in the twelfth century with access to a now lost version of the Chronicle, wrote that King William 'ceased not to lay waste the land, to murder the inhabitants and to inflict numerous injuries on them'. Hugh the Chanter, writing at York, said that the whole district round about was 'destroyed by the French with the sword, famine and fire'. Other sources insist that so many died that there was no one left to bury them and that over a wide area no village was left inhabited between York and Durham so the land remained uncultivated for years.

Some of the damage could, of course, have been the work of others and not just the Normans. The sources differ about whether all the damage at Durham, discovered by Bishop Aethelwine on his return from Lindisfarne, was the work of the Normans or of Earl Cospatric. The Bishop found the great crucifix, the gift of Earl Tostig and his wife Judith, thrown down, and the church plundered and stripped of its ornaments. Others attributed damage to punishment meted out to criminals and the Evesham Chronicle comments that the King had harried the north because he wished to 'extirpate outlaws and thieves who were infesting the woods', but as that statement might be referring to the 'silvatici', it could be Norman propaganda and Aethelwig of Evesham was a known collaborator. Some of the damage in the extreme north, however, was in fact down to King Malcolm of Scotland. In the Spring of 1070, after King William had returned south, the Scots devastated parts of Durham and Cleveland, so exacerbating the effects of the Norman harrying. King William's withdrawal and the fact that he did not attempt to occupy the debatable land between England and Scotland left a power vacuum. Earl Cospatric, on his own account, ravaged Cumbria. Sooner or later King William would have to deal with these problems, but he did not do so in 1070.

Northern sources insist that the villages were deserted and became the 'lurking places of wild beasts, and of robbers'. The harrying had led to an increase in banditry and disorder as the remaining people struggled to survive by any means available. There were certainly no more general risings though all opposition was not yet at an end and a last stand had still to be made.

Much land was also seized, especially in towns, for the building of castles, Cathedrals, Abbeys and other churches, or was given to Norman traders. At Shrewsbury the burgesses complained about how difficult it was for them to pay geld because Earl Roger's castle had occupied '51 mansurae' (town plots) and because fifty others lay waste, and forty-three French burgesses now held forty-three of the mansurae which had paid geld T.R.E. Also the Earl had given the Abbey which he built there lordship over thirty-nine burgesses who once paid geld like the others. York had suffered when the River Foss was dammed to form a moat for the castle to protect its south eastern flank. It drowned two mills and a whole carucate of land (i.e. 120 acres). Whole streets were destroyed to build the Baile castle and its construction split the communal district into two halves. Even in 1086 there were still 540 waste and 400 partially wasted tenements. Some had been destroyed in 1069 and the rest cleared to make a perimeter around the city walls. French settlers had occupied 145 manses once held by thegns and traders.[8]

There were consequences elsewhere after the events in the North. The Norman King's policy towards the English hardened and a much more determined effort was made to distribute their lands as fiefs for the Norman settlers.

The towns also suffered from Norman actions. At Winchester twelve burgesses lost their homes when the new royal palace was enlarged in 1070 and the castle took up space also. At Lincoln, half of the houses belonging to Toki Autison went to the baron Geoffrey Alselin (who 'inherited' Toki's lands in several shires), together with two churches and Toki's Hall, while the other half, thirty houses in all, were taken by Bishop Remigius for the building of Lincoln cathedral. This sort of thing happened all over the country, at Norwich, Nottingham, Canterbury and so on. All this seizure of property causes Norman accusations of misappropriation of Church land, in a handful of cases, by King Harold to pale into insignificance.[9]

Norman lords now also extended patronage over surviving English land owners, so increasing their own holdings, and then, if the English rebelled, the new lord seized the land for himself. At Evesham, Abbot Aethelwig, after 'the Kingdom had been conquered by the Normans and the region (around the Abbey) had been completely abandoned by the most important nobles, the Abbot himself received many men into his service, and so, little by little, the Abbot spread his protection, as many rich men of the province were drawn to him for protection against the Normans'. Yet this was an Abbot who collaborated with the new King and was given extensive powers of jurisdiction over seven western shires, most likely finalised in 1070. So surviving thegns who in King Edward's day, had possessed land and 'could go with their land to whatsoever lord they wished' (pre-Conquest England was a very mobile society as far as the relationship of lordship was concerned) now found it necessary to put themselves under a Norman lord for protection. But the new form of lordship meant holding land by some form of feudal tenure, either knight service or sergeanty. Most of the records of this come from Church records but must have applied also to men seeking Norman lay lords.

Several men of second rank who could not be made earls, became sheriffs; Simon of Senlis at Nottingham, Henry of Beaumont at Warwick, Robert of Mowbray in Durham and Walter Giffard in Buckingham are prominent examples. To these can be added William Ferrers at Derby and Hugh de Grandmesnil at Leicester. Others were rewarded with land, so Hugh de Montfort, for example, was given the lands of Gutmund, brother of Abbot Wulfric who had been Abbot of Ely before the Conquest. Gutmund held a Hall at Haughley which became the 'Caput' or centre of de Montfort's Honor. (An 'honor' is the great fief of a major baron). De Montfort's men were accused later of illegally holding lands belonging to Ely. Gutmund might have been involved in the resistance at Ely in 1071.

Elsewhere, fiefs were handed out by Hundred and Wapentake, especially in the area north of Watling Street and to the west of the Fens. Whole Hundreds were distributed as at Pontefract, Richmond and Holderness. Much of the distribution of lands was carefully controlled by King William, using all available information at his disposal, precisely in order to avoid the formation of vast compact fiefs which could provide a baron with a formidable power base, so avoiding the formation of feudal principalities as found in France. No Norman was to be allowed to be as powerful as the great English Earls, Godwine, Leofric and Siward, or Harold himself had been.

Even so, evidence elsewhere suggests that there had been in some areas a less controlled and planned settlement, especially in the Eastern Counties and East Anglia, which had, perhaps, been settled in 1067 while the King was in Normandy. Orderic makes dark hints about the extent of 'illegal' seizures of land, that is without prior royal approval, with stories of men who refused to accept ill-gotten gains. Norman barons and knights repeatedly and consistently encroached on Church lands (about which, naturally, written evidence has survived) on the flimsiest of pretexts. Much of the land held by lay lords must also have suffered in the same way as the lands of the Church, as the disputes recorded, (in the 'Clamores', or complaints, sections of the Yorkshire and Lincolnshire entries, or the Appropriations sections of Essex and Norfolk and the Encroachments listed for Suffolk), all indicate. They list over one thousand cases of illicit seizures of land and there were other cases noted throughout the entries in Domesday Book. So a woman called Alwynn 'a free woman, held Childerditch and it is not known how it came to be held by Robert fitzWymarc in King William's day'. Robert died in 1070. The reeve of William of Warenne seized a piece of land and two horses and refused to give them back. Another reeve, Lufa, claimed Farncombe and the Hundred reported that 'he held it when the King was in Wales, but Odo came to Kent and appropriated it'.

The Church fought long and hard to regain lands lost to encroachment and often persuaded the King to order their restoration, but even then, was not always successful. Instead, the Church was forced to accept Normans as tenants although the Abbots and Bishops did not want them and would have preferred to have been simply given back their lands. On the other hand, the Church had the documents, (Landbooks, charters or wills), which it could produce to support its claims whereas laymen mostly did not possess such evidence. The Church could launch anathemas against those who offended it and the psychological effects of such measures are demonstrated by the reports of men given nightmares, developing tumours or being driven mad.

St Aethelthryth of Ely was said to have given men heart attacks, reported as nightmares in which they were struck by the Saint wielding her crozier. She is reported to have so dealt with Gervase, the deputy of Picot, sheriff of Cambridgeshire. Bishop Wulfstan of Worcester fell out with the Norman sheriff of Worcester, Urse d'Abetot, over his encroachments and cursed him; 'Thou art called Urse, havest thou God's curse!'. No doubt much of this was either down to coincidence or to the psychosomatic effects of being cursed.[10]

But the descendants of men who had fallen at Hastings or in the rebellions, or had fled into exile, had little or no means of redress unless they had powerful Norman patrons. One man, Thorkell of Arden, managed to strike bargains with his Norman neighbours and did deals which protected the estates of members of his family. A thegn called Odo of Winchester did reclaim land from the Norman William the Archer at Compton. His story was as follows; 'He states that he held it T.R.E. (in King Edward's time) and was dispossessed after King William crossed the sea. He established his right to it in front of the Queen (Matilda). Hugh de Port is witness of this and the men of the whole Hundred'.[11]

The account of the trial held at Penenden Heath in Kent reveals that no one had been able to resist the depredations of Bishop Odo of Bayeux, so powerful was he, and that he therefore 'attracted to himself many men. These he annexed wrongfully to his own lordship'. There was also the case of the knight Peter de Valognes who was made to return to the Abbey of Bury St Edmunds the commended men of the abbey whom he held 'in captivity', according to the Conqueror's own writ. So the land of thousands of thegns fell into Norman hands and the survivors for the most part held their lands either under the king himself or one of his followers. Much of the transfer of land seems to have been finalised by 1071 but a great deal more changed hands after the fall of the Earls, Ralph de Gael of Norfolk and Roger of Hereford, in 1075.

According to the received tradition of the twelfth century, as recorded in the Dialogue of the Exchequer written by the treasurer Richard fitzNigel, King William and his magnates, after the overthrow of the rebels, which must refer to 1070 or 1071, made a tour of the whole kingdom and made careful investigation of the identity of those who had 'contended against the King in war and saved themselves by flight'. All hope of recovering the lands, estates and revenues they had previously possessed, even by the heirs of those who had fallen in battle, was precluded and it was thought 'too great a boon' to allow them to 'enjoy even the privilege of life under their enemies'. He says that those who had been summoned to war but had not actually taken part in the fighting, either because they had been preoccupied with their domestic affairs or held up by indispensable business, managed eventually to retrieve some lands for themselves by service to their lords, holding it only at their lords' pleasure. Even these, he says, were liable to lose what they had won back because they became hateful to their Norman lords, and were driven from their possessions. So the native English eventually laid a complaint before the King and after consultation with the magnates it was decreed that they should be granted inviolable rights to such land as they then held, but that they could not claim any land by hereditary right which they held at the time of the conquest.[12]

This was probably a statement of the law as it stood in Henry II's reign rather than a record of an actual decree. But it does acknowledge that there had been a general expropriation of the English for the benefit of the Normans.

Hereward Defies
the Conqueror But Ely is Betrayed:
Lent 1070 to Autumn 1071

On the advice of William fitzOsbern, 'In the Lent of this year the King caused to be plundered all the monasteries which were in England', as Florence of Worcester reports for 1070. He had them all searched in order to find money which richer thegns had deposited in them because of the severe treatment meted out to the English and the effects of the depopulation caused by the harrying of the North. No doubt some were hoping to withdraw this money and take it with them into exile. In the absence of banks, monasteries were regarded as safe places in which to store money and valuables, trusting that respect for such holy places would deter thieves and robbers.

A later writer, from the twelfth century, Gervase of Canterbury, records that the King also seized the charters and moveable wealth of the monasteries, which perhaps explains, in part, the need felt by so many monasteries to produce 'forged' charters to replace those which had been taken or destroyed. The intention was to produce copies of the records which had been lost and such charters may well contain some genuine information about the estates actually held by the monasteries. This report is also confirmed by the *Abingdon Chronicle* which explains the matter very fully.

According to the writer 'many treasures were deposited in the monastery... in the hope that, being protected by the custody of the Abbey, they might escape plunder'. But, he says, 'officers of the Court... obtained knowledge of this through informers... and everything that was found so stored was taken away and much that was contributed for the honour and use of the church was removed; gold and silver vestments, books and vessels. No respect was paid to the threshold of the holy places and no pity was shown to the distressed monks... and villages were also devastated.' The most prominent official involved was Froger, Sheriff of Berkshire but he was 'punished by God' because 'royal justice' removed him from his office 'which he had turned to a tyranny'.[1]

It was, of course, blatant theft on William's part, since the money deposited in monasteries was held in trust by them for the real owners and he had no moral right to it, although he justified his action by claiming that the thegns were rebels who had forfeited all right to goods and chattels as well as to their estates. The monasteries also were regarded as having aided and abetted the rebellions. The *Worcester Chronicle* calls the king's action a harrying.

The *Abingdon Chronicle* reveals the possibility that high-ranking individuals profited from the plundering of the monasteries. The *Chronicle* complains that 'in those days the ornaments of the Sanctuary itself were stolen'. It then goes on to explain that it was Queen Matilda herself who was responsible. She demanded that the most precious of the ornaments be sent to her so that she could have her pick of them. So the Abbot and monks sent selected items, not their best, but the Queen was not satisfied and demanded 'more precious treasures' which were, accordingly, sent. So the Abbey lost 'a chasuble wonderfully embroidered throughout with gold, and the best ceremonial cope; an alb with a stole and a gospel book, decorated with gold and precious gems'.

At roughly the same time, possibly at the Easter council held that year, the King also decided to provide Peterborough with a Norman abbot. The Abbacy was vacant at that time because Abbot Brand, the successor of Abbot Leofric, had himself died on 27 November 1069. The King's choice fell on a bellicose Norman from Fécamp, who was at the time Abbot of Malmesbury, called Turold (Thoraldr). William of Malmesbury says that Turold 'ruled his subjects' (at Malmesbury) 'like a tyrant' and so King William decided, no doubt after complaints by the monks, to remove him. Turold had been given Malmesbury after the removal of its English abbot, Brihtric, Turold being 'pushed in as abbot' as William of Malmesbury puts it. King William was recorded to have jested that 'as Turold is behaving more like a soldier than an abbot, by the splendour of God! I shall find for him a foe who is a good match for his attacks!' So he sent him to Peterborough, in its marshland site, which was said to be under attack from Hereward and his band of outlaws. 'He (Turold) can have Peterborough', the King said, 'as a field for his courage and generalship, and there he can practise his fighting!'[2]

According to the *Chronicles*, supported by the writings of the Peterborough monk, Hugh Candidus (the White), Hereward had been a tenant of Peterborough Abbey before 1066, or as Hugh put it, he 'was a man of the monks'. Hereward expected that a Norman would shortly be imposed on Peterborough and decided that in that case he would act to deprive the Norman of the riches of Peterborough, and prevent them falling into the hands of the King's men who had not yet reached the Abbey.

Before his death, Abbot Brand had, some time earlier, welcomed Hereward, (who was his nephew, son of the Abbot's brother, Asketil the King's Thegn,) back to England from his exile and campaigns in Flanders. Hereward had renewed his allegiance to the Abbey, presumably by an act of commendation (described in later reports as his having been knighted by the Abbot). He had also learned of the death of his father and other members of his family and the loss of his family lands. Abbot Brand would have told him that he had so far managed to keep the Lincolnshire lands of the family out of Norman hands by either transferring them to himself, as Abbot, so that they became Peterborough lands, or by repossessing those lands the family held as tenants of the Abbey. He had not been able to hang on to Hereward's lands and some of these had fallen into the hands of a Norman called Asfrothr and some into the hands of a Breton called Ogier. Lands in other shires had also fallen into Norman hands. Hereward was no doubt incensed by all this and that explains his determination to exact revenge. As the Normans claimed, he proceeded to 'commit many evil deeds to the injury of the king in various places'. Now, in 1070, Hereward had decided to prevent the rich treasures of Peterborough falling into Turold's hands.

Fortunately, or so it seemed to Hereward, the Danish fleet led by Asbiorn, brother of King Swein of Denmark, arrived in the vicinity of the Isle of Ely, after overwintering on the Humber, before deciding to return to Denmark. Asbiorn had, apparently, heeded the messages sent to him by King William who had not only granted him permission to forage for food and supplies along the sea-coast but also offered him a considerable sum of money as an inducement to leave England and cause no more trouble. He agreed to this and to leave the Humber at the end of the winter. But Asbiorn was a greedy fellow and decided to see if he could acquire more plunder in East Anglia. He accordingly came to Ely and there he encountered Hereward.

Much to the Danes' surprise, they were welcomed by all the local people (literally 'the folk'), that is the Fenlanders, who came to make peace with them, just as those around the Humber had done, in the expectation that they intended to conquer England. The monks at Peterborough were alarmed at the advent of the Danes and, on hearing that Hereward had joined forces with them, concluded that he intended to raid the Abbey, having heard of Turold's appointment. It was reported that in fact the new Abbot, who was 'a stern man', had already arrived at Stamford accompanied by a force of 160 knights.

Abbot Turold was then alerted to the intentions of the outlaws and their Danish allies by the sacristan of Peterborough, Yware by name. He collected up the Abbey's books containing the Gospels and Epistles together with a

Top of page: 1. King Edward grants an audience to Earl Harold who, as subsequent scenes show, was requesting the King's permission to embark on his voyage. No attempt is made to suggest that the King was sending Harold anywhere. The King's name is the work of restorers and is not spelt 'Eadwardus' as it is elsewhere, but no text has been lost as no space has been left for it.

Above right: 2. Earl Harold and his escort, in civilian dress, ride to Bosham accompanied by a pack of hounds. Earl Harold carries a hunting hawk, probably a falcon.

Right: 3. Earl Harold and his men feast in 'an upper room' at Bosham before setting out on the fateful voyage. Below, in the lower margin, the Fable of the Fox and the Crow is depicted, suggesting a warning of danger from the deceitful.

Bottom of page: 4. Earl Harold sets out on his voyage, wading out from Bosham Harbour with a hawk on his wrist, a sign of peaceful intent. Interestingly the Tapestry again fails to seize the opportunity to identify either his destination or his purpose.

Top of page left: 5. Earl Harold's vessel, blown off course by a strong wind, lands on the coast of Ponthieu. The voyage had a clearly peaceful purpose, no one is shown bearing arms.

Above left: 6. Earl Harold, having come ashore from his vessel, is taken prisoner by Count Guy of Ponthieu. It was the custom of Ponthieu to take anyone prisoner who made a forced landing on the coast, to be ransomed if rich or sold as a slave if poor.

Left: 7. At the castle of Beaurain Count Guy and Earl Harold discuss the Earl's plight. The Earl is in the act of surrendering his sword, a sign of submission, and it may be that the question of ransom is being discussed.

Bottom of page: 8. Duke William and his men return in triumph from the campaign in Brittany and arrive at the ducal castle in Bayeux. It was here that the designer of the Tapestry located Earl Harold's fateful oath.

Opposite page top right: 9. Duke
William confers arms and armour
on Earl Harold shortly after the
campaign in Brittany. This did not
necessarily mean that the Earl had
become the Duke's vassal, the Duke
is recognising Harold's prowess as a
warrior.

Top of page: 10. Earl Harold
is shown swearing his notorious
oath while touching the reliquaries
holding the bones of Norman saints.
Significantly, there is no attempt to
explain what it was that Harold
swore he would do.

Above right: 11. A submissive and
apologetic Earl Harold reports to
King Edward who admonishes him.
He cannot have sent Harold to the
Duke to renew the promise of the
throne because the Earl is apologising
for what he has done in Normandy.
One would expect King Edward to
have been pleased not angry.

Right 12. King Edward's body
is solemnly carried into his newly
consecrated Abbey Church of St Peter
at Westminster, accompanied by a
large crowd of clergy led by a bishop
with his crozier. The scene actually
precedes those showing the King's
death.

Bottom of page: 13. In a dramatic
manner the King's deathbed and his
actual death are shown one above
the other, and the deathbed scene
reproduces the description of it in
the Vita Edwardi Regis. Queen
Edith nurses the dying King's feet,
Archbishop Stigand stands in the
background, Earl Harold stretches
out his hand to acknowledge the
King's last words and his bequest of
the Kingdom and a figure of a retainer
supports the King as he strives
to sit up, this is probably Robert
fitzWymarc.

Top of page right: 14. King Harold, enthroned in state displays the symbols of kingship; Crown, Orb and Sceptre, while the Sword of State is held before him.

Top of page left: 15. An awestruck crowd points up at the 'hairy star', that is, Halley's Comet, while a servant urgently informs Harold, shown crowned and enthroned in his palace, of its coming. The scene is placed dramatically immediately after the coronation in order to emphasise that the judgement of God was upon him.

Above left: 16. A nobleman (possibly Count Eustace of Boulogne) supervises the construction of a Motte and Bailey castle at Hastings. The Normans took with them the means to construct the palisade and watchtower.

Below left: 17. The Norman Knights are shown riding 'manfully and wisely' into battle against the English. Note that the majority of them here, as elsewhere, carry their lances for use as spears, to be thrown, rather than 'couched'. Lances were used couched mainly for unhorsing other mounted warriors, a tactic of little use uphill against the 'war-hedge' or shield wall formation of the English.

Bottom of page: 18. The advance of the knights continues, lances at the ready for throwing, and the knights are supported by archers who act as skirmishers. The knights wear chain mail armour and carry kite shaped shields.

Above: 19. The Norman knights attack the English shield wall. The scene is set on level ground because the nature of the needlework of which the 'Tapestry' was composed rendered it impossible to show them riding uphill. Both sides attack each other with spears or other missiles. The designer does successfully show the depth of the English formation, possibly nine or ten ranks deep.

Below: 20. A dramatic visualisation of the intensity of the fighting as English thegns repel a Norman charge and men and horses fall. The Normans cannot overwhelm even a well defended hillock where a few Englishmen have formed a 'shield wall'.

Above: 21. Bishop Odo of Bayeux is the central figure here. He is encouraging the efforts of the younger knights while in the next scene the Duke raises his helmet to show his men that he still lives. The Bishop wears a quilted costume, not chain mail, and either a staff of office or a mace as priests were not supposed to shed blood.

Below: 22. King Harold, first wounded in or near the eye by an arrow, is struck down and slain by a Norman knight. The scene has been heavily restored; the 'arrow' might in fact have been a spear held by the King.

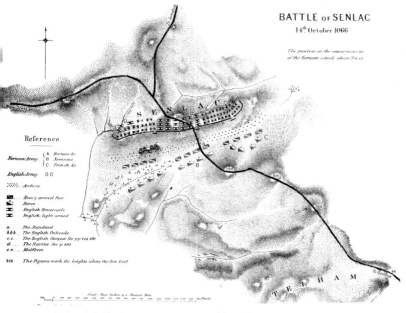

The position at the commencement
of the Norman attack about 9 a.m

Reference

Norman Army { A Bretons &c
              B Normans
              C French &c

English Army D D

⁝⁝⁝⁝ Archers

◼ Heavy armed Foot
◼ Horse
◼ English Housecarls
◼ English light armed

a.   The Standard
b.b.b The English Palisade
c.c   The English Outpost See pp 444 490
d.   The Ravine See p 490
e.s. Malfosse

325 The Figures mark the heights above the Sea level

Scale Four Inches to a Statute Mile

24. The battlefield of Hastings as envisaged by E.A. Freeman.

23. The Tower of Earl's Barton Church; a surviving Old English tower.

25. Ely monastery as it might have looked in the eleventh century.

27. Rougemont castle, Exeter, built in 1068.

26. King William's Seal; modelled for the obverse on that of King Edward the Confessor.

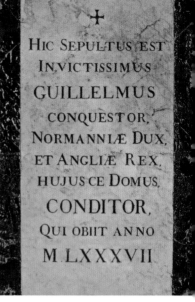

28. Abbayé aux Hommes, Caen. Built by the Duke as a penance for marrying without Papal approval.

31. Burial Place of William of Normandy, Caen.

30. The Norman gateway at Dover. It symbolizes Norman domination over the town.

29. Bayeux cathedral. Built for Bishop Odo, this was where the Bayeux Tapestry was originally displayed.

Top of page: 32. Bosham harbour. From here Earl Harold set sail in 1064.

Middle: 33. Bosham Church; used by the Godwine family. Here Harold prayed before his fateful voyage.

Below left: 34. Exterior of side aisles; All Saints, Brixworth. The old English arcading survived the Conquest. Most churches were replaced or altered to suit Norman religious ideas.

Below right: 35. Norman Doorway inserted into base of 'Saxon' tower, Campsall Church, Yorkshire.

36. Round Tower of Church of Burnham Deepdale, Norfolk. Within such towers the local population took refuge from marauding Norman soldiery.

37. 'Saxon' arch leading to Cloisters; Ely Cathedral. An example of how Old English architecture survived into the Norman period.

38. Tower and turret of Ely Cathedral, from the bailey of the Norman Motte. The Norman Church militant with crennellations and arrow slits, an example of Norman triumphalism.

39. Fortifications of the Warenne Castle at Castle Acre. This was the main residence of William de Warenne of Norfolk.

Top right: 40. Probable crossing point of the Norman Army on the 'Old West River' (now Great Ouse) at Little Thetford near Ely.

Middle and below: 41 & 42 Wicken Fen, Cambridgeshire; a fen restored to something like its condition in the eleventh-century. Such were the conditions the Normans faced in the fight against Hereward.

Top left: 43. Edward the Confessor. A painting from Ludham, Norfolk, c.1500, showing Edward in similar fashion and manner to later pictures of the saintly Henry VI.

44. Location of Duke William's army at the battle of Hastings. The Duke and his men must have been daunted at the prospect of charging uphill against a resolute foe.

45. Norman foot soldiers at the Battle re-enactment. Illustrates the body armour and weaponry of the infantry.

47. Battle Abbey.

48. Remains of the Episcopal Chapel built for Herbert Losinga, Norman Bishop of Norwich on the site of the former Saxon cathedral at North Elmham.

England on the Eve of the Norman Conquest.

Below: 46. Page from Simeon of Durham's *Historia Regum* (twelfth-century) describing the Norman Conquest.

Top: 49. England on the eve of the Norman Conquest.

Bottom: 50. The campaigns of 1066.

① Harald Hardrada's fleet invades.
② King Harold's advance on York and return to London.
③ English fleet returns to London.
④ Normans move from Dives to St Valery.
⑤ The Duke invades.
⑥ King Harold descends on the Normans.

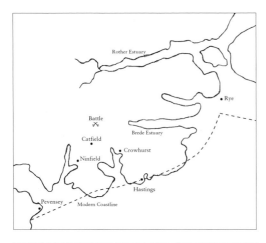

51. Pevensey and Hastings in 1066.

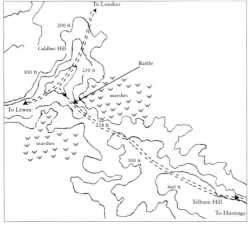

52. The field of Hastings 14 October 1066.

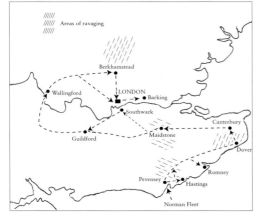

53. The march around London.

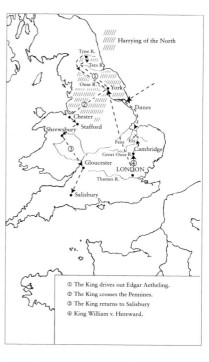

Above right: 54. The first stirrings of revolt 1067.

Below left: 55. The risings of 1069-70.

Below right: 56. The crushing of all rebellion.

Overleaf: 57. England and Normandy c.1070.

① William FitzOsbern occupies Norwich 1067.
② Eadric the wild attacks Hereford 1067.
③ Eustace of Boulogne repelled from Dover 1067.
④ King William subdues Exeter 1068 January.
⑤ Sons of Harold ravage Somerset 1068.
⑥ King William builds a chain of castles and subdues the Northern Rebellion 1068.

① English rebels capture York and join up with the Danes.
② King William retakes York, then returns South.
③ Local Norman commanders pacify the South West.
④ King William isolates the Danes on the Isle of Axholme.

① The King drives out Edgar Aetheling.
② The King crosses the Pennines.
③ The King returns to Salisbury
④ King William v. Hereward.

ENGLAND & NORMAN

CIRCA A.D. 1070
by W. J. Corbett

Natural Scale 1:3,600,000

20   0   25   50 Miles

EXPLANATION

ENGLAND. *William's conquests are full coloured, Pink, Blue &*
the districts assessed in carucates being further
with Red Lines. Districts allotted to the conqueror
principle of intermixed baronies are coloured **Pink.**
allotted on the principle of compact baronies are ce
Yellow. Important Ecclesiastical franchises are coloure

FRANCE *The Duchy of Normandy is coloured* **Green.** *The co*
Maine is hatched **Green.** *Districts assisting the Norn*
the conquest are edged **Green.**

The smaller place names entered in England are mostly
manors of baronies; those on the continent indicate t
from which the more important conquest families took
names.

number of chasubles, copes and other robes, and stole away by night and by dawn set out to reach Turold and 'sought his protection', that is attempted to ingratiate himself with the new Abbot whom he told of the coming of Hereward and his men. Yware acted, apparently, on the advice of the majority of the monks.

The sacristan had only just acted in time since, on the morning after his departure, Hereward and the Danes arrived 'in many ships' (probably in fact the flat-bottomed Fenland boats, forerunners of modern punts). They had approached Peterborough by sailing along the 'Wellstream' (which at that time was part of the river system around the Isle of Ely) which flowed down the western edge of the Isle to Wisbech (rather than down the eastern side to King's Lynn) and now set about getting into the precincts of the monastery from the south. The monks put up a stiff resistance, closing the gates and defying the raiders, but the attackers set fire to the buildings of the town lying outside the monastery walls and burnt down the whole settlement, all bar one building. By so doing they set fire to the Bolhithe Gate by which the Abbey was entered by water, and so breached the defences.[3]

Accordingly the monks, led by Prior Aethelwold, sued for peace, but the Danes insisted that the monks had to leave the abbey, though none were harmed. They all left except one, Leofwine the Long, who was lying sick in the infirmary and who was allowed to remain.

Meanwhile the outlaws and the Danes set about stripping the Abbey of its treasures, alleging that this was being done 'out of loyalty to the minster' to prevent the treasure falling into Norman hands. Both the Peterborough Chronicle and Hugh Candidus provide a very full account of the treasures that were taken. They were unable to remove the Holy Rood of Peterborough which was hanging before the High Altar, but did remove the gold crown from the head of the figure of Christ and the golden rest (the Scabellus) which supported the feet. They took two golden portable shrines (feretories) and nine others made of silver, fifteen great crosses also of either gold or silver, much other treasure in the form of books and robes (also encrusted with gems and precious metals), many other items made of gold and silver and a great deal of money. Climbing up into the tower they removed the great decorated altar frontal which had been hidden there by the monks. One item which was removed would have been regarded as even more precious, the Arm of St Oswald. Some of these items had most likely been given to the Abbey by Abbot Leofric in the days when Peterborough was known, because of its wealth, as Medeshamstead, 'the Golden Borough'.

Having taken everything they could, and leaving the monastery and surrounding dwellings a fire-blackened ruin, all but the Church, the Danes and the outlaws withdrew. No sooner had they done so than, on 2 June, Abbot Turold and his armed men arrived. Under his 'protection' the monks returned, a week after the attack. The Church, it was remembered:

> Before had stood full seven night
> Withouten any kind of rite.

Turold and the monks therefore, before all else, performed 'the service of Christ' in the Church and so re-sanctified it. It was also reported that Bishop Aethelric of Durham, who for some years had been resident at Peterborough before being arrested by King William's order and confined at Westminster, allegedly for having robbed the Church of Durham, on hearing of Hereward's assault on the Abbey issued a ban of excommunication against him on the grounds that some of what he had taken was the bishop's property. The bishop complained that they had sometime earlier 'carried off everything he possessed'. If he did, it had little effect on Hereward.

As Abbot, Turold proceeded to have a motte and bailey castle built within the minster precincts (the motte is still there adjacent to the cathedral in the prior's garden; it is known as 'Mount Turold'), he then 'evilly gave lands to his relatives and to the knights that came with him', and finally he demolished the original church (just as most other Norman abbots and bishops were to do elsewhere) to build a replacement.[4]

Meanwhile, the Danes and Hereward and his men had returned to Ely and there, for a time, the treasure remained. But King William, alarmed that the Danes had not yet left England, opened negotiations with King Swein of Denmark who was still lying with his main fleet off the coast of East Anglia. The two monarchs quickly reached agreement and Swein ordered the Danes at Ely to return to Denmark. That was when it all went wrong for Hereward. The Danes, having got their hands on the Peterborough treasures, refused to hand any of the plunder to the English, and, after pausing for two days in the Thames estuary, so rejoining King Swein, set sail for Denmark. With them, also, went Prior Aethelwold and several of his fellow monks, hoping to recover at least the relics which had been taken.

Unfortunately for the Danes, when they were halfway across the North Sea a terrible storm fell upon them and scattered the Danish fleet all over the North Sea, rather like the storm of 1588 which scattered the Spanish Armada. Some ended up in Norway, others were driven as far as Ireland, and a few staggered back to Denmark. So, very little of the treasure reached Denmark, only the altar frontal, some of the shrines and crosses and a few other treasures. Prior Aethelwold and his monks were among the survivors (no doubt praising God for taking vengeance on the Danes and for saving themselves) and the Danes reached a town near the coast, one of the King's royal manors, where they took refuge in the Church.

But the Danes, thankful for having escaped drowning, got drunk and, in their drunken stupor, set fire to the church. Aethelwold and the monks escaped, taking with them the relics and whatever they could carry. As had probably been agreed with Hereward, the monks were allowed to return to England with what they had managed to save and took refuge at Ramsey, where they left the relics, before returning to Peterborough. The relics were eventually restored to Peterborough, but only after Abbot Turold had threatened to burn down Ramsey Abbey.

Hereward's attack had not really been an act of random vandalism. This is shown by the fact that the Church was not destroyed and none of the monks were harmed. The list of treasures provides a good indication of the sort of wealth King William was hoping to acquire by plundering the monasteries. Of course, in the traditions of Peterborough and writings of William of Malmesbury, Hereward is criticized for his action as a 'latrunculus' or petty thief, whereas in the traditions of Ely and Crowland, he is their heroic defender. William's motive in so despoiling the monasteries was not only to enrich himself but so that he could enrich Norman monasteries with gold and silver plate, gold embroidered vestments and hangings (in the production of which English needlewomen excelled), reliquaries and books.

Hereward now had realised that the Normans would not let matters rest there. He was still an outlaw, based in the Fens, and he had now seriously offended King William. Hereward had no option but to hold out on the Isle of Ely and await the Norman response. It was not long in coming. Although the King himself took no part in the punitive measures adopted during the rest of 1070 and into 1071, he did order action to root out these remaining rebels. This was most likely the continuation of the policy of isolating Ely with a blockade during the risings of 1069. He is reported to have ordered 'brave and strong men... to gather together from towns and villages' and attack Hereward. Such attacks would have involved the King's local commanders in the area and no doubt men like William of Warenne, of Castle Acre, (who had his own quarrel with Hereward for killing his brother-in-law Frederick) and Ivo Taillebois, sheriff of Lincolnshire. Others involved would have included Richard fitzGilbert of Clare, in Suffolk, and the Cambridgeshire baron Harduin de Scalers. Hereward and his men are reported to have 'gone out against' these men, overwhelming and destroying any isolated groups of Normans they came across. Later it was claimed that

Hereward's name 'became known to all and the people told the story of his battles throughout the kingdom'. That perhaps explains why Hereward is introduced in 1070 by the scribe who wrote the Peterborough Chronicle as if he were a prominent magnate whose name would be familiar to all readers.

The attacks were fierce but strongly resisted, but some of Hereward's men, when reports came in of the strength of the Norman forces, despaired of being able to resist. Hereward, it is said, was enraged and fell on them in his fury, striking some of them so hard that they fell into the fens and drowned. Nonetheless, the Normans also found Hereward difficult to contend with and suggested to the King that Hereward should be offered terms under which he might be reconciled to the King. They argued that the Isle of Ely was too well fortified to be overcome merely in order to capture men who were now defending the 'heritage of their fathers'. This implies that the effort to deal with Hereward was proving costly in men, money and time. One report suggests that King William, who was now preoccupied with the reform of the English Church, agreed to this so that a truce was arranged whereby Hereward agreed not to continue raiding and attacking the Normans if he and his men were left alone. But that might only be a story concocted to explain King William's delay in dealing with Ely. It could also explain the story that Hereward was eventually reconciled to King William.[5]

However, deserted by his untrustworthy allies the Danes, Hereward remained at Ely supported by his outlaw band, described in fact as his 'genge', a word also used to describe the household troops of the English Earls. It was composed of members of his own extended family and by other tenants of Peterborough, together with a number of discontented Englishmen from all over East Anglia, that is men who had been 'condemned to be exiled and disinherited'. The Liber Eliensis insists that the outlaws carried out 'pillaging raids and depredations far and wide, a hundred men at a time or more than that'. Their offensives reassured the English people who lived in the Fens, which extended from the Fen edge to the south and east of Ely to the forest of Brunneswald in Northamptonshire, stretching in fact from north of Bedford to Ramsey, Oundle and Peterborough and then onwards into Lincolnshire.

Although recruits seem to have been plentiful, Hereward would not just accept all and sundry into his band. Instead he imposed a test on those seeking to join him. They had to pledge their loyalty to Hereward and his immediate companions by swearing an oath 'on the body of the most holy virgin Aethelthryth' (St Etheldreda) that they would devote all their strength and energy to the defence of the Isle of Ely. So the holy virgin became the patroness of the rebels, and Hereward could be reasonably sure that his recruits were not some kind of fifth column.

With the departure of the Danes, Hereward and his men and their Fenland supporters in the Isle of Ely continued to hold out, keeping a sharp lookout on all approaches to the Isle, determined to hold the Isle for as long as possible in the hope, perhaps, that King Swein would change his mind and decide to invade and drive the Normans out.

They had been invited to Ely in the first place because the people of the Isle trusted Hereward and his men to defend them. He therefore remained at Ely all through the autumn and winter into the spring of 1071. During this time he sent out messages to his kinsmen and friends, urging them to gather together all available fighting men whom 'the King had condemned to be exiled and disinherited, so that their company was strengthened in its opposition to their enemies'.[6]

Some of those who allied themselves to Hereward can be identified. He received a great deal of aid and support from a local thegn, Thorkell of Harringworth, known as Thorkell the Dane. He had lands in Northamptonshire and in the great forest area of the 'Brunneswald'. He had 'gone over to the Danes' on their arrival in England, having lost most of his lands to the Normans

His lands had been of what would later have been called 'baronial' extent, holding over two hundred hides or carucates in eight shires, and he was still able to rely on getting aid and supplies from his former tenants. It is thought that he could have been the son of Cnut the Great's Earl of East Anglia, Thorkell the Tall.

Others who rallied to the cause included King's thegns like Siward 'of Maldon' and Ordgar, sheriff of Cambridgeshire with lands in the 'Soke' or Liberty of the Abbey of Bury St Edmunds, or Thorbeorht of Freckenham. As Hereward was also joined by Earl Morcar, he had the additional support of relatives of the earl such as Godric of Corby and Tostig of Daventry.

Many members of Hereward's extended family were there; his paternal cousins Siward the Red and Siward the Black, his nephews, Outi and Douti and others more vaguely described as 'kinsmen'. There were also many East Anglian thegns, men driven out of their estates, such as Rahere, called 'the Heron' (because he could pass through the Fens on stilts), he was from Wroxham Bridge in the Broads, and even a monk from St Edmunds called Siward. These men formed part of Hereward's company or 'genge', his personal household fighting men, which was over fifty strong.[7]

Hereward was not content merely to sit in the Isle and wait for the Normans to attack. He took the offensive, carrying out pillaging raids far and wide, leading forces of a hundred men or more. Naturally the outlaws suffered heavy casualties and were often driven back to take refuge on the Isle, but they inflicted equally heavy casualties on the Normans and encouraged the fenlanders to continue their resistance to Norman rule.

Various people affected to a greater or lesser extent by the coming of the Normans also took refuge on the Isle. It is claimed that even Archbishop Stigand came there, presumably well before his arrest and trial leading to his deposition from office, possibly during 1067, in order to deposit his personal treasure and collection of relics with the Abbot of Ely, Thurstan, for safe keeping. Stigand is said to have urged Abbot Ecgfrith of St Albans to do likewise. Both were deposed in the spring of 1070.

Recruits came from quite remote parts of the country and one such party consisted of thegns holding lands under the Abbey of Abingdon in Berkshire. They set out to join the rebels at Ely but were intercepted and dealt with by the King's men. The Abingdon Chronicle is critical of them, saying that they ought 'to have sustained the cause of King William, but listened to the opposite advice and went armed to join the enemies of the King'. A result of that was the arrest and imprisonment of the Abbot, Brichtwine (also called Ealdred), who was deposed, and imprisoned at Wallingford. He was then moved to Winchester and put under the charge of Bishop Walkelin for the rest of his life. Aethelhelm then became Abbot of Abingdon 'by the express order of King William'. He was a monk from Jumièges.

Although recruits were plentiful, Hereward was unwilling to accept just anybody and, as has been mentioned earlier, he took the precaution of making his men swear loyalty over the body of St Etheldreda.

Despite the extent of Hereward's activities and the obvious concerns of his local magnates, King William as yet took no part in assaults on the Isle of Ely. Although the menace of the threat from the Danes had been faced and, for the time being, removed, William was more concerned about the situation in Maine and, even more so, about the incursions of King Malcolm of Scotland. But then, events took a turn which put the problem of Ely in a very different light.[8]

During Spring 1071 trouble began again. The Earls, Edwin and Morcar, despite having repeatedly been allowed to renew their submission, still resented their loss of power and the elevation over them of various Norman lords. Earl Edwin in particular had found that King William still showed no sign of giving him the daughter he had promised him in marriage. He had seen large areas of his earldom ravaged by Norman armies and authority within it granted away to the marcher Earls of Shrewsbury and Chester with wide powers over Mercian shires granted to the collaborator, Abbot

Aethelwig of Evesham. He and his brother Morcar no longer trusted the King's word. Morcar's earldom had, in effect, been split into two parts, the southern half governed from York by a Norman sheriff, and the northern half governed by the Norman Bishop of Durham, Walcher, along with Earl Waltheof, all of which was detrimental to Earl Morcar's power and influence.

Sometime that Spring, the two English Earls became aware of rumours that King William intended to have them actually arrested and imprisoned. Various Norman lords were casting envious and greedy eyes on the lands the two Earls still held and constantly whispered against them in the King's ears. So, once more, they fled from the King's Court where they had been held in some sort of house arrest, and sought to avoid recapture. They 'ran off, travelling here through woods and there over open countryside', dodging recapture for almost six months until they eventually parted company.[9]

During their travels they met and joined a party of nobles led by Bishop Aethelwine of Durham, now also on the run as an outlaw, and the wealthy Danelaw thegn called Siward Barn. These latter two had been among the remnants of the northern army at Wearmouth and, when others decided to join Edgar the Aetheling, in Scotland, they had decided not to do so but to take ship from Wearmouth and escape by sea to Cologne. They had been unable to make the crossing because of storms in the North Sea, which also prevented a return to Scotland or Northern England. Their ship was blown instead southwards and they had taken refuge in the Humber. The coming of storms suggests that it was now September and past the Equinox (16 September), so the refugees decided that they needed somewhere safe where they could spend the winter, before trying again in the following Spring.

Sailing down the coast to the Wash, all parties came together at 'Welle' in the Fens, in the vicinity of present day Upwell and Outwell, having sailed from Wisbech up the 'Wellstream'. This watercourse flowed into the Ouse River which, at that time, entered the Wash at Wisbech. There they were met by Hereward who had no doubt been warned by his lookouts of their arrival. He invited them to join him at Ely. Tradition at Ely insists that both Earls, Edwin as well as Morcar, took refuge there, but if Edwin did so, he did not stay long. Orderic Vitalis reports his movements and eventual fate, though his chronology is faulty and he was somewhat misinformed about the details. He thought Edwin was still alive after his brother Morcar had been imprisoned by King William, which was after the fall of Ely, and that he tried to organise his brother's escape. Orderic perhaps confuses events in 1071 with the escape of the Earls in 1070. But the continuing conflict at Ely must have occupied over a year, from 24 June 1070, when the Danes finally left England, until the October of 1071.[10]

Some of what Orderic says came to him as a result of a visit he made to Ely early in the next century where he found copies of a ballad about the unhappy fate of Earl Edwin. Apparently, the Earl decided not to wait out the winter at Ely but to make his own way, overland, to Scotland. He set off with his own household servants and some fighting men, about two dozen in all, and set out northwards through the Fens, probably using the Wellstream in order to pass the Wash and get into Lincolnshire.

But, on his way, he was betrayed by three of his own servants, who informed the Normans of the Earl's whereabouts, hoping to earn the gratitude of the King. The Earl and his party were trapped by a party of Norman knights 'between a rising high tide and a tidal estuary' (that is, 'ex aestuatio marina'), which aptly describes conditions for an attempt to cross the Welland or some other South Lincolnshire river leading into the Wash. There he was overcome and slain. His betrayers cut off his head and took it to King William, expecting to be suitably rewarded. Instead, the King, whose moods could be extremely volatile and unpredictable, was appalled by their treachery to their lord and wept at the news of Earl Edwin's death which had spread throughout England. He turned on the three disloyal and treacherous men and had them banished from the Kingdom in disgrace.[11]

Meanwhile, all the surviving leaders of English opposition, with, it was said, many hundreds of men, (other than those who were cowering in Scotland) were gathered together in one place, the formidable and almost impregnable island 'fortress' which was the Isle of Ely, with its equally defensible Fenland monastery. The rivers, meres and marshes surrounding the Isle made it a most formidable obstacle. It could not easily be taken by storm by an army as reliant on cavalry as that of King William. The most obvious mode of attack would have been by water, but any attempt to land on the Isle by boat could be countered and repulsed. There was also something of a ring of castles, mainly campaign forts or field works built in the course of the campaigns in the Fens; they were located at Aldreth, Wisbech and Peterborough and supported by the ones built earlier at Cambridge and Huntingdon.

The usual ways on to the Isle could also be watched and defended. The causeways (or causeys) through the marshes from Willingham, Earith, Soham or Downham were well known to the defenders and could be held by quite small forces. In addition the defenders constructed fortifications out of peat and wood, forming ramparts to deter attack on those places where an attack could be expected, and from which a barrage of missiles, stones from slingers, arrows, javelins and so on, could be launched.

Hereward and his men had already held out for some considerable time, many months in fact, as the Abingdon Chronicle hints, against the best efforts of local Norman magnates. The outlaws hid in the marshes and conducted a war of ambush and affray. Hereward had caused trouble for Abbot Turold of Peterborough, on one occasion allegedly capturing him and only releasing him after a large ransom was paid. He had confronted William of Warenne, based then at his fortress of Castle Acre, and the Sheriff of Lincolnshire, Ivo Taillebois. The Norman lords complained bitterly to the King about Hereward's 'many insidious stratagems' which caused them 'wearisome trouble'. Ely would not easily be taken, if at all. To rely on a long drawn out siege would be expensive in supplies and man power and the Isle was known to be well-stocked with food and water.

The Bastard had other important matters which would soon require his attention. His presence was becoming essential back in Normandy, where there was a threat from Maine and Anjou as well as Brittany. Malcolm III of Scotland was a constant thorn in William's flesh. The King had already had to pay a short visit to Normandy, earlier in the year, to negotiate with King Philip I of France in order to ease the situation there. On his return, William had learned of the flight of the Earls Edwin and Morcar and informants had reported on the gathering at Ely. He now knew that the Isle had acquired a large and dangerous fighting force, augmented by the warriors accompanying the rebel leaders. They were assisted by the dangerous outlaw, Hereward, a man with several years of successful military experience in northern France and Flanders, well-versed in Continental methods of warfare. He was a former Magister Militum in the service of Robert the Frisian. He alone was a magnet capable of attracting a growing number of disaffected and rebellious Englishmen. The Isle could, potentially, be reinforced from the sea, by the Danes or the thousands of English exiles on the Continent in Denmark and Flanders. King William could not afford to leave Ely to fester as it was likely to erupt and cause him considerable trouble. Taken together with the ever present threat from Denmark, the Isle had to be dealt with, and quickly. The Bastard decided on a major determined campaign and, as the *Peterborough Chronicle* reports:

> When King William heard of this, he ordered out naval and land levies and surrounded the district, building a causeway as he advanced deeper into the Fens, while the naval force remained to seaward.

Reports suggest that this 'causeway' was some two miles long and that the attack was launched more or less from the West, though south west would be more accurate. That there was a causeway is undeniable. A writ, addressed in 1082 to Archbishop Lanfranc, the Count of Mortain and Bishop Geoffrey of Coutances contains the instruction 'Lastly, those men are to maintain the causeway at Ely who, by the King's command, have done so hitherto.' Unfortunately it does not specify the exact location.[12]

The accounts of the struggle recorded in the Liber Eliensis (and elsewhere) insist that the King approached the Isle from the direction of the Royal Castle at Cambridge and that he made use of an existing track through the south western marshes from Willingham, leading to a place named as 'Aldreth' or 'Alrehede', that is, 'the landing stage of the alders'. The track is still there, leading by way of the Iron Age fort, 'Belsar's Hill', to the Old West River (now part of the River Great Ouse). It was a narrow and winding track, the most useful way to get on to the Isle, but would not have been wide enough or firm enough for William's cavalry and footsoldiers, so he undoubtedly widened and strengthened it and so built his causeway. He set up a base on the track, constructing a 'castellum', not a motte and bailey castle but a defensible palisade within which tents could be pitched and supplies stored. Logic suggests that, as at Anderida when he landed in 1066, the King made use of Belsar's Hill, repairing the earthwork where necessary and erecting a palisade.

The Old West River, in the eleventh century, flowed west not east, from a watershed near Stretham. The flow was reversed at some time during the thirteenth century so that the Ouse flowed east and then north to meet the Wash at King's Lynn, whereas earlier it had run from Earith to Wisbech. The causeway probably ended not far from the present hamlet of Aldreth where the Aldreth High Bridge used to stand.

While the causeway was under construction, the Normans tried to cross the River Granta (Gronte fluminis) just beyond Stretham, by making a ford with heaps of wood and sand, but the force of the waters there was too strong. This was where several streams flowed into the Granta and the river formed a sort of confluence with very turbulent water. The defenders were ready for them and repelled them from behind defences made of peat. The Normans could not cross a well defended ford in such marshy conditions.

The Normans had advanced from Cambridge over a fairly wide front, occupying Reach and Burwell and the prehistoric earthwork 'Devil's Dyke'. At Reach they set up a secondary base. Hereward and a small force of his best men attacked the base and killed all but one of the Norman garrison.[13]

But King William, having reached the river, had various materials brought up, intending to use them to build a rough and ready structure of timber and brushwood, supported on tree trunks and stones buoyed up by sheep skins filled with air. This jerry-built bridge was pushed out over the river until it reached the opposing bank. Then, as soon as it touched the bank, the Normans, eager to demonstrate their zeal and keen to capture Ely and its treasures, rushed pell mell onto the bridge. It is likely that the local peasantry, press-ganged into doing the heavy manual work required, had been more than careless in constructing it because, overloaded with the weight of men and horses, the bridge collapsed into the river. The leading soldiers and knights were thrown helplessly into its swirling waters and were 'swallowed up in the waters and the deep swamp'. Only one man, the first to cross, made it to the other side and he, a knight called Deda, was promptly seized by the defenders and taken to Hereward.

The number killed by the collapse is unknown but must have been considerable since the bodies of the dead were still being found, complete with rotting armour, at the time the account in the Liber Eliensis was first written, early in the twelfth century. Deda was well treated, shown exactly what Hereward wished him to see, and no more, and then released. He was shown enough to convince him that the defences of Ely were strong, that it had plentiful supplies of men, food and water, and could not be easily overwhelmed.

King William himself was alarmed and depressed by the disaster, though he could not yet afford to leave the pocket of resistance intact at Ely. He retreated to a royal manor, at Brampton where he sulked, like Achilles in his tent. His leading magnates pressed him to resume the attack, warning that defeat would encourage further English resistance and that Hereward, who had ravaged manors in Cambridgeshire and Norfolk, had to be stopped. The King, despite his anger, answered that the Isle seemed to be defended 'by the power of God' and that he was not sure he could capture it.

Ivo Taillebois and others insisted on a new attempt being made and wore down the King's resistance to the idea. Ivo himself advocated using a local wisewoman, a sort of witch or pythoness, to curse the English defenders in the hope of weakening their resolve. Another Norman, a young knight called Richard fitzOsbert, who had survived the attack on Reach, tried to argue for giving up the attempt but was overruled. The King then settled on a more considered approach. He ordered the construction of a more stable bridge, equipped with siege towers. All the local fen dwellers with boats were co-opted to ferry more materials to the riverbank, by way of a local watercourse called 'Cotingelade' (the watercourse of Cotta's people), near the vill of Cottenham.

Meanwhile, as fitzOsbert had reported, Hereward had not been idle. He and his men had made a foray from the Isle during which they burned down the vill of Burwell and attacked the garrison at Reach. Only fitzOsbert had survived. Hereward had let him go unharmed, saying that it was unfair for seven men to fight one young man. The account of Hereward's exploits, the Gesta Herewardi, includes the usual tales intended to embellish the reputation of its hero. Hereward is credited with having entered the King's camp at Brampton, disguised as a seller of oil lamps, in order to discover what he could of King William's intentions. More likely, however, he had been kept informed by local peasants recruited to work for the Normans. But the story claims that the 'pythoness' or witch was seen making preparations for her task of putting a curse on the defenders. She was seen to go into the marshes to consult 'the Watchman of the Springs', her guardian spirit from which she was alleged to derive her magical powers. She appears to have tamed a giant Eel, probably by feeding it and making it her pet. From this Hereward was able to reassure his men that she was quite harmless. The story, of course, ends with Hereward being unmasked by one of the King's servants, having to fight his way out of the camp and return to Ely by way of Somersham. The tale conceals, behind the heroic trappings, the fact that Hereward and his men had spied on the Normans and been kept informed of the King's plans by local supporters.[14]

The building of the new bridge proceeded apace. Again it was made of tree trunks and timbers but supported this time by sheepskins filled with sand and stones. The two siege towers were to be brought up to the river bank so that missiles could be launched to drive the defending English back from their defences. The witch was made to stand on the top of one of the towers to begin casting her spells. She began her ritual incantations 'forecasting destruction and uttering charms' designed to instil fear in the hearts of the King's enemies. She is even said to have insulted the English by baring her naked buttocks at them.

But Hereward and his companions had made their own counter-measures. They infiltrated the Norman side of the river, moving through the marshes by paths well known to them and mingling among the workers recruited to build the bridge. So now, just as the witch was reaching the climax of her ritual and as the towers were rolled forward to begin their bombardment, they threw off their disguises, revealing hidden armour, and attacked the Normans, throwing them into confusion by setting fire to the siege towers and the timbers of the bridge. The whole structure went up in flames as the Englishmen threw burning rushes and reeds soaked in oil onto the bridge. The unfortunate witch herself was trapped on her burning tower and, choking with the fumes and smoke and hysterical with fear, 'as if by a whirlwind' was made to fall from the tower and break her neck. She who had intended the death of others herself perished.

The fire grew fiercer, fanned by the wind, and spread into the surrounding reeds for a distance of two furlongs. Hereward's men aided the spread by throwing burning brands into the reeds. So the fire spread through the fen with the peatbog below also catching fire, below the surface of the marsh, spreading out of sight and then rising to the surface in unexpected places, engulfing the fleeing Normans. Some attempted to escape on foot, others on horseback, along paths in the marsh, stupefied by the terrifying raging fire and the noise of the inferno as the reeds and willows crackled in the flames. The Normans were driven almost insane with fear, especially of falling into the pits of fire when they erupted.

Hereward's men, more familiar with the spread of fire in the Fens, pursued the Normans, firing arrows and throwing javelins. So, as the Liber Eliensis boasts, 'a hundred men were routed in terror by one man and a thousand from confrontation with ten of his followers'. So calamity, inspired by the tactics of the defenders, struck the Norman army once more. The fire continued to burn in the peat long after the Normans had once more retreated to Brampton, rendering any further attempt to cross the river at Aldreth impossible.

As for the Normans and their King, they were thrown into both fury and grief and the Bastard decided upon a more deceitful strategy. The Isle was already blockaded from all sides, especially by water as King William's 'butsecarles' (the fighting boatmen) had been set to prevent any escape by boat and to prevent the arrival of reinforcements. The King redoubled the watch on the Isle to prevent all escape. Butsecarles were used to harry the defenders, probing for weak points in the defences. Weapons have been found in the Ouse at Braham Dock, Dimmock's Cote and Rollers Lode, suggesting fierce fighting all along the river.[15]

King William now announced that all lands nearest to the Isle belonging to the Church at Ely would be forfeited to the royal demesne and then bestowed on his followers. This announcement was leaked to the monks at Ely by the King's agents and greatly worried the Abbot, Thurstan, who decided on seeking the King's favour if he could to prevent the loss of church lands and safeguard the interests of his monastery. It seems that the Abbot had visited a vill in Bottisham called 'Angerhale' where he had hidden much of the abbey's treasure and while there had learned of the threat to confiscate the abbey lands.

In order to win back the King's favour, the abbot decided to advise him how he might most successfully breach the Isle's defences. Thurstan assured the King that the people of the Isle would cease all resistance if told to do so by their Abbot.

King William also sought to deceive Earl Morcar and the other leading nobles at Ely by promising them, through 'crafty messengers', who put to them 'treacherous terms', that if they were to surrender, the King would allow each of them to be 'received in peace as a loyal friend'. They also pointed out the risks involved in holding out until they were forced to attempt an escape by water.

Earl Morcar and his companions were deceived and agreed to lead their men out, seek out the King and surrender. These messengers also negotiated with Abbot Thurstan and he and his fellow monks, after praying for guidance at the tomb of 'Christ's beloved betrothed, Aethelthryth', sent envoys to the King promising submission. All these specious promises had only one aim, to weaken the resolve of the defenders, and to foster dissension between the Earl and his company, the Abbot and his monks, and Hereward and his men. The Liber Eliensis glosses over the Abbot's part in all this, suggesting that he drove a hard bargain with the King and obtained a guarantee that the lands of the abbey would be restored.

On the Abbot's advice, King William retreated to Cottenham and from there followed a winding and perilous route through the fens, bringing his supplies and men by boat along the lodes south of the Isle from Cottenham to Stretham, avoiding the more treacherous areas of the marsh, masked as they were by beds of Flag Iris which looked solid but were liable to split open and swallow up the unwary traveller.

At times the Normans found themselves walking over the bodies of dead men or horses which had perished in the fens, struggling across the many streams and meres, some deep, some shallow. At one point even the King found himself having to wade up to his neck through marshy water. But at last the Normans came to a point on the Old West River where there was a spur of higher ground which met the river opposite Little Thetford, not far from a stream then known as the Alderbrook and its crossing point 'Alderforth', the ford of the alders. (That has caused a great deal of confusion over the exact location at which the Normans crossed onto the Isle.)

Once there, the King brought up more of his men by boat, using the wide, flat-bottomed Fen craft, ancestors of the modern punt, to ferry engineers and ballista men who could use catapults to bombard the enemy. The area of conflict was to be known in later centuries as 'Hereward's Reach' where his men made their last stand.

Finding himself once more opposed by the defenders who had concealed themselves behind barriers made of peat, the King ordered his men to bombard the defences and drive the defenders back from the river bank. So fierce was the bombardment that 'the unstable ground shook, threatening everyone supported by it with drowning' until the defenders eventually gave way and fled.

The Normans then put together a floating bridge composed of fen boats lashed together and overlaid with reeds and planks. It literally formed a 'pontoon bridge' and across this 'weak and shaky bridge' the Norman knights and footsoldiers swarmed over the river and up the opposing shore past Little Thetford onto firmer ground near what is now Bedwell Hay Farm. It is not that far from the site believed by archaeologists to be that of 'Cratendune', whose inhabitants were moved by St Aethelthryth to the higher ground around her church at Ely.

> Then the resounding cry of victory drove the enemy from the Isle... so that few escaped and they only with difficulty.

The Norman force swept onto the Isle and divided into two columns; one driving directly along Akerman Street (roughly the line of the A10) towards Ely, the other swinging round through Witchford to approach the town and the abbey from the West. Thus the remaining forces of the Earl Morcar and his companions found themselves surrounded and taken prisoner.

The Bastard then proceeded to vent his rage on the leaders of the resistance and their thegns and Housecarls. The armed men were led out; first the leaders, then a considerable number of men who were prominent because of their reputation or some mark of distinction. He sentenced some to imprisonment, some to loss of eyes, hands or feet; but he released unpunished the mass of common people.

The plentiful goods found in the Abbey precincts were confiscated to compensate the King for the horses lost in the struggle and the time and trouble he had expended in overcoming resistance. Earl Morcar was thrown into gaol and left in the charge of Roger the castellan, of Beaumont, to be kept in prison for the rest of his days. On his own deathbed, King William ordered Morcar's release, as well as that of other noble prisoners, but King William Rufus had Morcar re-arrested and imprisoned and he died in prison.[16]

Bishop Aethelwine of Durham was arrested and imprisoned at Abingdon where he died shortly after his incarceration, on 15 October. That helps to date the conclusion of the struggle at Ely, towards the end of September 1071. The Bishop was buried in the side-chapel of St Nicholas at Abingdon and Orderic Vitalis says that he had asked to be buried still wearing the fetters of his imprisonment as a mark of his suffering. Siward Barn was also imprisoned and was eventually released in 1097. He was believed to have gone into exile at Byzantium, like so many others, and to have taken service in the Varangian Guard. Of the fate of other prominent men little more is known, though many must have suffered mutilation. Their estates were confiscated, as Domesday Book shows. Thorkell of Harringworth's lands, for instance, went to Earl Waltheof, who, in his turn, lost them in 1075. Sheriff Ordgar of Cambridgeshire was deposed from office and replaced by the dreaded Picot of ill-repute, who was 'a hungry lion, a ravening wolf, a cunning fox, a dirty pig, an impudent dog' as the monks of Ely put it. Siward of Maldon lost his lands to Rannulf Peverel although the Abbey of Ely later claimed in its lawsuit for the recovery of some of its lands that Rannulf held Siward's lands (he held some as a tenant of Ely) illegally. That would mean that Rannulf had not troubled to obtain the King's writ and seal to validate his land grab.

The one exception was Hereward himself. He and many of his men had been absent from Ely at the time of the King's final attack, perhaps because they had been deceived by Abbot Thurstan. Hereward went out on one of his forays against the Normans and returned to find that they had got onto the Isle and were approaching Ely. He was at first tempted to set fire to the abbey and the town, perhaps intending a final act of defiance, but was persuaded instead to escape. He and those who were willing to go with him took to their boats and escaped into the fens to freedom. His fate thereafter became the stuff of legend.

He was alleged to have hidden in the Brunneswald and to have continued to cause the Normans trouble as an outlaw, a forerunner of Robin Hood. A well-born Lady, influential at Court, was said to have persuaded the King to allow him to be reconciled and be restored to some of his family lands. But there is no evidence for this in Domesday Book, and it probably arises from confusion between Hereward the thegn of Lincolnshire and another man of that name with lands in Warwickshire and Worcestershire. Hereward was, in this version, said to have lived to a ripe old age and to have died and been buried at Crowland.

The alternative version, found in Geoffrey Gaimar's works, also alleged that he was reconciled to the King, but in this version he went with the army to Maine and, during his return home, was betrayed by his own servants and murdered in an heroic struggle against a gang of Normans led by 'Ralph of Dol' who beheaded him. The poet is giving his hero a hero's death and possibly had confused him with Earl Edwin who was killed in a similar manner. As Hereward was later, erroneously, believed to be the son of Earl Leofric, it is likely that the poet had heard or read a ballad about Earl Edwin's death in which his name was not actually used, and Geoffrey jumped to the conclusion that it was describing the death of Hereward. 'Ralph of Dol' is an echo of Earl Ralph de Gael of East Anglia who rebelled in 1075.

Hereward's most likely fate was probably that of so many other Englishmen at that time, to go into exile, perhaps back to Flanders, and eventually to have died there. His name lived on in Lincolnshire and East Anglia and during the twelfth century it was quite common for parents to name their sons after him. He certainly had no connection with the Wake family, Barons of Bourne from the reign of Henry I onwards, though their claim to be descended from him resulted in his nickname of 'the Wake'.[17]

The account of the fall of Ely ends with King William fining Abbot Thurstan and his monks extremely heavily because of their involvement in the resistance, over 1000 silver marks. It was so heavy that they had to surrender everything of value in the Abbey, even a gold and silver statue of the Virgin Mary, enthroned and holding the Child Jesus in her arms, and all the ornaments on the tomb of St Aethelthryth.

King William himself visited the Church at Ely, posting guards so that he would not be disturbed by the monks (who were then chided by Richard fitzGilbert for ignoring the king's presence!). William did not dare approach too closely to the tomb of Saint Aethelthryth, fearing, it was said, the judgement that God might pass on him for capturing the holy sanctuary and for the violence used by his men. Instead he merely threw a gold mark onto the High Altar and hurriedly left.

His fearfulness did not prevent him from extracting money from the Abbot or imposing the burden of at least forty knights on the Abbey, to be kept in a garrison there at the monks' expense. They were used to provide a castle guard at Norwich as there was no castle at Ely. (The Motte and Bailey Castle at Ely was more likely the work of Bishop Nigel, the first Bishop of Ely, appointed by Henry I).

The Abbot, Thurstan, is reported to have tried to plead the ancient rights of his abbey, the Liberty of St Etheldreda, with its freedom from royal interference. But King William spurned the Abbot's prayers and gifts, refusing to revoke his demand that knights be retained to garrison the Isle of Ely since they were 'well-born adherents of the King'. The Abbot had to bestow arms on these men and maintain them, according to custom, and let them live in the hall of the Abbey within its precincts. They were paid daily wages and given their provisions by the Cellarer.

Eventually this proved such a burden that the Abbot had to provide these 'intruders' with fiefs carved out of the Abbey's lands and men like Picot, sheriff of Cambridgeshire, Harduin de Scalers, Roger Bigod and Hervey de Bourges came to hold fiefs under the Abbot. That enfeofment might well have been carried out by Theodwine of Jumièges who was made Abbot in place of Thurstan in 1072. He used his appointment as an opportunity to demand the restoration of the Abbey's 'gold and silver and precious stones' which the King had taken from St Aethelthryth. No doubt this was a means of gaining the obedience and loyalty of the monks.

Having defeated the last remnants of English resistance, King William withdrew, most likely via Cambridge, to London to consider his next moves.[18]

The Normanization of England Begins:
Autumn 1071 to December 1074

Having dealt with the last flickers of rebellion in East Anglia, King William set about sorting out a number of pressing problems. The Aetheling, Edgar, still represented a possible focus for the activities of 'renegade' Englishmen such as Eadric the Wild. The 'marcher' lands facing Wales and Scotland had to be brought thoroughly under Norman control and there were problems arising back in Normandy. Above all, however, the King needed to satisfy Rome that he would carry out his promise to reform the English Church.

Ever since 1066 when Malcolm III, Canmore (his cognomen means 'great chief' rather than 'bighead') had given sanctuary to the exiled Earl Tostig of Northumbria, Scotland had served as a refuge for men regarded by the Norman King as renegades. Edgar Aetheling had been an honoured guest at Malcolm's Court and, by 1071, King Malcolm had married Edgar's sister, Margaret. King William's campaigns in the North in 1069-70 had brought, as might have been expected, a reaction from King Malcolm. He was now the most immediate threat to the stability of the Anglo-Norman Kingdom.[1]

It was a question of frontiers. Events in Maine and Flanders had no doubt worried King William more than the continuing resistance led by Hereward in the Fens, though the King had realised that he could not afford to leave such a source of trouble unquenched and had accordingly dealt with it in his accustomed manner. Furthermore, an earldom had been established in Norfolk to provide some protection against the Danes. Even in Britain there were other matters requiring urgent attention. The other Celtic region, Wales, was also a challenge to William's hegemony.

King William probably dealt with Wales first, after settling the problem of Ely. Just as the potential threat of an invasion from Flanders had been dealt with by appointing his half brother, Odo, Bishop of Bayeux, as Earl of Kent in 1067 and his right-hand man, so William fitzOsbern had been made Earl of Hereford, to keep an eye on the South Welsh princes. FitzOsbern had contended in South Wales, with the aid of Caradoc ap Gruffydd ap Rhydderch, against the troublesome Princes of North Wales. There had been at least one battle, on the river Rumney. That began the gradual acquisition of territory in Wales by the Normans. There are reports of 'French' harrying in Ceredigion, Menevia and Bangor. Roger of Montgomery made incursions into Dyfed and Ceredigion, aided by a knight called Warren the Bald, and William fitzOsbern fought Rhys Cadwgan and Meredydd.[2]

Now fiefdoms were established at Chester and Shrewsbury to defend Offa's Dyke. They did not immediately become earldoms. Chester was handed to Gerbod, brother of Frederick Oosterzele-Scheldewindeke (who married Gundrada, sister of William of Warenne), but he decided, in 1071, to return to Flanders, allegedly uncomfortable with the impact of constant English attacks. Perhaps he was actually disappointed not to have been given the title of Earl. He was replaced sometime before 1077 by Hugh of Avranches who, with Robert of Rhuddlan was certainly fighting the North Welsh from 1073 onwards. Shrewsbury became an Earldom for Roger II of Montgomery by 4 November 1074. It looks possible that both were given extensive estates in these areas, perhaps at the Christmas Court of 1071, with a view to promoting them to their Earldoms in due course.

During the rebellions of 1069-70, King Malcolm also gave refuge to Earl Waltheof, and to many other English exiles. He assisted them by providing a base, a 'snug nest for tyranny', from which English and Danish troops could 'cut to pieces William's generals'. King Malcolm had also, for Edgar the Aetheling's sake, 'ravaged the neighbouring provinces of England with robbery and arson', not because he thought it would further Edgar's hope of becoming King, but simply to annoy William as it would anger the Norman King to see his own lands exposed to Scottish forays. It was that which eventually provoked King William into invading Scotland. But, as William of Malmesbury, whose account of these events is somewhat confused, implies, part of King William's motive in ravaging north of York after he had taken it in 1069, was to deprive King Malcolm and his men of supplies and sustenance when they raided England. Having routed the rebels, with the loss of many of his own men, King William had ordered the region to be devastated, in the first instance in order to deprive the Danes led by King Swein's son Cnut of food and support. He intended to 'leave nothing near the seashore which a raiding pirate could find and carry off… or use for food.' The writer confirms other accounts of the ravaging, saying that the province was hamstrung by fire, rapine and bloodshed; the ground for sixty miles and more left entirely uncultivated, the soil quite bare even down to the writer's own day in the twelfth century.

William of Malmesbury appears to think that some of this harrying occurred during 1072 when William passed that way to invade Scotland

and it could be that the passage of the Anglo-Norman army made matters worse. However, also during 1070, King Malcolm had ravaged as far south as Cleveland, destroying what little the Normans had left there. He reached the mouth of the Wear and burned St Peter's Church. He had invaded via Cumberland, over the pass of Stainmore into Teesdale, circling around rather than penetrating into Northumbria proper. His raid had petered out before the walls of Durham, and he lost most of the booty he had taken. This caused Earl Cospatric to respond by devastating Cumbria (then held by the Scots) before returning to Bamburgh. Malcolm took English people into slavery in Scotland. Consequently, Bishop Walcher was sent by King William to be Bishop of Durham, after Bishop Aethelric had died, and was welcomed by the surviving nobility and Earl Waltheof was appointed to rule English Northumbria.

The harrying had made the North even more uncontrollable and it proved to be impossible to prevent the Cumbrians and the King of the Scots from raiding in the North. The area was only finally occupied and tamed after Yorkshire had been redeveloped many years later.

King William, on the other hand, now felt reasonably satisfied that he had overcome all meaningful opposition in England. The years 1070-1071 had seen the end of the organised rebellions and the last flicker of Danish intervention on land in alliance with Hereward and his men. King William had 'pacified' the North, Roman style, 'make a desert and call it peace'. The process of distribution of the estates of fallen or exiled thegns to William's Norman followers was well under way and the King could turn his attention to the 'cleansing' of the English Church. The Danes had been bought off with 'Danegeld' in time-honoured fashion, and the Norman regime had survived its first major test. The king could also take steps to ensure the resumption and continuance of regular government. It was most likely that it had been late in 1070, perhaps at the midwinter Council held in Gloucester at Christmas, that, as the various compilations of laws made in the twelfth century all agree, King William renewed 'the Law of King Edward', with such additions from Norman practice as he thought would prove most useful.

At Easter, 4 April, in 1070 King William had welcomed the Papal legates at a Synod held at Winchester. These were the Cardinal Bishop of Sitten, Ermenfrid (holding the See of Sion 'in partibus infidelium'), a cardinal deacon, John Minutus, and another cardinal priest, Peter the Bibliothecarius. The legate presided at a solemn 'crown-wearing' and placed the crown on William's head. This was seen by the Normans as Papal approval of William's accession, and by the Papacy as an indication that William was the Pope's vassal (a delusion of which the Papacy was to be disabused a few years later). John and Peter returned to Rome at Pentecost, after the Synod held at Windsor on 23 May, but Bishop Ermenfrid remained to complete his inspection of the English Church. The main business of the synod had been the deposition, beginning on 7 April and ending on the 11 April, of Stigand, who had retained his hold on Canterbury despite losing Winchester, and the elevation of Lanfranc of Bec to replace him.[3]

Stigand was accused of pluralism, because he had retained the bishopric of Winchester after his appointment to Canterbury, and of simony, although no proof has been found that he bought his church appointments. William of Malmesbury accuses him of buying and selling sacred offices but produces no examples. He admits that in his own view Stigand's fault was to be mistaken rather than to sin deliberately. More seriously Stigand was accused of intrusion, that is, of having occupied the See of another Bishop (Robert of Jumièges) while that Bishop still lived, contrary to Canon Law. Yet Archbishop Robert had also breached the Canons by deserting his See and leaving it without a Shepherd. Finally Stigand was accused of having accepted a pallium from an Anti-Pope, Benedict X, despite the fact that he could not have known that Benedict would be rejected by the majority of the cardinals. Stigand, dismayed at these charges protested that the sentence against him was unjust. Then he called on King William to come to his aid since the King had treated him as a friend ever since 1066. In the end, Stigand rejected the authority of his judges. Nonetheless, he was deposed and sentenced to life imprisonment.

Other Bishops and Abbots were deposed and replaced (no longer was William prepared to wait until they died). Stigand's brother, Aethelmaer, Bishop of Elmham fell with him, as did Leofwine, Bishop of Lichfield (who resigned, jumping before he was pushed and retiring to Coventry) and Aethelric, Bishop of Selsey. It is possible that Abbot Ecgfrith of St Albans was also removed. But this did not satisfy the King and the process continued until only seven English bishops remained in office (and most of them did not last long). Of the seven survivors five were foreigners, mainly from Lotharingia, one was a Norman and the last an Englishman, Bishop Wulfstan of Worcester. Overall William was to make sixteen Episcopal appointments to the twelve sees, mainly Normans with two Lotharingians and one from Maine. In accordance with established Norman practice, soon to be condemned by the Papacy, he invested his bishops with ring and staff (though it is not certain that King Edward had done so). The abbots fared no better and only three remained in office by 1087. In these early years Aethelsige of St Augustine's, Canterbury, Aethelnoth of Glastonbury, Godric of Winchcombe, Sihtric of Tavistock (who fled into exile and became, to the Normans, a pirate) and Wulfric of New Minster, Winchester were all removed, not forgetting Bishop Aethelwine of Durham's brother Aethelric, and, after 1071, so was Abbot Thurstan of Ely. All were replaced by men from overseas. Many of the depositions were clearly political rather than purely canonical and seem to reflect knowledge of, or the suspicion that, those deposed had given support, open or tacit, to the rebellions.

Bishop Aethelric's brother, Aethelwine, had been allowed to return to his see of Durham during Lent but at the Whitsun synod he was declared an outlaw and so set off to flee to Cologne, ending up instead, because of a storm, in Scotland before ending up at Ely. Bishop Wulfstan of Worcester, who was to be the great survivor (he lived to hold the See of Worcester until 1095), demanded the return of the Abbey's lands, those retained by Archbishop Ealdred when he was confirmed as Archbishop of York in 1062 and which had been held by the Norman King since the Archbishop's death, but a decision on this was deferred, because the See was vacant, until Thomas, Treasurer of Bayeux, had been appointed to York. Bishop Aethelric of Selsey appealed to the Pope, Alexander II, arguing that to depose him from his bishopric was, as Florence of Worcester reports, contrary to the canons. The Pope appears to have agreed because he wrote to King William demanding that Lanfranc rehear the case and, as a result, Aethelric was deposed by Archbishop Lanfranc, although the grounds on which he did so are unknown. Aethelric had, however, been the candidate chosen (to become Archbishop) by the monks of Canterbury in 1050. He was a relative of Earl Godwine and had been rejected by King Edward in favour of Robert Champart, Abbot of Jumièges and Bishop of London, who was driven out by Earl Godwine in 1052. Aethelric was, after the Conquest, detained by King William, as a prisoner at Marlborough, and his See went to a cleric called Stigand. The motive for his removal seems to have been political.[4]

But a few 'collaborators' survived the wholesale changes in the Church after the Conquest, though only at a cost. For example, Abingdon was allowed to 'redeem' its treasures, so avoiding the plundering which applied elsewhere, and faced an extra burden in the shape of 'the geld on every hide which no one but God can reckon', apparently referring to the geld levied in 1070.

Among the foreign clerics promoted in the early 1070s were Walkelin of Rouen, a royal clerk, who replaced Stigand at Winchester, and Herfast, another clerk, who was given East Anglia (Elmham). It also appears that King William now began the practice of 'Investiture', by which a newly consecrated Bishop received his ring and crozier from the hands of the King and, in effect, became his vassal. Pope Gregory VII was to launch an attempt to stamp this practice out, though he made no real attempt to make King William comply as he needed his support against the Emperor of Germany. Eadmer the Chronicler reports that 'from the time that William, Count of Normandy, subdued this land to himself by warfare (which points to 1066) investiture had not been practised in England'. That statement leaves open the question whether King Edward had exercised a right of investiture as there is no direct evidence either way.

After Lanfranc had become Archbishop he insisted that all bishops in future make canonical submission to Canterbury. Bishop Wulfstan of Worcester, who had never made such a submission to Canterbury (he was the sole surviving English Bishop), was expected to do so also. However, there is a contradictory legend, that Wulfstan refused to submit and Lanfranc demanded that he surrender his ring and staff. Wulfstan demurred and dramatically cried out that he would return his staff to he who had given it to him and, advancing to the tomb of King Edward, he thrust his staff into the stone over the tomb and it stuck fast! No one was able to remove it until Wulfstan himself did so after Lanfranc had agreed to confirm his possession of the See of Worcester. It is quite probable that Wulfstan did in fact insist that he had received his bishopric from King Edward, and that no one could take it from him. He probably did lay his crozier on the tomb and no one had dared to remove it.[5]

Lanfranc proceeded to introduce canons forbidding and condemning simony (the purchase of ecclesiastical office) and pluralism (the holding of more than one office by the same cleric). He required clerics to be chaste (that is to abandon the custom of marrying or else keeping a concubine) or to surrender their office. In practice, as a synod of 1076 shows, those who were married were allowed to remain so. Celibacy could only be insisted on for new candidates. The intention was not only to 'cleanse' the English Church but to Normanise it because Bishops and Abbots were among the closest advisers of the King and, in the Anglo-Norman Realm, great tenants-in-chief. William of Malmesbury relates that the King refused absolutely to appoint any Englishman as Bishop or Abbot and that he therefore 'deposed some of the clergy legally during their lifetime' in order to appoint any 'competent man of any nationality except English'.

The King's efforts did not always meet with the expected gratitude. William offered a bishopric to a prominent and celebrated theologian who, after 1073, left Normandy to join the entourage of Gregory VII. This was the monk Guitmund of La Croix-St Leuffroy. But he rejected all offers of preferment alleging that he did not wish to govern men of strange customs and barbarous speech 'whose friends and ancestors', he said, 'have been put to the sword, driven into bitter exile, and unjustly imprisoned or enslaved'. He told William that the King could not avoid sin while he still profited from the spoils he had seized by war and bloodshed. 'The sacrifice of injustice', Guitmund said, 'is a polluted offering. I deem all England to be the spoils of robbery and shrink from it and its treasures as from a consuming fire.' He also said that it was wrong anyway to impose on Christians a Pastor chosen from among their enemies and that Edgar the Aetheling had a better claim to the throne! No sign here of any recognition that William had a legitimate claim to be King. The offer was made shortly before William fitzOsbern went to Normandy 'in the fifth year of the reign' to be regent there alongside Queen Matilda.[6]

It had been in 1070 also that King William imposed the obligation of providing soldiers by knight-service on the bishoprics and abbeys. The number required from the various sees and monasteries varied immensely. The Churches of Canterbury, Winchester, Peterborough and Glastonbury all had to provide sixty knights but the Bishopric of Chichester, at the opposite extreme, was only required to provide two. Simultaneously, the obligation was being steadily imposed on the lay lords also. At first many ecclesiastical and lay lords simply discharged the obligation by hiring stipendiary knights who were housed in castles or retained in their households. In time this proved onerous and inconvenient, especially in the case of the abbeys, and the process of granting out estates to be held in return for a stipulated number of knights (known technically as sub-infeudation) began. Individual knights might receive an estate in return for their personal service, while richer men might have much larger endowments and be required to produce numbers varying from ten to sixty or more knights.[7]

This is further illustrated by the records of Abingdon which report that in the early years of the Abbacy of Aethelhelm, the abbey was required to provide a garrison of knights for Windsor, which was a royal palace. After the 'disturbances' (sic!) had died down 'it was noted in the annals how many knights were to be exacted from Bishops and Abbots for the defence of the realm', so Abbot Aethelhelm assigned some of the monastic estates to knights in return for stipulated military service. For this purpose (like Turold at Peterborough) he chose his own relatives, using for this the estates formerly held 'by those called thegns who had fallen in the Battle of Hastings'.

The rebellions of 1068 to 1070 had been so serious that King William had been forced to remain continuously in England and was unable to return to Normandy to recover his authority over Maine and the city of Le

Mans which had rebelled against him. Not until 1070 had he been able to discharge his mercenary troops. But for Abbot Aethelhelm, the Abingdon Chronicle relates that he was still concerned for his own safety. It says that 'he deemed it necessary never to go about without an armed retinue for, in the midst of the conspiracies which broke out almost daily against the King, he (Aethelhelm) felt compelled to take measures for his own protection'. The Abbot was not alone in doing this and the English, watching the Norman lords, lay and ecclesiastical, passing by accompanied by their armed escorts, remembered how English Earls and King's Thegns, and the Bishops and Abbots, had gone about with a 'genge' or retinue of riding men, called 'cnichts', now applied the same word to the escorts of Norman mounted warriors and so they came to be called 'knights'.

It was during 1070 also that King William ordered the building of the Abbey of Battle, which was to be completed by 1094. As the decision was not made until the Legate, Ermenfrid, had imposed penances on those who had fought at Hastings, and afterwards, it looks as though the building of the Abbey was William's own penance for the slaughter at Hastings, rather than, as the foundation myth of Battle alleges, the result of a vow made on the field of battle in thanksgiving for victory.

There was a disagreement between King William and the monks recruited to build Battle Abbey. They went to the site and began work, digging foundations well down the western slope of the battlefield, because there was no water supply on the hilltop. But the King, hearing of this and desirous that the Abbey and its Church occupy the place of King Harold's last stand, ordered them to stop and to build the Abbey on the crest of the hill, locating the High Altar on the very place where Harold was said to have been killed and where his Standard of the Fighting man had been found. He promised to supply the monks with plenty of wine to replace their drinking water. They also objected to the lack of local building stone, so the King ordered stone to be brought from Caen.[8]

The King appointed, as first Abbot, Robert Blanchard of Marmoutiers, but he, rather unfortunately, drowned while returning from Marmoutiers shortly after his appointment. He was replaced by Gausbert who continued the building work. It took twenty years and was consecrated in 1094. The site had presented serious problems to the builders, quite apart from the lack of water. There was little space for further development once the area occupied by the English army had been used up. The dormitory range had to be projected out over the steep slope and supported on a series of vaulted arches or barrel vaults. These were gradually reduced in size as the hill rose, which shows how steep it was. The area occupied by the English shield wall must have been flattened and lowered to accommodate the Church and other buildings, so reducing the overall height of the hill.

The Archbishopric of York still remained vacant and King William now decided on Thomas of Bayeux. Lanfranc, who had conducted the earlier synods, was consecrated as a Bishop on 24 June and installed as Archbishop, at Canterbury on 15 August, the feast of the Assumption. Thomas of Bayeux then sought consecration at the hands of Lanfranc but was presented with a demand that he acknowledge Lanfranc as his superior. Thomas refused and deadlock ensued. The quarrel between the two Archbishops derived from the confusion arising from the arrangements for the government of the Church in England originally made by Pope Gregory I in the seventh century. Earlier archbishops of both Sees had cooperated quite well, but Lanfranc was a canon lawyer and was insisting on a clear definition of the relations between Canterbury and York. After considerable wrangling, Thomas grudgingly agreed to make a profession of obedience to Lanfranc personally rather than to the See of Canterbury itself, reserving the right to protest should any successor of Lanfranc make the same claim. But the point at issue remained unsettled. The King therefore decided in the autumn of 1071 that the two Archbishops should go to Rome for their palliums, hoping that the Pope would decide the matter.[9]

Lanfranc was well received at Rome and the Pope referred settlement of the dispute back to the English Court to be settled in accordance with English law and custom. It remained unsettled until 1072 when it was decided in favour of Canterbury. King William now no longer needed the services and support of the Papacy after 1070 (it was rather Gregory VII after his accession in 1073 who needed William's support) and from 1073 onwards the King no longer allowed Legates to enter the Kingdom without his consent.

King William, satisfied that the English rebels would remain quiescent and that the realm was now peaceful, seemed content to carry on with the government of the country along the same lines as those attributed to his predecessors. It was, however, believed, in the twelfth century, that William actually formally re-issued the 'Laws of King Edward' but there is no contemporary evidence that he did so. In the light of that belief various lawyers in the twelfth century compiled collections of laws which they attributed either to King Edward or to King William In fact the King merely issued a decree, by writ, that the laws of King Edward were to be upheld and King Henry I added a clause to his 'Coronation Charter' in 1101 which states 'I restore to you the law of King Edward with all the reforms which my father introduced with the consent of his barons... with the additions which I have made as being most useful for the English people'. That 'law' of King Edward was essentially that embodied in the Codes issued by Cnut the Great which Edward himself had confirmed, through the agency of Earl Harold, in 1065 in order to comply with the demands of the Northumbrian rebels. If there was any such decree, then 1070 is considered to have been the most likely time for it to have been issued.[10]

One version of the decree, from the 'Laws of William I', laid down that all free men were to swear loyalty to him (as they had been required to do by previous English Kings since the early tenth century), in return for which he promised them his protection. The harrying of the North shows how much that 'protection' was worth. Despite this, all forms of these 'Laws' of King William insist on this promise of protection. The Laws also say that William introduced the system later known as Frankpledge (though in fact it was an enhanced version of the Tithing System in use in England before the Conquest). This required every man to be 'in pledge', that is, to have sureties who would pay what was charged against him in the event of his escape from arrest when accused of a crime. The system eventually meant that the previous state of affairs by which all free men were members of a tithing (a group of ten men) had added to it a requirement that they should induce a lord to stand pledge for them and the lords then insisted that they seek surety among their neighbours. In effect all free men had to join a tithing and could no longer choose their own sureties. The duty of a tithing was to produce for trial anyone accused of wrongdoing or be fined for not doing so. They also had to compensate the injured party. In effect the tithing became identified with the territorial unit of the 'vill' (which played a part also in the collection of the geld), a subdivision of the Hundred, which was already required to raise the 'hue and cry' in pursuit of felons.

King William also abolished, probably after 1076, capital punishment, by hanging or beheading, and replaced it by blinding or castration. Other punishments included that hands and/or feet be cut off, 'so that the trunk remains alive as a sign of his treachery and wickedness'. So this was essentially a barbarous and savage rather than a merciful act since those so dealt with subsequently died. The purpose was that those who had been mutilated should live out their days and serve as a deterrent to others.

William is thought to have issued his decrees at a Council held at Gloucester. The decrees are not further dated, but the Gloucester Councils were usually held at Christmas whenever the King was free to be present in England, which suggests Christmas 1070. One decree laid down that if a 'Frenchman' (i.e. Norman) summoned an Englishman and charged him with 'perjury, or murder or theft, homicide or 'ran', by which the English mean open robbery', then the Englishman could choose whether to accept trial by ordeal of hot iron (the former Old English method) or trial by combat.

The King insisted that all men should enjoy royal protection and then introduced what became known as the 'Murdrum' fine; 'If any man is slain, his lord shall arrest the slayer within five days if he can. If not, however, he shall begin to pay me 46 marks of silver from the property of the lord as long as it lasts out. When, however, the property of the lord fails, the whole hundred in which the murder was committed shall pay in common what remains.' This was further elaborated as follows; 'If a Frenchman is slain and the men of the Hundred do not seize the slayer and bring him to court within 8 days, in order to prove who has done it, they shall pay the murder-fine, namely 46 marks. Of these 46 marks, forty of them went to the king, who had lost a vassal, and six to the relatives of the dead man.'

Now, the Dialogue of the Exchequer, written in Henry II's reign by his Treasurer, Richard fitzNigel, Bishop of Ely, recording the traditions then current about King William's reign, claims that the context of these regulations was the need to deal with terrorist assassinations. These murders had become very frequent, so William simply resorted to the unpleasant and dubious method of making the law abiding citizens in conquered England responsible for restricting the activities of the wild men, the silvatici. The word 'murdrum' meant 'concealed' or 'hidden' and so referred to cases where the death of a man had been concealed and the slayer's identity was unknown. Richard fitzNigel comments that 'the remnant of the conquered English secretly laid ambushes for the Normans whom they distrusted and hated, and far and wide in woods and remote places, when opportunity presented itself, they slew them in secret.'[11]

This fits well with Orderic's remarks about the activities of the silvatici and the allegations against Hereward of carrying out secret attacks and assassinations, which led to the authorities taking 'for some years, violent measures against the English... with various refinements of torture... and yet the latter had not altogether ceased their attacks'. According to the locality the fine varied from thirty-six pounds to forty-four pounds as well as the forty-six silver marks, according to the frequency of homicides. It was hoped that 'each man might hasten to punish so great a crime and to hand over to justice the man by whose fault such an enormous indemnity was imposed on the whole neighbourhood.' The burden becomes clearer if these sums of money are converted into the coinage in circulation, the silver penny. Thirty-six pounds is 8,640 pennies, forty-four pounds is 10,560 pennies and, as a mark is thirteen shillings and four pence, forty-six marks is 11,960 silver pennies, very large sums indeed for ordinary men to find. It is from 'murdrum' or 'le murdre' in Norman French, that the modern term 'murder' is derived.

One way to avoid the fine was to show that the victim was an Englishman, and this evolved into the procedure called 'Presentment of Englishry', by which the kin of the deceased identified the victim as English and so avoided the fine.

Another tradition was that King William, in line with his renewal of the Law of King Edward, required the people to accept the written laws and customs of the realm in a threefold form, that is that Mercian, West Saxon and Danish customs were to apply to the three varieties of men and that of these customs some were rejected by the King while others were approved, and that he added to them 'those laws of Neustria (Normandy) overseas which seemed most efficacious for preserving the peace of the realm'. One other change that was made was that William authorised the Sheriffs to see to it that all men accepted the authority of the new Norman bishops.

King William 'subjugated and distrusted' the English and after the rebellions had been put down, sought out all those who had waged war against him, and their heirs also, and deprived them of all hope of ever recovering their estates. So the Bastard 'hardened his heart' and, as the harrying of the North shows, revealed the worst side of his character. Yet he also still tried afterwards to deal with the English according to his own idea of justice. He attempted to learn English so that he could deal with cases involving Englishmen himself rather than relying on interpreters (known as 'latimers'). But he was unable to persist in his efforts and never managed more than an understanding of the formulae used in charters and writs.

William, in his efforts to find out what the Law of King Edward actually was, demanded that groups of twelve men in each shire declare on oath what the laws were. It is likely that the Shire Courts were asked to declare what they knew about the law. But, despite all claims that peace now reigned in England after 1070, the 'murdrum' procedure reveals a very different picture.

The year 1072 had seen changes in the government of the Church. At Winchester in April of that year, at a 'general council' of the Church, Archbishop Lanfranc had set out the grounds for Canterbury's primacy over York, in the presence of the Papal legate, Hubert. Lanfranc was acting under the commission, given him by the Pope, to settle the matter of the Primacy over the English Church. He based his case on the text of Bede's Ecclesiastical History, on the acts of early English councils and the professions of obedience of early bishops, testimony of living witnesses and of Papal Letters. The Papal Letters are now recognised to have been forgeries or genuine letters amended to support Canterbury's claims. The brief Lanfranc used had probably been prepared for him by the monks of Canterbury. The Council, at Easter, 8 April, accepted the documents presented to it at face value and ruled that the Church of York should be subject to that of Canterbury. In future the Archbishops of York and their suffragan bishops were to attend synods summoned by the Archbishop of Canterbury. The several Sees claimed by York (Lichfield, Worcester and Dorchester) were assigned to Canterbury and York was left only with Durham and such bishoprics as existed in Scotland. The Council further ruled that it had now been established that Canterbury had a right to a sworn profession of obedience from York but 'out of love for the King', released Thomas of Bayeux from the obligation to take the oath. The result of all this was that Lanfranc became, in the words of Eadmer of Canterbury, 'Primate of All Britain and Patriarch of all the Islands on this side of the Channel'.[12]

There was, however, a more political dimension to the demand by Lanfranc for a profession of obedience from York. Hugh the Chanter, one of the church historians of York, provides the rationale; 'It was expedient for the unity and solidarity of the kingdom that all Britain should be subject to one Primate; it might otherwise happen, in the King's time, or in that of one of his successors, that someone from among the Danes, Norwegians or Scots, who used to sail up to York in their attacks on the realm, might be made King by the Archbishop of York and the fickle and treacherous Yorkshiremen, and so the Kingdom might be disturbed and divided.'

This was a real possibility. The Archbishop of York, Ealdred, had consecrated and crowned two kings already, that is both Harold II and William I. The Danes were actually able to capture York in 1075 and to prepare an expeditionary force for an invasion in 1085 which was only frustrated by the death of the Danish King. In the year 1070 itself, the very year in which it was decided to nominate Thomas of Bayeux to replace the deceased Ealdred, King Swein Estrithson had entered the Humber to take command of the remnants of his fleet, intending to break Earl Asbiorn's promise of the previous winter to depart in peace. In fact the Danes had accepted overtures from King William, and a payment of Danegeld, and so had left the East Anglian Fenlanders in the lurch to face King William's wrath. But the people of the Fens had greeted the Danes with enthusiasm, expecting that King Swein would 'win all that land'.

A further move to strengthen control was made when a Lotharingian cleric from Liége, called Walcher, was appointed as Bishop of Durham, (after the final arrest, deposition and imprisonment of Bishop Aethelwine, captured at Ely). Bishop Walcher was endowed with Waltham Abbey and its lands, worth one hundred pounds a year by 1086. The North was still too insecure to allow King William to appoint one of his royal clerks. Bishop Walcher was sent specifically to bring the Clerks of St Cuthbert under Norman control, with the assistance at first of Earl Cospatric (until his fall from grace). The new Bishop had to be given a military-style escort commanded by the Housecarl Eilaf, who took him as far as York and then handed him over to the protection of Cospatric to be taken to Durham.

At the same time at Winchester, Lanfranc deposed Wulfric, Abbot of New Minster and confirmed a number of canon laws, of which only the headings survive. One decreed that Bishops were to hold a diocesan synod once a year and empowered them to appoint Archdeacons and other ministers in Holy Orders, so authorising the formation of Cathedral Chapters. Further Councils were held in the 1070s by Lanfranc; one in 1075 pledging the English Church to adhere to ancient Canons directed against various alleged abuses, simony, marriage within prohibited degrees of kinship and such like and, more importantly, authorizing the transfer of several Sees, from small towns and villages to larger ones, that is Lichfield, Selsey and Sherborne to Chester, Chichester and Salisbury; the other, in 1076, was almost a comprehensive reform of the English Church in line with the decrees issued at Rome by the new Pope, Gregory VII, particularly as they concerned clerical celibacy.

That Lanfranc's legislation depended on its being in harmony with the King's wishes is demonstrated in 1072 by the ordinance then issued in a famous writ which survives in two separate copies, reflecting its general distribution throughout the country. The King announces his intention to amend the Episcopal laws of England because they were contrary to the precepts laid down in the canons. He says that from then on no Bishop or Archdeacon (who acted as Vicars General to the Norman Bishops) was to hold pleas relating to Episcopal, (that is ecclesiastical), law, in the Hundred Courts. (It was now not thought fitting that secular judges should have a say in deciding ecclesiastical cases. Instead the bishops were to hold their own Episcopal courts for the cases of clerks who offended against Church Law). Clerics were to be judged by God and the Bishop and not by the secular law of the Hundred Court. Nor were sheriffs, reeves or royal officials to interfere with the administration of Episcopal Laws. Bishops could fine offenders and, if necessary, excommunicate them, and the King would see to it that excommunication was effective. Lanfranc was to spell out the details at his Synod of 1076.

The Archbishop was also free to recover, for Canterbury, estates it had lost during the upheaval of the Conquest. He needed to re-assert the authority of the Archbishopric, damaged by Stigand's long tenure, and to retrieve control over estates, though he might also have to accept the sitting Norman tenants as his vassals. Lanfranc was very successful, recovering, for example, twenty-five estates from Bishop Odo alone. He was also able to begin the rebuilding of Canterbury cathedral which had burned down, by accident, in 1067. The process of retrieval was begun at the trial on Penenden Heath (near Maidstone), presided over by Bishop Geoffrey of Coutances. Even the aged Bishop Aethelric of Selsey was brought to court to give evidence. So feeble was he that he had to be brought there in a cart. Archbishop Lanfranc won lands back from Hugh de Montfort and Ralph Courbépine as well as Bishop Odo.

Lanfranc had truly become an almost fanatical supporter of the King. He wrote a letter, sometime between Christmas 1072 and 21 April 1073, to Pope Alexander II, saying:

> I urge you to entreat God mercifully to grant long life to my lord the King of
> the English. While the King lives we have peace, of a kind; but after his death
> we expect to have neither peace nor any other benefit.

King William was now free to make use of many of the more valuable Churches as endowments for his Clerks. He exploited in particular the English Old Minsters, which were now annexed to Cathedrals, by using their lands to provide prebends or livings for the canons. Other Minsters were engulfed by royal or baronial castles and, in effect, became castle chapels. A few were moved to new sites and others were simply suppressed. There are examples of this process at Dover, Clare, Taunton, Pontefract, Newark and Hereford. Roger, Earl of Shrewsbury, similarly exploited churches, by systematically annexing them and their lands to Shrewsbury Abbey. Robert, Count of Mortain, the King's half brother, acted similarly in Cornwall.

It was also from this period onwards that monasteries were rebuilt, and many new ones founded. One effect of this was to offend and dismay many devout English monks (who regretted the loss of ancient buildings and objected to the rule of Norman Abbots) and many of them were in effect driven out of their monasteries, preferring to remove themselves elsewhere and found new houses of their own. Monks from Evesham and Worcester, for example, moved north in 1074 to found new northern houses (which were actually re-foundations) at Jarrow, Wearmouth, Tynemouth, Whitby and Melrose.

King William Deals With Scotland

So, most likely at Court, either at Easter or Pentecost 1072, the King decided to settle accounts with Scotland. He had been unable to do so earlier because of the trouble in Maine followed by the need to deal with the remaining nest of rebels at Ely. Now he was free to act. He could take action beyond the Tees in order to consolidate his control over the rest of England and at the same time punish King Malcolm for his insolence. He might also have intended to attempt the conquest of Scotland. It was at this point that Eadric the Wild, the great Shropshire landowner, who had rebelled against William mainly in protest at the incursions of Norman settlers into his lands, was reconciled to the King.

It is said that when Eadric made his submission, he was summoned to see King William at Court and that he came accompanied by his wife. Now, Eadric was to become the focus for many legends, he was even associated after his death with the fabled and ghostly Wild Hunt, possibly simply because he was known in life as 'the Wild'. But one legend concerned his wife. Eadric was said to have come across a band of 'fairies' dancing in the woods and to have fallen in love with and married one of them, or so says Walter Map, author of De Nugis Curialium (or 'Courtier's Trifles', miscellaneous anecdotes of Court life written c.1200). King William, says Walter, heard of Eadric's marriage and ordered the thegn to bring her to Court. As Professor David Douglas remarked, 'a conversation between William the Conqueror and the Queen of the Fairies would have been worth hearing!' It could be that the truth behind this was simply that Eadric had encountered a group of Welsh wisewomen, with a reputation for knowledge of magical arts, who were still celebrating some pagan festival and that his wife had been one of them.

Reporting events shortly after the defeat of the rebels at Ely, and probably with reference to Spring 1072, the Liber Eliensis claimed that 'the whole of Scotland with her hordes of soldiers sought to rebel against King William and to overthrow him', that is, that there was yet another Scottish incursion into Northern England. King William had for a time returned to Normandy at the end of 1071, returning in Spring 1072 only to learn of Malcolm's incursion. This seems to have made the King determined to act. As all sources report, he gathered together a ship army (the 'ship fyrd') and a land army and led it to Scotland (exactly the same sort of language had been used by the Worcester Chronicle to describe the decision to besiege the Isle of Ely).[1]

It must be to the gathering of this army that the writ, which is itself undated, addressed to Abbot Aethelwig of Evesham (and accepted as dating between 1072 and 1077) would seem to refer. It commands the Abbot to 'summon all those who are under your administration and jurisdiction (sub baillia et justicia tua)' to attend the King at Clarendon 'with all the knights which they owe me, fully equipped'. They were to meet the King on the Octave of Whitsun. The Abbot was also to bring 'those five knights which you owe me from your abbacy'. It was witnessed at Winchester by Eudo the Dapifer. So from Whitsun onwards the King was preparing to attack Scotland. As the writ to Aethelwig shows, the Bastard was now making increasing use of the imposed 'servicia debita', the defined number of knights owed to his service by Abbots, Bishops, Barons and even wealthy knights in return for holding their English estates. The Abingdon Chronicle also reports this imposition of knight service on the Church. Many of these burdens had, it would seem, been steadily imposed as opportunity arose from 1066 onwards and particularly after the defeat of the English risings.

However, the Liber Eliensis points to 1072 as the defining moment when King William attempted to quantify the amount of service due to him. Not only did he command the Bishops and Abbots (and, as is obvious from the context, his barons and knights) to send him their due knight service but the Liber Eliensis claims that 'he established from that time onwards the contingents of knights to be provided by them for the Kings of England in perpetual right for military expeditions'. That might only have applied to the clergy but there is no reason to think that King William was not, wherever possible, also defining the obligations of his lay vassals.[2]

One illustration of the process is provided by the foundation charter for Eye Priory, in Suffolk. Robert Malet, successor to the now-deceased William Malet, endows the Priory and refers to 'all the other liberties which my lord, William, King of England, granted to me when he gave me the Honor' (that is, his great fief).

The summons to the host was carried out with remarkable speed and completed by the summer, most likely by 15 August. Eadric the Wild was one prominent Englishman who accompanied the royal army which included English as well as Norman levies. The land army travelled by way of Durham, through Lothian to Perth, crossing the Forth by a ford near Stirling and then turning eastwards to the upper reaches of the River Tay. The fleet, which moved up the coast in conjunction with the land army, sailed as far as the estuary of the Tay and made contact with the King. It was a bold move and a hazardous one. Much could have gone wrong and the two prongs of his force might not have made contact. But the King moved against King Malcolm in vain. The Scottish King preferred to retreat as the Anglo-Normans advanced hoping for a decisive battle somewhere in Lothian where the cavalry could be deployed effectively. King Malcolm simply refused to give King William the opportunity, he had no wish to suffer the fate of King Harold Godwinson.

Nonetheless the invasion was a daunting one and King Malcolm was driven into negotiation. The two Kings met at Abernethy, and not far from the Norman ships. The usual diplomatic protocol was followed. King Malcolm surrendered hostages to William, including, it was claimed, his son Duncan, and became William's man, just as his predecessors had done to Kings Aethelstan and Edgar. It is likely that the homage was purely personal and it remains uncertain whether it involved the 'Kingdom of Alba' itself or merely some territory in Cumbria and Lothian. The 'principality' of Scotland was probably not involved on this occasion, since, in 1079, when King William sent a second army into Scotland, commanded by his son, Robert Curthose, with more or less the same result, it was then claimed that the hostages were given 'in surety that the principality of Scotland should be subjected to the Kingdom of England'. That had been of little practical significance in 1072. The real point was that the Scottish King had now recognised the new regime in England and, as an indication of this, Edgar the Aetheling was expelled from Scotland. Malcolm III remained a greater threat to the peace of Northumbria than any Scottish King before him and his raids on England certainly did not cease, recurring in 1079, 1091 and 1093.[3]

But in 1072 he had been both overawed and wooed into submission. King William, 250 miles from his nearest base at York, had now settled for assurances from King Malcolm. There was in any case little food available for his army, so the Norman King returned, travelling by way of the Roman site of Pons Aelii, then known as Monkchester (pausing long enough for his men to plunder the area), south to Durham, taking the precaution of ordering a castle to be built there, as a home for the Bishop. He was acutely aware that any Norman bishop would need protection, not least from his own flock. In addition, Earl Waltheof was made Earl of Northumbria, to hold it along with his existing Earldom in Huntingdonshire and Northamptonshire (just as Earl Tostig had done in King Edward's day). The Church at Durham was to concoct a miracle story to explain the King's withdrawal from Durham. They implied that King William feared for the safety of his soul because of the guilt he felt for ordering the harrying of the north. In fact the King confirmed the ecclesiastical privileges of St Cuthbert (the rights to land and jurisdiction held by the canons of St Cuthbert) and restored to the Church at Durham the manor of Billingham.[4]

Durham sources do make it plain that the situation in the north was far worse than political and military events alone can explain. Bishop Walcher himself needed protection 'ab incursantibus', that is from insurgents. That meant either continued Scottish raids or the sort of attack characteristic of the northern rebellion. Most of all, it meant the attacks of indigenous thieves and robbers. The area was prone to large scale brigandage (as Earl Tostig had found out in the 1050s). For example, Bishop Aethelwine and his escort for St Cuthbert's body when returning to Durham in 1070 had been harassed and plundered by a brigand called Gilmichael who was said to be 'very powerful beyond the Tyne'.

The whole area remained quite uncontrollable and lawless and was probably excluded from the great Survey of Domesday Book in 1086 because the Normans did not really have sufficient control over it. Archbishop Thomas of York took the precaution of making his Suffragan, Bishop Wulfstan of Worcester, perform the Episcopal functions in the unsubdued parts of the York Archdiocese.

It could well be that it was in connection with the lawlessness and rebelliousness of the Northumbrians, that Earl Waltheof took action against the family of the Yorkshire thegn Karli. In doing so he also involved himself in an ancient feud between his own family and that of Karli Thorbrandson. Earl Waltheof's maternal grandfather, Earl Ealdred of Bamburgh had killed Thorbrand the Hold because he had slain Ealdred's father Earl Uhtred, at the behest of Cnut the Great. The thegn Karli Thorbrandson had then killed Earl Ealdred. The feud had lain quiescent since 1038 and it is inherently unlikely that Earl Waltheof now deliberately revived it. It is more probable that he was seeking to curry favour with King William by removing what he believed to be a source of disaffection. Most likely at Christmas 1073/74, the Earl sent a party of men to find and kill the sons of Karli. They were reported to be holding a feast at Settrington in the North Riding, a manor belonging to Thorbrand Karlison. Also present was his brother Gamal who had lands at Duggleby and Heathfield, and the youngest brother, Cnut. The third brother, Sumerled, luckily for him, had not yet arrived. Earl Waltheof's men attacked and killed all present but spared the young man, Cnut, because he was young and well loved in the area. (This was done while King William was absent in Normandy). Earl Waltheof might well not have been unwilling to eliminate the members of this troublesome family.[5]

While at Durham the King, said to be sceptical about the claim for its incorruptibility, demanded that he be shown the body of St Cuthbert, threatening dire trouble for the assembled prelates should the body of the Saint not prove to be intact. The feretory containing the Saint's body was brought forth for the King but, despite the fact that it was now November, it was said that King William was overcome by a sense of intolerable heat which caused him to give up his intention of viewing the body. Instead he speedily took horse and began to ride back into England, hastening as far as the Tees in his anxiety to get away from the saint's body. What really happened is now impossible to know but the background events cast some light on the general situation.

It was more credibly reported that King William had decided to tax the Bishopric of Durham, Saint Cuthbert's land, and that would have violated the Saint's patrimony and privileges. He is said to have sent an agent, a tax official called 'Rannulphus' (Ralph or Randolph; and it has even been suggested that this was in fact the infamous Rannulf Flambard) to set in train the collection of the tax. However, the official had a dream in which he saw Saint Cuthbert who struck him with his Staff, telling him to leave the area immediately. The official awoke to find himself paralysed and remained so until he had promised to do no wrong to Saint Cuthbert, imploring his forgiveness for his temerity and offering gifts to the Shrine of the Saint. He did not recover from his paralysis until he had been carried in a litter out of the boundaries of the bishopric. Once outside them he duly recovered.

Informed of all this, the King, in amazement, duly confirmed Saint Cuthbert's privileges. The story is intended to provide an explanation for the immunity from taxation granted to the Bishopric. More likely, the King for his part decided to allow the Bishop to keep the royal revenues from his Bishopric to defray the costs of governing what was later termed the Palatine Bishopric. Like the Welsh Marcher Earldoms, the Bishopric of Durham had the onerous duty of defending Northumbria against the Scots.

Such stories (there are others from other parts of England) reflect the strength of local feelings of hostility towards the Norman regime which must have frequently forced the King to recognise local rights and privileges in order to win over the inhabitants to his rule. It reflects the practical limits to royal authority. There is a possibility of a psychological aspect to such tales, given the strength of religious belief. It is only too likely that a man threatened with the displeasure of a local Saint might well have nightmares or even suffer hysterical paralysis.

Bishop Walcher of Durham, working in the early 1070s with Earl Waltheof, had effectively replaced Earl Cospatric who had been deprived of his Earldom in 1071, charged with complicity in the risings, including the death of Robert de Commines and the killings at York. His Earldom had been given to Earl Waltheof and Cospatric himself was exiled, dividing his time between Flanders and Scotland. He eventually took service with King Malcolm and became Earl of Dunbar. Eventually some of his Yorkshire lands were restored to him and he still held them in 1086. That did him little good as most of it was still waste land and he had to hold it as a vassal of Alan of Richmond.[6]

Having concluded his dealings with Scotland, King William was now free to turn his attention to Maine and, after wintering in England during a time when the country remained quiet, (the peace and quiet of exhaustion one suspects), King William returned to Normandy to deal with the problem of Maine and, after a three month campaign, was back at Bonneville-sur-Touques by 30 March 1073. The summer of that year put him in a stronger position with respect to the threat from Anjou and he was content to remain in Normandy. Overall, the King was to spend most of the rest of his reign in Normandy. The English position can perhaps best be illustrated by the case of the thegn called Aethelric who had held Marsh Gibbon, in Buckinghamshire, under King Edward, a four hide Manor worth seventy shillings a year, but who, by 1086, held it as the tenant of William fitzAnsculf, holding it 'at farm of William in heaviness and misery'. At Nottingham, men complained that they were no longer permitted even to go fishing in the River Trent.[7]

At Thetford in Norfolk, men complained that there used to be a market held there every Saturday, but that William Malet (who was dead by 1072) had built a castle at Eye (in Suffolk) and that there he had set up another market in the castle on Saturdays and 'thereby the Bishop's market had been so far spoilt as to be of little value'.

In contrast, of course, some men did rather well. The thegn Aelfsige of Faringdon (in Berkshire) who held land there which had previously belonged to Earl Harold, some thirty hides, is a good example. He had been given more land by King William at Barcote (another five hides of Harold's land). He had two hides at Rycote and another two hides at Shipton-under-Wychwood (both in Oxfordshire) plus eight hides there of the King's own land, which Aelfsige held at farm for him, in effect, as his reeve. He was the King's reeve at Sutton Courtenay (Berkshire) and farmed Great Barrington (Gloucestershire). A 'farmer' held land on the basis that he would manage the estate and render to the lord an agreed amount, in cash, and was then free to recover his outlay from those who worked the land. As the farmer could demand more from those on the estate than he paid to the lord, this could be very profitable. The lord gained a guaranteed income and had no need to manage the estate himself.

By now, the disturbances in Normandy and in Maine had encouraged King Philip I of France to support the candidature of Edgar Aetheling as pretender to the English throne. It is certain that Edgar was in Scotland in July 1074, on St Grimbald's mass day, 8 July, in order to visit his sister Margaret, now, following her marriage, Queen of Scotland. He was received – the word is 'underfon' implying diplomatic recognition – by King Malcolm who paid him great honour. While Edgar was in Scotland he received an embassy or a letter from King Philip with a remarkable offer. He was to receive custody and control of the castle of Montreuil and its garrison, on the river Canche in the Pas de Calais, between Le Touquet and Hesdin. This was to be his base for future operations against King William, in pursuit of the Aetheling's claims to the English throne. The offer was part of King Philip's avowed aim, in conjunction with Count Robert the Frisian of Flanders, to cause trouble for the Norman King.

Edgar accordingly set out to return to France to take up the offer, probably accompanied by other English exiles, only for a storm to arise and wreck both his fleet and his chances. He was driven ashore, most likely on the North East coast of England, as some of his party were captured by 'Frenchmen' (Francigenae), that is, Normans resident in England. Edgar himself managed to make his return to Scotland and was, for the time being, stranded there.

King Malcolm then persuaded him that the storm was a sign of the verdict of providence, that it was God's Will that he should not accept King Philip's offer. Possibly this interpretation of events came from the devout Queen Margaret. More realistically, King Malcolm advised the Aetheling to send an embassy to Normandy to seek peace with King William. If that is so, then one can see here the operation, in William's favour, of the terms of the treaty of Abernethy; King Malcolm neither wanted to encourage Edgar to accept King Philip's offer nor to continue to offer him sanctuary in Scotland.

King William was only too pleased to frustrate King Philip's designs, thinking it better to bind Edgar to him in honourable captivity; not imprisonment but something more like house arrest. He had used the same tactic with the Earls Edwin and Morcar and even with Earl Harold during his sojourn in Normandy. The Aetheling therefore set out on a journey to Normandy to see King William so that he could present himself to him as no longer the vassal or ally of King Philip. King Malcolm and Queen Margaret loaded Edgar with gifts to replace those lost in the shipwreck, and possibly to enable him to make suitable gifts to King William.

Under King Malcolm's protection he set out and was escorted as far as Durham, an indication of the extent of Malcolm's influence. There he was met by Hugh fitzBaldric, the successor of William Malet as Sheriff of Yorkshire. Hugh then escorted him through England, travelling from castle to castle through the conquered land, and across the Channel to Normandy. King William received him with honour (again the word used is 'underfon' so he was probably accepted as a vassal), and made him a permanent resident at Court, as a member of the King's 'hirede' or household, providing him with a modest endowment of land in England. Domesday Book credits him with two estates in Hertfordshire, totalling eight and a quarter hides in Barkway and Great Hormead, together worth ten pounds a year. His pre-Conquest lands in Huntingdonshire, at Upton and Coppingford, had passed to Hugh, Earl of Chester. A thegn called Godwin held Great Hormead under Edgar and Godwin was in time father of a knight named Robert who went with Edgar in the First Crusade. Edgar lived in this manner for the rest of King William's reign and made no further attempts at resistance.

In discussing the Conqueror's reign, Peterborough Chronicle, under the year 1087, comments that it was thought that had he lived perhaps two more years he would have won Ireland without fighting. What basis, one might wonder, did this have in fact? The answer perhaps lies in a curious episode in 1073. In that year the Irish Kings and Bishops, representing both Irishmen and Danes settled in Ireland, approached Archbishop Lanfranc. They wanted his assistance in obtaining Episcopal consecration for a successor to Bishop Donatus (also called Domnald) who had died or was dying. As a result the Bishop-Elect of their choice, called Patrick, came to England with letters from the clergy and people of Dublin and from another figure whom Lanfranc calls 'King of Ireland', possibly Godred or Godric by name.[8]

Patrick was then consecrated Bishop at London and is alleged to have made canonical submission to Archbishop Lanfranc. If he did, then his diocese in Ireland was considered to be part of the Province of Canterbury. Patrick ruled as Bishop for the next ten years, until he drowned in 1084. Lanfranc then consecrated his successor, Donach. This might well have kindled King William's interest in Ireland, leading to speculations about his intentions. But if he had any ambitions in that direction they came to nothing.

The real area of foreign policy in 1073 of interest to King William was Maine. His dealings with Maine do not directly impinge on English History at this time except in so far as it meant that King William was preoccupied with that problem and out of the country for most of 1073 and 1074.

Interestingly, however, he took with him, to the war in Maine, a large contingent of English soldiers who distinguished themselves in the fighting. Geoffrey Gaimar, in his L'Estorie des Engles, alleged that Hereward, last heard of at Ely, had been reconciled to the King (like Eadric the Wild), and accompanied the King to Maine. Gaimar only introduces this story because it allows him to present his own late and unverified account of the death of Hereward. He alleges that, like Earl Edwin of Mercia, Hereward, who was returning from Maine, was betrayed to a band of jealous Normans and, in an heroic struggle against overwhelming odds, was slain. It could be that he has confused Hereward with Earl Edwin since, by the 1140s when Gaimar was writing, Hereward was believed to be descended from Earl Leofric.[9]

Anglo-Norman involvement on the Continent had led to the death, at the battle of Cassel in 1071, of Earl William fitzOsbern. As a result his Norman lands had passed to his elder son, William, while his Earldom of Hereford and English lands had passed to the second son, Roger. The latter does not appear to have been happy with the division of lands nor with the degree of respect that he received from King William. He never played the major part in the King's Councils that his father had played. That was to have tragic consequences for him.

So, early in 1073, King William had, then, crossed to Maine via Normandy, where he held an assembly at Rouen of clerical and lay lords to settle outstanding problems concerning the Norman church. He then launched his attack on Maine and, in a three month campaign, regained control. King William and his mainly English army dealt harshly with the County. 'The land of Maine they mightily wasted and vineyards were destroyed, and it was all brought into William's hands, and then they went home to England'. During the campaign Fresnay-le-Vicomte castle was besieged and was 'foredone', with the result that Beaumont-le-Vicomte and Sillé surrendered. The host approached Le Mans where the 'magistrates' surrendered the city. King William received the keys of the city and the inhabitants threw themselves on his mercy. He in turn swore to observe the city's customs and its rights of jurisdiction. The rest of Maine capitulated. King William went on to attack the border stronghold of La Flèche and confront the Count of Anjou, Fulk le Rechin. There was a stand off until the Church stepped in and a Cardinal Priest from Rome negotiated a peace treaty at 'Blancheland' (Bruère). William's son, Robert Curthose, did homage to Fulk for Maine and honour was satisfied on both sides.[10]

The Army commanded by the King was said to number 60,000 men, (the number is not realistic and means only that it was huge), but King William seems to have been less than confident of victory and preferred to avoid further fighting, especially against a combined Breton-Angevin force.

It seems likely that the state of affairs in England during his absence resembled that of 1067 when he had left Bishop Odo and Earl William fitzOsbern in charge. But this time the King had entrusted effective regency to Archbishop Lanfranc, a more disciplined character. Nonetheless, the King's continued absence was to lead to trouble.

14

The Revolt of the Earls:
January 1075 to December 1076

King William spent the whole of 1074 in Normandy, dealing with the security of the Duchy and its dependent territories. Charters at Rouen show his presence there in May and a visit to Lillebonne, and he was back at Rouen in November. He was accompanied by Bishop Odo of Bayeux and Roger of Montgomery, which suggests that he was satisfied with the degree of calm and peacefulness obtaining in England. He used his time attempting to dismantle the continental coalition which had gathered against him and in neutralizing the threat represented by Edgar the Aetheling. In many ways 1074 was the high point of William's career. His friendship was courted elsewhere in Europe. He was, for example, received into the membership of the Confraternity of Cluny, the great reforming Abbey in Burgundy. He is reported to have actually refused to intervene in German affairs though it was rumoured that he contemplated an attack on Aachen on behalf of the Archbishop of Cologne. But the rumour proved to be false. Henry IV of Germany was said to have sought his aid but if so nothing came of it.

A prominent Englishman with whom King William had contentious dealings was Earl Waltheof, son of the great Earl Siward. He had been involved in the revolt of 1069 but had made his peace with the King in 1070. So successful was the Earl's submission that William was led to trust him sufficiently to appoint him as Earl in Northumbria where he worked harmoniously with Bishop Walcher. But well before that he had been twice passed over for his father's earldom which included the whole of Northumbria and Yorkshire. Waltheof's northern Earldom really only meant Bamburgh as Yorkshire was governed by its Sheriff, Hugh fitzBaldric. Waltheof might therefore have felt that he had a grievance as his earldom was much reduced compared with that held by his father, Earl Siward. As Earl Waltheof had rebelled previously he could also have been willing to listen to seditious talk. If so, that led him to become an accomplice if not an active participant in the revolt of the Norman Earls.

Waltheof had been a King's Commissioner between 1072 and 1075, dealing with the perennial problem, in this period, of encroachments on Church lands, particularly those of Ely. Among others, he restored the lands of Thorkell of Harringworth to Crowland Abbey, and, as a result, his name and that of his wife, Judith, were recorded in the Abbey's Liber Vitae so that prayers could be said for them after their death. Earl Waltheof gave Leighton Bromswold to Remigius, Bishop of Lincoln, and Countess Judith, the Earl's wife, founded a nunnery at Elstow in Bedfordshire. But Earl Waltheof was in dispute with Peterborough Abbey and Abbot Turold over land left to Peterborough by his stepmother, Countess Godgifu (Lady Godiva).[1]

Early in 1075 two of King William's Earls, each the son of an Earl appointed shortly after the Conquest, agreed on a marriage alliance. One of these young Earls was to marry the sister of the other. The sources for the period disagree about the legality of the marriage. The Anglo-Saxon Chroniclers at Worcester and Peterborough (based on a Canterbury original) thought that King William had actually given Emma, (daughter of William fitzOsbern and sister of that Earl's son, Roger, Earl of Hereford), in marriage to Ralph 'Guader' or de Gael, son of Ralph the Staller, Earl of East Anglia, (that is of Norfolk and Suffolk) and nephew of the pre-Conquest thegn Godwine of Field Dalling. But the Worcester 'Chronicle of Chronicles' by John of Worcester (usually cited as Florence of Worcester) corrects this version of events, as he does on a number of other significant occasions, and says that Earl Roger gave his sister in marriage to Earl Ralph 'against the command of the King'. King William was already vetting the marriages of his barons.[2] Perhaps the Earls allowed their guests to assume that they had the King's consent. John of Worcester was also better informed than the Chroniclers since he asserts that the marriage feast – the bridale – was held at Exning near Newmarket rather than at Norwich. It could be that the betrothal had taken place at Norwich and that the actually wedding was at Exning. It was a splendid affair by all accounts, attended by many adherents of the two Earls, some Bishops and Abbots and especially Bretons holding land in East Anglia and was held while the King was out of the way, in Normandy. 'Then was that bridale, to many men's bale', as the Chronicler lamented over the dismal fate of the participants.

Having contracted their alliance, the Earls now 'planned that they would drive their royal lord from his kingdom', taking counsel together how they might do so.[3]

Exactly why the Earls felt driven to such an extreme decision still remains somewhat vague. The motives ascribed to them at the time seem inadequate. Perhaps it was the boastfulness and arrogance of two young, and powerful, men, their vanity fed by the flattery of their followers. Orderic Vitalis in his account, set out in his customary manner in the form of speeches attributed to the participants (as was the style in vogue), alleges that they raked up the matter of King William's bastardy, saying that it would please God to get rid of him! Furthermore they said that he was a 'degenerate' man who had robbed William of Mortain, poisoned Count Walter of Mantes and his wife Biota as well as Count Conan of Brittany, and unjustly seized the Kingdom of England and killed or cruelly exiled the genuine heirs to estates. Above all he had not sufficiently honoured the companions of his victory as he ought to have done and he had given wounded men barren lands wasted by the enemy.

So, the Earls said, 'All men hate him and will rejoice at his death!' There was no time like the present to take action because the King was out of the country along with his army, overwhelmed by rebellions and discord among his own family. Some of those present thought, perhaps hoped, that he would never return! 'The English', they said 'are a peaceful race, much given to feasting rather than fighting but they would surely rise up in vengeance!' So they turned to Earl Waltheof, hoping he could rally the English, as his participation would make the revolt part of the English resistance to the Conquest.

The proposal put before the Earl was that one of the three of them, Waltheof, Roger and Ralph, would be King and the other two would be his Earls in as powerful a position as the great Earls of King Edward's time, and the three would be a triumvirate ruling the kingdom together. It was left rather vague which of the three would wear the crown! Waltheof might have thought that the English would not want another Norman as King instead of William, and that it was intended that he should wear the crown. The Earl later claimed that he protested about all this, saying that he was King William's man. It was then concluded that he had taken care to conceal his own part in the affair. He was after all King William's Earl and the husband of his niece Judith. He allegedly told the two Earls that he would not break faith or be a traitor to them and that anyway an Englishman who was a traitor could lose his head under English law and so he was taking a greater risk than they were.[4]

It is unlikely that Waltheof said anything of the kind to the Earls. Had he done so they would surely never have let him go free to blab what he knew. These arguments are almost certainly those that Waltheof used later in his own defence. It is far more probable, as other accounts allege, that he was beguiled by the two Earls and consented to the conspiracy, only to develop cold feet afterwards and, as John of Worcester alleges, repent. But while he was privy to the plot he might well have made his own important contribution to it. Not only did Earl Ralph manage to bring into the plot most of the Breton lords in Eastern England, but the conspirators, perhaps at the suggestion of Waltheof (whose name would have carried weight) sent east to Denmark seeking the support of a raiding ship-army.

While the two Earls returned to the centre of their Earldoms to prepare, Roger to Hereford and Ralph to Norwich, Waltheof took himself off to see Archbishop Lanfranc to whom he made a clean breast of it. But while he was doing so the other Earls acted, mobilising their forces. Waltheof approached Lanfranc as both his spiritual and temporal superior, since the Archbishop had been left, in effect, as regent in England. The Earl confessed to the Archbishop that he had taken an illegal oath, to the conspirators, and sought absolution from it. Lanfranc's response was to impose as penance that he go to the king and confess. Waltheof accordingly set off for Normandy taking rich gifts with him with which he hoped to appease the King's wrath.[5]

King William let it appear that he was satisfied with Waltheof's ready confession and required only that he remain in Normandy until he himself decided to return to England. Waltheof was for the moment left unpunished and at liberty though no doubt forbidden to communicate with the Earls.

It is not known whether Archbishop Lanfranc made any attempt to deal with Earl Ralph and it may be that he did not, since he seems to have had a deep contempt for all Bretons. But three letters have survived among his correspondence addressed to Earl Roger. The earliest charged him with disloyalty to King William and accused him of illegal invasion of royal lands and of the lands of other barons. The Archbishop urged the Earl, 'Remember the ways of your father and turn away from your errors. Come to me and accept my fatherly counsel'. When the Earl failed to come to him, Archbishop Lanfranc told him that if he did not do so, he would be excommunicated. 'I will not absolve you from the chains of anathema unless you seek the mercy of my Lord the King and do justice to him and his men for your unjust depredations'.

The Earl appears to have taken illegal control of several castles, as another letter runs; 'Our Lord, the King of the English, greets you and yours as his faithful men in whom he has great trust and commands that as far as possible we (that is, Lanfranc) may have the care of his castles, lest, – which God forbid! – they fall into the hands of his enemies.' He urges Roger to be 'scrupulous in this matter' and to 'do your duty as a vassal.'

Again Earl Roger is urged to behave like his father Earl William, a man of prudence and goodwill 'who allowed neither perjury nor fraud to affect his lands'. To Roger, the Archbishop says that he should return to his senses and 'come and see me'. The King has further ordered that none of his sheriffs shall hold any pleas of the crown in Roger's lands until the King himself has crossed the sea, so that he can hear the case between the Earl and the Sheriffs himself. The third letter is less temperate.

'The Devil's prompting and the advice of evil men have led you into an enterprise which under no circumstances should you have attempted... therefore I have cursed and excommunicated you and all your adherents... cutting you off from the holy precincts of the Church and the assembly of the faithful'.

None of Lanfranc's letters made the slightest difference to Roger, a peculiarly obstinate and most proud individual. He set out to cross the Severn with the aim of joining forces with Earl Ralph who was advancing from Norwich. The aim appears to have been to isolate the north of England by deploying their forces from both east and west but Archbishop Lanfranc seems to have anticipated this and deployed two groups of barons to confront the advancing rebels. Then, to their chagrin, neither the English nor the 'Francigenae', the mixed French and Norman element in the population, joined them.[6]

Earl Ralph advanced through Norfolk into Cambridgeshire and moved on towards Whaddon, one of Earl Ralph's own manors, a few miles east of Cambridge. Falling back before him the King's local justiciars, William de Warenne of Castle Acre and Richard fitzGilbert from Clare, called in vain for assistance. The involvement of these two men, who supported King William at the siege of Ely perhaps explains the Ely tradition that men from Ely, even Hereward the Exile, had taken part in the revolt of 1075.[7]

Despite the military threat presented by the two Earls, Archbishop Lanfranc wrote to King William pleading with him to leave the matter in the hands of his loyal vassals in England; the Archbishop's sycophantic tone is striking. 'It were with great pleasure and as a messenger from God Himself that we should see you again among us. Do not, however, hasten to cross the sea at this moment, for you would be offering us a grave insult were you obliged to come to our assistance in subduing such perjured brigands'.

Earl Roger, meanwhile, advanced from Hereford, only to be confronted by the King's agents in the west, Bishop Wulfstan of Worcester and Abbot Aethelwig of Evesham, supported by Urse d'Abitot, Sheriff of Worcestershire, and the baron Walter de Lacy, who all prevented him from crossing the Severn. They advanced against the Earl and very shortly afterwards he was taken prisoner. It rather looks as though many of his men failed to support him.

In Cambridgeshire the King's men rallied to the support of the two justiciars and Bishop Odo of Bayeux, Bishop Geoffrey of Coutances and Robert Malet, with their levies and castle garrisons, attacked Ralph at 'Fagaduna' (Fawdon in Whaddon). There was a brief skirmish and the Earl made a hasty retreat. He was, as Archbishop Lanfranc gleefully reported to King William, pursued all the way back to Norwich. The Archbishop told William that the rebel Earl would soon be either captured or driven out of England. He hoped he would be taken – dead or alive! All prisoners taken in the conflict were mutilated, having their right foot cut off.

Ralph managed to get back into his castle at Norwich but did not dare remain there to withstand a siege as the King's men set about mounting one with 300 men-at-arms equipped with siege engines. Instead, Earl Ralph set sail for Denmark, leaving his wife Emma, a redoubtable lady by all accounts, (she was, after all, a fitzOsbern), to hold the castle for him!

Emma held out for three months, until granted terms for her surrender, giving her husband time not only to reach Denmark but to return to his paternal inheritance at Dol in Brittany. Perhaps the barons were unwilling or too embarrassed to have to make war on a woman. Archbishop Lanfranc announced to King William; 'The castle at Norwich has fallen! The defenders have agreed to leave England within forty days. The castle itself has been occupied by Geoffrey of Coutances, William de Warenne and Robert Malet. Thanks be to God, the noise of war has completely ceased in England!' He carefully forgot to mention that the castle had been held by Emma as King William too would have been appalled that the daughter of William fitzOsbern should have defied him. But Lanfranc and the barons had extinguished the revolt and the English had signalled their acceptance of the Norman regime by refusing to join the revolt. They had shown that they were unlikely to support rebel barons against the King's authority. In any case, too many areas of England had been depopulated and the heart had gone out of the resistance.[8]

The Archbishop now rejoiced at the defeat of the revolt. 'Glory be to God on High!' he wrote, 'whose mercy has cleansed your Kingdom of the filth of the Bretons!' He also referred to the Bretons as dung. They had been given safe conduct for life and limb if they left within forty days, but the mercenaries in Ralph's pay were given only thirty days. Bishop Geoffrey and his companions occupied the Castle and garrisoned it with their men-at-arms and engineers. Emma took advantage of the safe conduct to accept exile in Brittany where she joined her husband.

Archbishop Lanfranc and his supporting barons maintained a careful watch in expectation of the arrival of the Danes (of which Lanfranc had possibly been informed by Waltheof). Even Bishop Walcher of Durham was alerted and ordered to prepare to hold Durham Castle against them. Lanfranc told him that 'the Danes are indeed coming as the King told us'. Too late to participate in the revolt, the Danes, led by King Swein Estrithson's son Cnut and Earl Hakon, arrived with 200 ships. But they did not dare to confront the King's men. Instead, they went, as they had frequently done previously, to York and there once again 'broke into St Peter's Minster and there took much property, and so went away', and took ship to Flanders (where they would sell their plunder). No battles were reported during their stay nor attacks on castles. Earl Hakon and those with him were reported later to have perished, but no details are recorded. Some have speculated that this was Earl Swein Godwinson's son, the former hostage, but Hakon is a common enough Scandinavian name and there is no proof. As for Cnut, he, sometime later, married a daughter of Count Robert the Frisian and eventually succeeded his brother Harald Sweinson who himself became King of Denmark in 1076 when King Swein Estrithson died.

King William took time out from his preoccupations in Normandy and returned to England. He only did so once Lanfranc had assured him that peace had been restored and the leading Bretons expelled. He brought Earl Waltheof back with him and the Earl was now placed under arrest. Earl Waltheof was placed in a prison; (the text uses the foreign imported word 'prisun', a new name for what, in England, was a new concept). Earl Roger, too, was imprisoned. Both men were so dealt with because of the threat from the Danes. The King spent midwinter at Westminster and as Queen Edith had died, seven days before Christmas (18 December), King William ordered her body brought from Winchester to Westminster and, with great honour, she was laid to rest alongside her husband, King Edward.

King William then proceeded to the punishment of all those still in England accused of participation in the revolt. All the Bretons who had attended the bridale suffered dreadful punishments and loss of their lands. They were, as the Chronicler wrote, 'fordyde' (ruined).

> Some of them were blinded,
> Some driven from the land,
> Some were brought to shame.
> Thus were traitors to King William laid low.

as the rhythmic epigram puts it.[9]

The King in Council now proceeded with the trial of the three Earls.

Earl Ralph was included, despite his absence, and sentenced formally to outlawry and the forfeiture of all his English lands. He was condemned as 'a man of disposition foreign to any good.' His men, especially those who had attended the bridale, were put to shame and mutilated, except for those who had fled into exile, simply because King William could not get his hands on Earl Ralph.

Earl Roger was unable to offer any defence to a charge of treason and was condemned to loss of his Earldom and all his lands and sentenced to perpetual imprisonment. The Earldom of Hereford ceased to exist and another Earl was not appointed. Earl Roger had been judged 'according to Norman laws'.

Earl Waltheof presented a different and more difficult problem. He had tried to atone for his original complicity in the revolt by a speedy confession to Archbishop Lanfranc and an impressive display of repentance. King William's leniency towards him in Normandy had probably raised his hopes. Unfortunately he had many enemies among the Normans and even his own wife, Countess Judith, sought his destruction.

She accused her husband of favouring and of being an accomplice in the revolt, despite the fact that he had taken no active part in it. Earl Waltheof's defence was that he had not really consented to the crime. Orderic Vitalis actually uses the word 'delated' for Judith's testimony, often used by Roman historians for the act of denunciation of an accused to the authorities. But the Earl's defence failed, possibly because of the oath he had sworn, as demanded by the conspirators, even if unwillingly; as in making confession to Archbishop Lanfranc he had in fact broken his oath, which perhaps made matters worse. But the Council was unable to reach a decision immediately and the Earl was, in effect, remanded in custody to a prison at Winchester.

King William was left free to re-distribute the lands of Earl Roger as well as those of Earl Ralph and his Bretons. He also had Queen Edith's lands at his disposal. These included lands in Herefordshire at Stanford Regis, Leominster and its dependent estates, Westhide, Leinthall, Shobdon, Orleton and Stoke plus Martley in Worcestershire. Then in Hampshire a group of manors at Anstey, Greatham, Selborne, Upton and Wootton. The king proceeded to enrich those who had supported him, so that Ralph de Tosny, for instance, received two of Queen Edith's manors. and, in Norfolk, Roger Bigod was rewarded with land. But the greater part of all these lands became part of the royal demesne and made the monarchy even more powerful and wealthy.

Of Earl William fitzOsbern's lands, as held by his son Earl Roger, known as 'of Breteuil', the family estate in Normandy, some were reserved for the

King and others used to reward his supporters. Alvred of Marlborough, for instance, was given the castle of Ewias Harold which Earl William had restored, refortifying it. King William confirmed the gift of lands made to Alvred by the Earl and gave him the lands of Ralph de Bernay which the latter had held with the castle. But few of Earl Roger's supporters can be identified, which, as they are not named, suggests that many of his vassals had been unwilling to join the revolt. Only six can be positively identified, Ralph de Bernay, who had been Earl William's sheriff in Herefordshire, Eon the Breton and Turstin the Fleming, together with three lesser men holding small estates near Monmouth. Turstin's land at Downton on the Rock was held in 1086 by Roger de Lacey, son of Walter who had helped lead the resistance to the rebellion. Walter de Lacey himself also got the lands of Eon the Breton at Street and King's Pyon. Ralph de Bernay's lands at Monnington, which Ralph had unjustly seized went to Alvred of Marlborough. Alvred d'Epaignes was given seven vills in Wales which Earl William and his son had kept in demesne.

But most of the forfeitures remained in King William's hands. Earl William's lands in Gloucestershire, held by his son Roger, were forfeited to the King as well as land at Tewkesbury belonging to the castle at Hanley, and large estates at Forthampton, Dymock, Arlington, Beckford, Tockington, Hempsted and Shenington. At Ashton under Hill the tithes of the land had been given by Earl William to the Church of Cormeilles, but King William took back the estate because the Shire Court testified that it had never seen the King's writ giving the land to the Earl.[10]

Earl William fitzOsbern had been immensely powerful in his day as his possession of at least five castles shows. He built the castle at Chepstow (Estrig Hoiel) and others at Clifford and Wigmore and refortified Ewias Harold to form a castlery commanding all the routes into the Black mountains. He also had a castle which he had built on the Isle of Wight during a separate campaign of the Conquest, on his own initiative. The juxtaposition of the Earl's land holdings with those of Queen Edith suggests that he had some sort of duty of supervision over her, to ensure that she did not become a focus of discontent. His son, Earl Roger, had succeeded his father in 1071 because Earl William had died at the battle of Cassel. Orderic Vitalis comments on the death of the Earl; 'Where now is William fitzOsbern, Viceroy, Earl of Hereford, Seneschal of Normandy and England? He who was the first and greatest oppressor of the English, who through ambition and avarice encouraged the fatal enterprise in which so many thousands of men perished; he fell in his turn and received his just reward. He who killed so many men with the sword, died by the sword and, after his death, the spirit of discord made his son and his son-in-law revolt against their lord and kinsman.'

Orderic Vitalis further comments on the fall of the House of fitzOsbern, especially because Earl Roger had no heirs. He says; 'Truly the world's glory droops and withers like the flowers of the grass. It is spent and withered like smoke… the race of fitzOsbern has been uprooted from England so that there is now no corner in which it can set foot'.

Earl Ralph could have had a history of disaffection. It is thought he had supported Count Conan of Brittany back in 1064 and that he only came to England after the Conquest was an established fact, possibly in 1070 or a little later, after his father, Ralph the Staller, died. The fall of Earl Ralph led to the fall of his brother, Harduin. He and others were replaced shortly after 1076 and Domesday does indicate that much royal demesne came into the King's hands after 1076 rather than in 1066. There are entries such as 'The lands of Earl Ralph which Godric the Steward has custody of in Suffolk in the King's hand.' The Steward also held land in Norfolk on the same terms. This Godric had previously been Ralph's steward and was now a royal officer. Lands previously held by Earl Gyrth and Archbishop Stigand had passed through Earl Ralph's hands and were then re-distributed after his fall.

A number of thegns, such as the Englishman, Wihtgar son of Aelfric, and Finn the Dane, who had managed to retain lands after 1066, were found to have joined the revolt and now lost them. So did Fathir, a thegn of King Edward, in Norfolk. So it was not always the Conquest which brought men lands and wealth in the form of vast East Anglian estates, but the revolts and rebellions of 1069-70 and 1075.

In Little Domesday, 120 entries use the term 'forfeited' and many of them reflect the results of the revolt of 1075. Of these entries, twenty-six relate to the forfeiture of a whole Hundred or of a Borough or some Liberty. A second set of entries, some seven cases, result from a specific legal case. But the rest, eighty-seven entries, relate to 1075. They name the forfeiture of a specific individual in ninety-three per cent of these cases; over ninety per cent are Earl Ralph's own losses of course, and the rest relate to his brother, Harduin, to Walter of Dol, Humphrey of St Omer (in Brittany), Lisois de Moutiers and to Wihtgar son of Aelfric.

Great Domesday provides much less evidence about Earl Ralph, possibly an effect in part of the way the entries have been summarized. Two entries for Hertfordshire refer to Earl Ralph as land received 'after Earl Ralph's forfeiture' and 'not on the day on which he forfeited'. One Cambridgeshire entry says Earl Ralph lost the estate 'because he had offended the King'.

Earl Ralph, on his lands in Brittany, prospered and eventually became a crusader, dying, along with his wife Emma, on the way to Jerusalem. Earl Roger spent the rest of his natural life a prisoner, constantly insulting and cursing the King. On one occasion, moved to make one of his periodic gestures of benevolence, King William, aware that it was a particularly hard winter, sent Earl Roger a rich Christmas gift of silk garments and furs. But the Earl simply made a heap of them in the middle of his chamber and set fire to them.

King William, when told of this, said, 'The man is too proud who scorns me so. By the Splendour of God! He shall never leave prison while I live.' The Earl was ordered to be freed at the King's behest on his deathbed, only to be re-arrested and imprisoned by King William Rufus. He eventually died, still a prisoner.

Earl Waltheof spent the whole winter and then the spring of 1076 in prison, occupying himself with acts of penitence, possibly repenting for his many sins, including the deaths of the sons of Karli.

Each day he recited the whole Psalter, which he had learned by heart. Archbishop Lanfranc was a witness to his claim to innocence of the charges laid against him and of his genuine repentance. But the Norman baronage feared to release him and coveted his lands and honours. King William himself was in England for Easter, 1 April 1076, to attend a Council held by Lanfranc at Winchester, and it is thus possible that he was still in England and at Winchester when Waltheof was executed. It was at this time that he allowed Bishop Walcher of Durham to purchase the Earldom of Northumbria as it was when Earl Waltheof held it, so that Durham became, in effect, a Palatine Bishopric.

Earl Waltheof's case was reviewed at Pentecost, 15 May 1076. This time, he was sentenced to death under English Law because he had listened to men who had plotted to kill the King and had not immediately opposed them and revealed the plot to the King. He was sentenced to be executed, a result without precedent in England or Normandy. There is no evidence that King William ever passed a similar sentence against anyone else as his usual policy was to sentence men to exile or prison, though he was also fond of ordering mutilation (which usually resulted in death). But Earl Waltheof was English and, it was maintained, had to be treated like an Englishman. Precedents were sought in English law from King Alfred's time onwards through to the laws of Cnut. A Code of Aethelred for example, reads; 'And if anyone plots against the King, he shall forfeit his life, unless he clears himself by the most solemn oath determined upon by the authorities'. Another expands this, adding, 'if it is proved against him; and if he seeks and is able to clear himself, he shall do so by means of the most solemn oath, or by the triple ordeal.' In the absence of oath helpers who would support the Earl's word, Waltheof could not clear himself and so was sentenced to execution.

This condemnation taken of the part played by Earl Waltheof in the revolt reflects traditional English opinion about treason; 'A full great treachery it is in the world that a man deprive his lord of his life or drive him in his lifetime from the land'.[11]

So on 31 May, the Feast of St Petronella, 1076, the sentence was carried out. Earl Waltheof was taken to the place of execution early in the morning, lest any of the citizens of Winchester should seek to prevent the execution. He was taken to a hill outside the walls (the site of the later St Giles' Church). He had clothed himself in the full dress of an English Earl and gave gifts and relics to various poor clerks and other men. Then he knelt and prayed with tears of penitence, until the headsman intervened, saying, 'Rise, we must do the bidding of our master'. Earl Waltheof said, 'Wait yet, let me at least have a little moment to say the Lord's Prayer for me and for you.'

He was allowed to do so and had almost finished when as he said the words, 'Lead us not into temptation', the headsman's sword flashed. Bystanders testified afterwards that they heard the severed head say, 'But deliver us from evil.'

The body was at first buried at the site of execution. The citizens, on hearing the news, lamented with grief. But that was not quite the end. The people of Winchester saw his death as a martyrdom and the story of how he met his end with Christian resignation became widespread and eventually reached Crowland Abbey in Lincolnshire when the body was taken there for a more respectful burial. The Earl had been a benefactor of the Abbey so that St Guthlac's foundation was a suitable place of rest. As was not unusual in the eleventh century, given the circumstances of the Earl's death, miracles were reported at the grave. Most of this comes from traditions at Crowland. There was also a focus for his cult at Romsey Abbey, near Winchester, where he was held to be a saint by the nuns.

The English, especially those who were Anglo-Scandinavian, continued to consider Waltheof a saint and the story of his holy death reached Scandinavia itself, as Snorri Sturlason testifies in the Heimskringla. But Earl Waltheof's skald, Thorkell Skallason, sang not of his sanctity but of his prowess as a warrior. He boasted that the Earl had once burned a hundred Normans in a wood, (allegedly after the battle of Hastings but more likely, if at all, at York during the rebellion of 1069). He composed a poem on the Earl which has survived.[12]

William, who reddened steel and cut through the icy sea from the south,
has indeed betrayed the doughty Waltheof under a truce;
Truly the slaying of men will be a long time ceasing in England;
But no more glorious lord than was my gallant chief shall die!

Crowland Abbey was ruled from 1062 to 1086 by Abbot Ulfcytel, with whom Hereward had quarrelled shortly before his exile, and while Ulfcytel was Abbot, Earl Waltheof had given the Abbey an estate at Barnack, a major source of building stone, so enabling the Abbot to rebuild the Church at Crowland. It is thought that Countess Judith, perhaps dismayed at the results of her action, persuaded King William to allow the translation of the Earl's body to Crowland which was done on 15 June, a fortnight after the execution. The body was then buried in the Chapter House. Abbot Ulfcytel was eventually deposed by Archbishop Lanfranc at midwinter, 1086, simply because he was English, though it was alleged at the time that he was accused of superstition and idolatry, probably for allowing the development of the cult of St Waltheof. The Earl would not have been seen as a saint by the Normans!

The Crowland tradition was that Ivo Taillebois, sheriff of Lincolnshire, had complained about Ulfcytel in 1076, though more likely in 1086. This may be a genuine piece of tradition from the time when Ingulf was Abbot, 1086-1109. It was Abbot Ingulf who moved Waltheof's body a second time, giving him a benefactor's grave near the High Altar. Miracles were reported there well into the twelfth century. Much of what is known of the Earl's death and the fate of his body was recorded by Orderic Vitalis who visited Crowland and other Fenland Abbeys during the abbacy of Abbot Geoffrey, 1109-1124. Orderic composed an account of the Earl's death in verse. The cult of the Earl can best be interpreted as evidence of English resentment against Norman rule.[13]

The evidence of the aftermath of the revolt and the treatment accorded to the rebel Bretons is recorded in Domesday Book, while the rather vague causes of the revolt were described by Orderic. But there could have been much more to the affair than appears. The Danes, led by Cnut of Denmark did actually appear off the Northumbrian Coast with 200 ships (representing some ten or even twelve thousand men), but, as the North was seriously depopulated and its remaining population thoroughly cowed, no popular support emerged. What cannot be known is whether the revolt would have taken a more serious turn if the Danes had arrived early enough to affect events. It is also possible that King Philip of France might have had a hand in the Earls' revolt since he was certainly pleased when Earl Ralph escaped to his castle at Dol. When King William besieged Ralph at Dol in 1076; King Philip came to his assistance and drove King William off. The Normans lost many men and horses and much treasure. Earl Ralph had also had the support of soldiers provided by Count Fulk le Rechin of Anjou.

The Earl's hostility, therefore, possibly had its roots in Breton antipathy towards Normandy. Ralph had inherited his father's Breton lands and was the natural leader of all the Bretons who had come over with Duke William in 1066. The Gael barony was to the west and north-west of Rennes and included Montfort and Montauban-De-Bretagne. At the time when the revolt was being planned, and when Ralph either agreed or suggested that the Danes be called in, his fellow magnates in Brittany were preparing to revolt against Count Hoel or perhaps rather to launch a raid against Normandy. The appeal to Denmark therefore makes sense, giving the revolt a wider significance, which explains why the King ordered Lanfranc to put the East Coast on alert. Ralph in fact continued his part in the struggle from Brittany, which suggests that if the revolt had succeeded King William would also have had a hostile power established to the west of Normandy. As it was, there was war in 1076 when Earl Ralph joined up with Geoffrey Granon, bastard son of Count Alan III with a power base around Dol, to attack Hoel, so that Ralph had held Dol with reinforcements from Anjou. King William's defeat by King Philip was his first failure for twenty years and counter-balanced the successful repression of the revolt in England. Ralph remained powerful in Brittany and William failed to prevent King Philip from occupying the Vexin which lies between Normandy and the Île de France.

Count Fulk le Rechin attacked Maine, against John de la Flèche, and the result was a truce which produced a pact between King William and King Philip at Blanchelande in 1077. The need to hold down England was to hamper King William's struggles against King Philip for the rest of his reign. The fall of Earl Roger had its own side effect. It drove William of Breteuil, Roger's elder brother, to join the King's son, Robert Curthose, in his rebellion against his father. In a sense the revolt of the Earls had reflected the general air of discontent affecting the sons of the first generation of Normans in England.

It was not only Bretons who were 'purged'. The Flemings holding land in the north were eclipsed also and Gerbod, the first Earl of Chester, preferred to return to Flanders rather than remain in England. Flanders itself became very hostile to England and Normandy, as did Brittany. One Breton lord who became less important was Count Brian of Brittany, and he was replaced in Cornwall by Robert, Count of Mortain, the Conqueror's half-brother.

The overall effect of the revolt and the treatment meted out to the rebels was that the Norman element became much more dominant in England. It could be that one effect of the revolt was the holding of an enquiry by Commission, composed of Archbishop Lanfranc, Count William of Eu and Richard fitzGilbert, into the conduct of sheriffs throughout England during 1076 or 1077, which ordered many of them to make restitution of any lands seized from the Church.

With the defeat of the revolt of the Earls, one can say that the era of Conquest had come to an end and the reign of the Conqueror as King in England had begun.

Epilogue

So the period of the actual Norman Conquest came to an end. King William was to rule England for another eleven years and three months, starting from the day on which Earl Waltheof was executed, 31 May 1076 (the last act in the drama of the revolt of the Earls), and ending on the day William the Bastard died, 9 September 1087.

The Anglo-Norman State thus created was the fruit of a double conquest; that of Western Neustria (Frankish northern France) by Rollo, and that of England by Duke William II. It owed to this origin a structure much more regular than that of other principalities built up piecemeal or other monarchies burdened, like that of King Edward the Confessor, with a long and sometimes confused tradition. That might be why it has for so long been considered to be the start of the development of Modern Britain.

The conquest had taken place at the very moment when the transformation of economic and intellectual conditions throughout Western Europe began to favour the struggle against the disintegration of society. Hence the significance of the fact that the Norman monarchy, born of a successful war, had at its disposal at an early date an educated personnel and bureaucratic machinery.

The War of Conquest and the harsh suppression of the subsequent rebellions removed from the scene the native aristocracy and all danger to the unity of the State posed by such an aristocracy seemed to be at an end. Yet, the idea that it was possible for the King to govern his whole realm effectively and directly was still so alien to men's minds that King William had found it necessary to create a number of regional commands. However, the very faithlessness of two of the great barons to whom they were assigned, Ralph de Gael and Roger of Breteuil, quickly led to the suppression of two of those units, leaving only Shrewsbury, Chester and Durham which were needed to contain the Welsh and the Scots. Even the Earldom of Kent disappeared after King William fell out with his half-brother, Bishop Odo.

Although his rule in England remained virtually unchallenged, King William's control over Normandy was never secure. He spent most of the next eleven years at war with his royal rival, King Philip I of France, who was to be the real victor in the campaigns of 1076 to 1078. He impaired King William's position as Duke of Normandy, placing a limit on the growth of the Duchy. Orderic Vitalis remarks that after Hastings the Bastard 'never once drove an army from the field of battle'. He had never done so before Hastings either. King William then fell out with his son, Robert Curthose, who was now demanding independent control over Normandy and Maine. Robert became the focus of support from fractious Norman barons, especially William of Breteuil, brother of the imprisoned Earl Roger, and other members of the rising new generation.

The King's enemies abroad took full advantage of the situation and, in the fighting which followed, King William was defeated and humiliated at Gerberoi, January 1079. This was the worst defeat of his career and he was forced into a reconciliation with his son. That was to lead, after King William's death, to the separation of Normandy from England.

King William suffered the defection of his half-brother, Bishop Odo of Bayeux, in 1082 and a further rebellion by Robert in 1083, the year in which Queen Matilda died. Warfare was still going on in September 1087 when the King died.

His rule from 1067 to 1087 had therefore been carried on against a background of incessant warfare. Of King William it was never more certain than that 'uneasy lies the head that wears a crown'. The defeat at Gerberoi had emboldened King Malcolm of Scotland to break the Treaty of Abernethy and ravage northern England. That was dealt with when King William dispatched his son Robert with a large army to offer the Scots the choice of renewed peace or war. Peace if they submitted, war if they did not.

King Malcolm carefully chose, as in 1072, not to offer battle. He came down into Lothian but retreated at the sight of the Anglo-Norman army. He offered hostages and accepted once more, perhaps more plainly this time, that Scotland should be subject to England. Robert effectively renewed the terms of Abernethy and hastened joyfully to report his success to his father.

All hope of England ever being liberated from the 'Norman Yoke' (the phrase is that of Orderic Vitalis) had now vanished though some Englishmen still dreamed of it and hoped for aid from Scandinavia which never came.

Orderic, although he is quite laudatory, especially in the earlier sections of his work, about William's achievements, provides a mordant summary of the reign. He reproaches the King with his bastardy, and accuses him of using poison to dispose of his enemies, of disinheriting men without due cause, of resorting to murder, of avarice and of failing to make an equitable distribution of the spoils of conquest.

More tellingly, in 1080, Bishop Wenric of Verdun and Trier wrote to Pope Gregory VII accusing him of giving support to Rudolf of Swabia (against the Emperor Henry IV) despite the fact that Rudolf was guilty of perjury, homicide and adultery. He told Gregory that he was guilty of supporting others 'who have usurped kingdoms by the violence of a tyrant, themselves paved the road to a throne with blood, placed a blood-stained crown on their heads and with murder, rape, butchery and torment established their rule'. That is an obvious reference to King William.

Overall, in a reign of nineteen years and one month, King William spent only seven years and ten months in England and was virtually an absentee ruler from 1072 to 1087. Orderic, writing of the King's dying moments, puts into his mouth a speech amounting to a deathbed confession which reflects the atmosphere around the dying King. Orderic had close contacts with many of those who were present. He makes William admit that he did not 'attain that high honour' of kingship 'by hereditary right, but wrested it from the perjured King Harold in a desperate battle with much shedding of human blood' and 'by the slaughter and banishment of his adherents I subjected England to my rule'. He is made to admit to cruel oppression and that he caused innumerable numbers, especially in Yorkshire, to perish through 'famine and the sword'. 'I fell on the English of the northern shires like a ravening lion,' he says, and 'became the barbarous murderer of many thousands, both young and old'.

William of Poitiers comments that many thousands had fallen on evil days and that the sons of royalty and nobility 'fettered with manacles and irons are in prisons and gaols... have lost their limbs by the sword or disease... or been deprived of their eyes'.

In the light of such comments, one might well ask what effect the numbers that died might have had on the overall population of England. Just how many were killed, just died, or were exiled, during the period of the conquest must remain unknown, but their disappearance must have caused large numbers to remain unborn. Estimates derived from the number of persons recorded in Domesday Book and its satellite documents, as to the size of the population in 1086, vary from one and a quarter to two and a half million, depending on how many individuals are reckoned to have been listed and what multiplier is used to estimate the size of the population on the assumption that the Domesday Commissioners were recording heads of households. (F.W. Maitland's estimate was 1,375,000.) It is not beyond the bounds of possibility to suggest that the figure for 1086 might, had these losses not occurred, have been some three million. An unknown number of persons inhabited fens, moors and hills and Domesday does not include mercenary soldiers or landless knights. It omits London, Winchester and some other towns and fails to record burgesses, drengs, king's sergeants, monks and nuns. The North of England was not surveyed and there are few population figures for Yorkshire.

It is known that the Old English Kingdom's administrative and governmental structures, as King Harold's brief reign shows, were still in good order on the eve of the Conquest. Thereafter they fell into the hands of a ruling class which subverted, possibly because it did not fully understand, them.

However, King William's success can be accounted for by the theory put forward by H.W.C. Davis, who argued that well-governed countries, such as eleventh century England, can more easily resist invading armies than less well-governed states, but, should they fail, they are also more easily controlled. This is because they do not lend themselves easily to successful guerrilla resistance because efficient governments can remove the opportunities for such activities.

King William took over a country in which well-trained officers were in charge of both local and central government. The Shire and Hundred system, together with the efficient transmission of the King's will by means of the Writ, gave the new Norman King the degree of control he needed as soon as the Bishops, some Abbots, the Sheriffs and other Reeves had agreed to collaborate. Every man owning land in England was already expected to have a lord and was reachable by justice and the taxation system. Every village belonged to a Hundred with a court which met monthly and there were Shire courts which met twice a year. King William also had at his disposal a unique tax system, the geld, which enabled him to levy a tax across the whole country for the support of his government and his army.

The only areas to offer resistance after Hastings were precisely the less well-governed border areas or wilder areas such as the Fens. Once crowned King, William could demand the obedience of his 'civil service' of Bishops and Abbots and Sheriffs and use the geld 'exactors' to raise the taxes he needed. Documentary evidence, such as Geld Rolls, was available which recorded exactly how many taxable hides or carucates there were in a shire and from whom the tax could be demanded.

King's messengers, accompanied by a military escort, could be sent to courts of Shire and Hundred, bearing the King's writ and seal, to transmit his wishes and collect his taxes. King William used the system for the first time as early as January 1067 and imposed a geld which shocked the country. Thus the Old English system of government itself became an instrument of oppression once it was in Norman hands.

William the Bastard used it to effect a massive transfer of English-held lands into Norman hands. He took over the estates of those slain in the battles of 1066, especially that of Hastings, and went on to seize the lands of all those who could be condemned as rebels if they opposed him. He could do this simply by asserting his rights as the duly crowned king and by claiming to be the legitimate successor of King Edward (which automatically made rebels of all those who had fought against him).

The higher clergy, especially the Bishops, many of whom were foreign born, were more than willing to collaborate with the Norman King in order to secure their continued possession of the estates of the Church. William persuaded them that he fully intended to create a genuine Anglo-Norman realm, with equal rights and protection for both Normans and Englishmen. But this never became a reality because William also had to satisfy the avarice of the 'motley crew' of adventurers who had helped him conquer England and who expected to be well rewarded for doing so.

The situation in the early years was quite chaotic and many Normans and other supporters of the King took advantage of this to secure vast estates, beyond the dreams of avarice, while others complained of receiving barren farms and domains depopulated by war and famine. Much land was seized by the use of force and few Norman lords did anything without the support of armed soldiers. In several shires it is possible to summarise the effects of the Conquest. Kent is shown in Domesday to have few English survivors among the land holding classes since it bore the brunt of the first stage of the Conquest. The thegns of Dorset lost heavily because of their participation in the Battle of Hastings and also because of involvement in the revolt at Exeter or the fighting at Montacute. Cambridgeshire suffered from the impact of the revolt of the Earls. Shropshire fell into the hands of Roger of Montgomery and its thegns suffered a reduction in wealth and status. Such examples can easily be multiplied especially as 'King William implanted the customs of the French throughout England and began to change those of the English' as the monks of Bury St Edmunds observed.

Any opposition, however feeble, constituted rebellion and provoked the use of force, resulting in the loss of even more land. Most of the English noble and military class was either slain, exiled or mutilated. It became almost impossible to organise a really effective regional resistance and the rebellions, when they came, were vigorously crushed.

Castles became another instrument of oppression. They were smaller than the Old English 'burhs', the fortified towns, but they made it possible for a few hundred well-armed men to hold down a subject population, forming a real army of occupation. This military aspect of Norman rule was even reflected in the architecture of the Cathedrals and Abbeys constructed after the conquest and built in stone with crenellated towers like the castles they imitated. They were huge buildings and, like the castles (especially after these, too, were built in stone), also dominated the countryside in which they stood. This military appearance was maintained even in later centuries as surviving gateways show, such as St Osyth's in Essex, that of Battle Abbey, and the many towers. This was in marked contrast to the English churches which, unlike the Norman, and though smaller and less imposing, were provided with wall paintings and tapestry work, vestments embroidered in gold or silver and jewel-encrusted altar vessels. Unlike the Normans, the English excelled in craftsmanship and their women were skilled in embroidery and cloth of gold.

As for the legality of the transfer of land, the best right proved to be the sword of conquest.

Appendix 1

The English Succession

The successful invasion of England by William the Bastard, Duke of Normandy, is naturally, because of its outcome, known as the Norman Conquest of England. William of Poitiers, however, refers to the events of October 1066 as 'The War between Duke William and Harold, King of the English'. Yet it was, most certainly 'the War of the English Succession'.

King Edward's foreign policy, throughout his reign, is best interpreted as a series of diplomatic manoeuvres aimed at preventing a foreign invasion, and much of his internal domestic policy had the same aim. As no invasion came until after the King's death, his policy must be accorded a certain amount of respect.

The policy was very simply put into effect by playing the various possible or probable pretenders to the throne off against each other. Edward can be said to have behaved rather like the proverbial rich uncle, who promises his inheritance first to one nephew and then to another or even to a third, so that they will do their best to win his favour. King Edward's decision to do so could have been stimulated by the first steps in a diplomatic quadrille taken by his Danish half-brother, King Harthacnut. He, it appears, had secured his throne in Denmark, against the claims of King Magnus of Norway, by agreeing with Magnus that should either of them die, and without an heir, the survivor would inherit his rival's throne. Such an agreement seems to have been a common feature of eleventh century peace treaties between rival rulers.

King Magnus seems to have assumed that the deal included England as well as Denmark as both were inherited from King Cnut the Great. When King Harthacnut died, King Magnus not only seized Denmark, in the face of the claims of Cnut's surviving nephew, Swein Estrithson, but also went on to make preparations to invade England. That indicates that all such agreements depended on the ability of the survivor to enforce his claim, if necessary by war. King Magnus was only prevented from carrying out his intention by his own premature death.

The heir to the claims of King Magnus was King Harald Sigurdson, or Hardrada. Having secured Norway, King Harald spent the next twelve years at war with King Swein Estrithson over the throne of Denmark. The English appear to have been permanently anxious lest either of these two should defeat the other and then turn against England. But, in the event, neither was free to press their claims to England.

On the death of Harthacnut, his half-brother, Edward was chosen by the Witan to be King of England, as the heir to the line of Cerdic and Alfred. King Swein is alleged to have put forward his own claim, in a protest to Edward, and to have agreed with Edward that he would not enforce his claim (not that he was free to do so) provided Edward agreed to the usual arrangement, that should either of them die without an heir, the other was free to claim the dead man's throne. In 1066, knowing that both Duke William of Normandy and King Harald of Norway intended to mount an invasion, Swein Estrithson very carefully did nothing.

As for King Edward, after 1051, when it became clear that he was not going to have an heir, concluding that God had decided that Edward's Queen, Edith, daughter of Earl Godwine of Wessex, was not going to provide an heir, the King resorted to balancing the claims of the pretenders against each other. A passage in the Vita Edwardi Regis, in which Queen Edith, in a poem written by the anonymous author, is made to praise her newly rebuilt Church at Wilton, and the convent of nuns it contained, as the 'peerless mother' of 'blessed babes... conceived immaculate from sin' (that is the many nuns the Church of Wilton will bring forth) and will 'celebrate each day the many births', and do so without experiencing 'slow birth by ordered lapse of those long, lazy months'. At the bringing forth of these nuns the Church will 'feel no pains' and, significantly 'nor will one fashioned in your womb expire'. This invites the possible solution to Edward and Edith's childlessness; that Queen Edith had born a child but that it was stillborn, and Edith proved to be unable to have further children.[1]

King Edward's policy had developed in the 1040s after he had become king, and became aware of the threat from King Magnus of Norway. King Edward sent out a fleet in 1045 because of the threat from King Magnus but he refused Earl Godwine's demand in 1047 that fifty ships be sent to the aid of King Swein against Magnus (fearing no doubt to provoke the latter's anger against England), and both the King and his Earls took ships to sea as a precaution. King Magnus then died that year on 25 October. Edward was now free to use his fleet to support the German Emperor against Count Baldwin of Flanders, in a blockade. He also sent it after the exiled Staller, Osgod Clapa in 1049, who had gathered a fleet with the intention of invading England. Fortunately, the Staller's fleet was wrecked by a storm in the following year and the threatened invasion never came. King Edward was then able to disband the mercenary element of his fleet, most in 1050 and the rest in 1051. They were a Scandinavian force inherited from the Danish Kings and he did not trust them. That allowed him to abolish the 'heregeld' or army tax, that part of the common geld which paid for them.[2]

In 1051 came the great quarrel between King Edward and his premier Earl, Godwine of Wessex. The King had been edging him out of any position of dominance in the royal council, the Witan, and had ignored the candidate he favoured for archbishop, Aelric (or Aethelric) a monk of Canterbury elected by his fellow monks and a kinsman of the Earl. Instead, the King had chosen to make an old acquaintance from Normandy, Robert Champart, Archbishop of Canterbury, after the death of Archbishop Eadsige. Robert was a former Abbot of Jumièges and currently Bishop of London. The Earl then defied the King, refusing to punish the people of Dover who were blamed by the King for an assault on his kinsman, Count Eustace of Boulogne. The Count and his men had behaved appallingly at Dover, billeting themselves on the townsfolk by force and attempting to take control of the burh. There had been an affray in which there were some twenty casualties on each side and the Count had complained to his kinsman the King, demanding that the townsfolk be punished.[3]

There was a confrontation between the Earl and his supporters on the one hand and the King and his men on the other. Open war had been avoided but the Earl had been outlawed and he and his family forced to flee for their lives to Flanders and Ireland. King Edward needed to prevent Earl Godwine, if he could, from using the Channel ports to recruit mercenaries and ships, and so made overtures to the young Duke William of Normandy, no doubt reminding him of his father's generosity towards Edward when he was an exile in Normandy. No effort had been made to involve the Duke any earlier. In the mid 1030s William had been a minor and no Norman interest in English affairs had been possible.[4]

As a result (if the notice of his visit found in the Worcester Chronicle is genuine) the Duke made a brief state visit to England, taking time out from his campaign against Anjou, and was formally received by the King. It is possible that some sort of treaty was arranged between them, possibly to deny Earl Godwine access to Norman ports and possibly to counteract the influence of Godwine's ally, Count Baldwin of Flanders, and the Duke returned home. The background to this lies in the fact that English kings had searched for a Norman alliance ever since the 990s, hoping thereby to eliminate raids by Viking pirates. No use was ever made of this visit by the Duke by Norman writers, despite their anxiety to prove that the Duke was King Edward's chosen successor, which suggests that the succession question was not raised on this occasion, the only time the King and the Duke could have met after Edward became King.[5]

Norman writers later claimed that the King had caused the three great Earls, Godwine of Wessex, Leofric of Mercia and Siward of Northumbria, together with Bishop Stigand (identified in the Norman sources by his later title of Archbishop) to swear to accept the Duke as his heir and that Archbishop Robert was sent to Normandy to inform the Duke of this.

The problem is that there are only two occasions on which Robert could have done so. The first was before the quarrel with Earl Godwine, when Robert went, in 1051, via Normandy to Rome to fetch his pallium from the Pope. But in that case, it should have been Archbishop Robert who swore the oath and not Stigand who was only Bishop of Winchester. If there had been such an oath, then it should have been Archbishop Robert who swore alongside the Earls. The second possible occasion was after Earl Godwine's triumphant return to power and influence, in 1052 and Stigand had replaced Robert as Archbishop. Just as the Earl returned to London, and negotiations were going on to persuade the King to receive him into his peace and friendship, Archbishop Robert had fled the country, in a somewhat leaky tub of a vessel, and taken refuge in Normandy.[6]

Some argue that it was then that the King informed the Duke that he had been chosen as his heir. The difficulty is that Robert had already arrived in Normandy before the Earl was restored and Stigand had been appointed as Archbishop, and so could not have known of any promise by Stigand and the three Earls to accept the Duke as the King's heir. This part of the Norman claim makes no sense. The triumphant Earl would never have agreed to such a promise in 1052 and there is no reason to suppose he would have agreed in 1051 in an atmosphere of fear and distrust between himself and the King. There is, of course, no evidence for any of this in English sources. What the Norman writers were doing was transferring the Norman custom, under which the Dukes of Normandy nominated their successors, to England where that custom was unknown.

It is possible that Edward did at one time think of making the Duke his heir, but it is less clear that he did anything about it. In any case, the King only had a powerful, but by no means decisive, voice in the question of his successor. Before 1051 it was still hoped in England, possibly even by the King himself, that Queen Edith would give birth to an heir. There is no sign in the 1040s that anyone doubted that there would be an heir. It is then possible that during the 1050s, before 1054 when Bishop Ealdred of Worcester went to Germany in search of the son of Edmund Ironside, after it had become clear that Queen Edith would never produce an heir (having, perhaps had only a stillborn child), King Edward briefly considered adopting the Duke as his heir, but there is no evidence that he did so.[7]

The question of Edward's lack of children only becomes a problem for historians if it is accepted that the King was known to be celibate, for which there is no pre-Conquest evidence. If his marriage, as seems probable, was perfectly normal, then the problem only arose gradually when it became apparent that he was not going to have an heir.

Nonetheless, the Duke did apparently develop an idée fixe and convince himself that he was Edward's chosen heir. How could this have come about? The only possible solution, if the concept of an embassy headed by Archbishop Robert, while still only Bishop of London, being sent to Normandy to convey the promise to him is discounted because of the difficulties about it outlined above, is that Robert, a refugee for a time at the Ducal Court, either immediately after his flight from England or after his return from Rome (where he had gone to complain to the Pope about his rejection by the English), told the Duke that King Edward had authorised him, because he was in the King's most secret counsels, before his flight, to inform the Duke that he was his chosen heir. Edward might well have dropped hints about the succession question to the Duke during his state visit, without being explicit, and so the Archbishop's words fell on fertile ground. William of Poitiers does in fact assert that Robert, as Archbishop of Canterbury, was Edward's 'ambassador in this matter', sent to inform Duke William of Edward's 'resolve to make him the heir to the throne obtained by his efforts'. He adds that King Edward sent hostages by the agency of that same Robert. It could well be that Archbishop Robert, when in exile, allowed the Duke to believe that King Edward had entrusted him with such a mission. Duke William then convinced himself that he was Edward's favourite. Was he not the great-nephew of the King's mother? Did the King not owe a debt of gratitude to the Duke's father, Duke Robert, and his uncle, Duke Richard? Duke William readily accepted the notion and the idea remained in his mind and solidified into certainty over the next fourteen years.

It is possible that the idea received verification from the fact that, as is likely, the Archbishop had kidnapped the son of Earl Godwine, Wulfnoth, and the Earl's grandson, Hakon son of Swein, and had now given them to the Duke as evidence of the King's promises.

None of this can be proved and these suggestions rest only on possibilities. It is unlikely, given the absence of any English evidence, that Edward actually made the Duke his heir. The Norman claims that he did so only emerged after his death when he could no longer deny them. No chronicler, Norman or English, connects the quarrel with Earl Godwine to any offer of the succession to Duke William. Norman sources know nothing about the quarrel between King Edward and Earl Godwine. Had the King made any offer of the throne to Duke William, then he would certainly have invited the Duke to England and presented and recommended him to the Witan. Of such an act there is no sign. What King Edward did do was to permit the Witan to seek out the Aetheling, Edward the Exile, son of King Edmund Ironside, with a view to making him Edward's heir. He was in fact recalled from Hungary but unfortunately died before he could be installed as the King's heir.

During Earl Godwine's enforced exile, Archbishop Robert had attempted to get the King to divorce Queen Edith, that is to allow him, as Archbishop, to annul the marriage. No reason was recorded as being given at the time for the divorce, since it was never an accomplished fact. The obvious grounds for that would have been adultery on the part of the Queen (of which she was to be scurrilously accused in late and unauthoritative sources), or on the grounds of her childlessness. If the latter was the problem, then the Archbishop probably hoped to persuade the King to seek another wife who would bear him a son, who was not related to Earl Godwine. The third possibility, a divorce on the grounds that the marriage had not been consummated would have made no sense from Archbishop Robert's point of view. A new marriage would have involved the same problem if non-consummation had been a deliberate choice on Edward's part.[8]

The idea that Edward remained a virgin throughout his life remains doubtful. It rests on a peculiarly mediaeval deduction; Edward's body, forty-six years after his death, was found to be incorrupt, there was a tradition already in being that he was a saint, miracles had been recorded about him, therefore it was fitting to claim that he had lived not merely a chaste life but a celibate one and that therefore he had never consummated his marriage, of which the proof was that he had not had children. It suited the religious climate of the day to be able to produce a celibate king who was therefore a saint.

The section of the Vita Edwardi Regis which dealt with the King's marriage is now missing, vital pages having dropped out of the manuscript, and what remains is ambiguous. The work was written by a monk who only knew the King during the last few years of his life when he most likely did in fact abstain from marital relations. By the 1060s he was growing old (by the standards of the age) and devoted himself almost entirely to his pet project, the building of his Abbey of Westminster. The Vita describes his relations with Edith as more like those of father and daughter than of man and wife.

In 1053, Earl Godwine had died, of a stroke, and the King had given his Earldom of Wessex to his surviving eldest son, Harold. He became even more powerful than his father, second only to the king himself and seen by some as the 'sub-regulus' or under-king. Edward, now over fifty years of age and weary of the duties of kingship, seems to have accepted that he and Edith would never produce an heir. He became increasingly devout and pious, despite a continued love of hunting, and devoted his time increasingly to the construction of his favourite project, the Abbey of St Peter at Westminster. The business of government was increasingly left to Earl Harold, especially after the deaths of the senior Earls, first Siward and then Leofric. Those who succeeded them were lesser men.

One of the earliest decisions of the Witan, after Harold's succession to the Earldom of Wessex, was to seek out the son of King Edmund Ironside, another Edward (known as the Exile) with a view to his return to England and possibly his adoption as King Edward's heir. Bishop Ealdred of Worcester made the first overtures in 1054 and Earl Harold himself, who was certainly in Flanders in 1056 and probably accompanied Pope Victor II on his journey back to Rome, by way of Cologne and Regensburg, seems to have successfully arranged the Exile's return in 1056. He may even have escorted him to England.[9]

Unfortunately, either disease, the rigours of the journey or a weak constitution caused Edward to die shortly after his arrival, in 1057, even before he could meet his kinsman King Edward. The Worcester Chronicle records his unfortunate demise in a passage full of poetic rhetoric and laments his death, bewildered by the workings of Providence. But the writer emphasises that he had 'a fine family', one member of which, the Aetheling Edgar, was subsequently brought up at Court by Queen Edith. Had King Edward lived a few years longer it is likely that Edgar would have been the Witan's choice, succeeding, as the Chronicle observed and some people thought, 'as was his natural right'. Duke William could not, then, have mounted a challenge acceptable to the Pope and the European Powers.

Certainly, King Edward made no known contact with Duke William between 1052 and his own death, preferring to leave the outcome of the succession to God.

But, in 1064, Earl Harold made one of his customary journeys to the Continent, as the Vita Edwardi testifies, to study the character, policy and strength of the princes not only through his servants but personally. He is said to have studied them in order to work out what he could get from them and acquired an exhaustive knowledge of them so that 'he could not be deceived by any of their proposals'. On this occasion his vessel was blown off course by strong winds and he had to make an unplanned landing in Ponthieu.[10]

The County of Ponthieu was a somewhat uncivilised area, known, like the neighbouring County of Guînes, for the practice of holding those who landed unexpectedly on its shores to ransom. There Earl Harold fell into the hands of the Count, Guy, at that time a vassal of William of Normandy. Somehow the Duke learned of Earl Harold's imprisonment by Count Guy, and promptly ordered that he be released into the Duke's hands as his 'guest'. The diplomatic courtesies of the time demanded that Earl Harold accede to his rescuer's bidding and he accompanied the Duke on a campaign against Brittany, where he distinguished himself by rescuing some of the Duke's men who had fallen into quicksands. As a result, the Duke bestowed on Harold a set of Norman arms and armour. The Bayeux Tapestry shows this being done in a manner which implies that this meant that Harold was in some sense the Duke's vassal. Norman accounts of Harold's sojourn in Normandy insist that he did homage to the Duke in the customary manner, that he agreed to become the Duke's son-in-law and that his sister was to marry a suitably noble Norman, then furthermore that he swore an oath on the relics of Norman saints to do all in his power to ensure that William was accepted as King in England if King Edward died without an heir of the body. Strictly speaking, Edward did have an heir, Edgar the Aetheling, though he was still too young and lacking in support to be a force to be reckoned with.[11]

The Norman account was later embellished to an unacceptable degree; Harold was alleged, in one source only, to have promised to act as William's 'vicar', probably meaning 'proxy' or representative, at Edward's Court, use his wealth and influence to ensure William's acceptance as King, garrison a castle at Dover with the Duke's knights at his (Harold's) own expense, and place similar garrisons in other castles elsewhere in England. The Duke then graciously agreed to confirm Harold in the possession of his own Earldom and lands!

Harold in fact made no attempt to do anything of the sort. No castle was built at Dover, nor were Norman garrisons placed there or elsewhere. This passage seems to depend on hindsight, in that a castle was built and garrisoned in 1066, after the Battle of Hastings, and there were a number of Norman castles, one in Essex, held by the Breton staller Robert fitzWimarc, and several on the Welsh Marches held by followers of the, now deceased, Earl Ralph, of Mantes and Hereford, King Edward's own nephew. No marriage was ever contracted between Harold and a daughter of the Duke, nor did any sister of his marry a Norman. Again, English sources, albeit they are very patchy for the period 1057-1065, know nothing of any of this, and the story only emerged in full after both King Edward and King Harold were dead, when neither of them could deny any of it.

Whatever the commitments Earl Harold entered into when in Normandy, they in fact did little to determine the outcome. Whatever they were, they were sufficient to permit Duke William to brand Earl Harold as a perjurer and an oath-breaker and so a faithless vassal, in the eyes of his Norman barons, the princes of north west Europe and the Pope Alexander II. But none of this transpired until 1066 after King Edward had died and Harold, as his nominated successor, had been chosen by the Witan and anointed and crowned King by Archbishop Ealdred of York.

The Witan had accepted the dead King's nomination of Earl Harold, convinced of the need for a King who could confront the pretensions and ambitions of the rival pretenders to the throne, especially Duke William the Bastard of Normandy, King Harald Sigurdson called Hardrada of Norway and King Swein Estrithson of Denmark. They also needed someone who would keep out the exiled Earl Tostig.

Earl Tostig tried, unsuccessfully, to attach himself to Duke William's coat-tails, failed just as miserably to persuade King Swein to make a claim, and finally fired the ambitions of Hardrada. Therefore, not only did Duke William threaten invasion and make preparations to do so but Harald Hardrada did likewise. King Harald, to his cost, actually beat Duke William to the punch, landing in the Humber in late September. He defeated the northern Earls, Edwin of Mercia and Morcar of Northumbria at Gate Fulford but was himself crushed a few days later by King Harold II at Stamford Bridge.

No sooner had King Harold defeated the Norwegians than news came of the landing of Duke William and his motley collection of Normans, Bretons and other miscellaneous Frenchmen at Pevensey. King Harold made a speedy return to London, called up a second army and confronted the Duke near Hastings. After a nine hour battle, ending in his own death, King Harold was defeated and Duke William went on to make himself King of England. So ended the first stage of the War of the English Succession or, as William of Poitiers puts it, the War of King Harold and Duke William.

The second and much more long drawn out stage was a guerrilla-style conflict between the Norman King and various unco-ordinated groups of rebels which lasted until 1071, ending only when the last flickers of resistance had been quenched by a policy of 'thorough', that is the elimination of all opposition in a series of devastating campaigns culminating in the 'Harrying of the North', an act which might well deserve the name of genocide. This was combined with the expropriation, imprisonment and/or exile of all land-owning opponents, bar for a select band of collaborators, and the punishment of all lesser rebels by blinding and mutilation, such as was seen after the fall of Ely.

The last English Earl to oppose King William, in alliance with the rebel Earls, the Norman Roger of Hereford and the Breton Ralph de Gael of Norfolk, was Waltheof, by then nominally Earl of Northumbria. Earl Roger was condemned to perpetual imprisonment and died a prisoner, Earl Ralph, condemned to a similar fate in his absence, remained an exile. As for Waltheof, he was simply beheaded.

Appendix 2

A Note on Castles

What the Norman Motte and Bailey castles were like is described effectively in the Vita Johannes Episcopo Tervanensis, a Life of a bishop of Térouanne.

> They make a mound of earth as high as they can, and encircle it with a ditch as broad and deep as possible. They surround the upper edge of the mound not with a wall but with a palisade of squared timbers firmly fixed together, and with such turrets set around it as is fitting. Within they build their house, a citadel that commands the whole.
>
> The gate can only be reached by crossing a bridge which springs from the outer edge of the ditch and, gradually rising, is supported by double or even triple piers trussed together at suitable intervals; then, ascending, it crosses the ditch and reaches the mound at its top level with the threshold of the gate. A palisaded bailey is then added.[12]

It has been estimated that there were as many as 400 castles in England built before the year 1100, in less than thirty-five years after the Conquest. Many were to be temporary structures, built in the course of military campaigns and which did not become permanent homes for barons or their knights, but a large number survived and were added to in subsequent decades. The number of major, mainly royal, castles has been put at eighty-six by 1086, of which forty were constructed before 1076. Some twenty county towns had a castle, while York had two and London three. Another ten substantial boroughs also had their own castles. The building of them was a burden imposed on the local population, employed to construct the 'motte' and lay out the surrounding 'bailey' as well as to dig ditches and pile up earthworks around the bailey.

Following the Conqueror's own example (he began the White Tower in about 1078), the barons also soon began building in stone. The White Tower, which was designed by Gundulf, Bishop of Rochester (who also went on to build the similar tower keep of Colchester), was intended to be fortress, palace and seat of government all in one.

But the early castles were of wood. They consisted first of a central tower, the 'donjon', about twelve feet square, which was used as a look-out post and placed on the summit of a hill or artificial motte, often standing on stilts, while around the motte, if possible, lay a moat or at least a deep ditch lined with a palisade. Beyond that lay the 'bailey', a large open courtyard, often of grassland, containing the out buildings. That was surrounded by a ditch and an earthwork surmounted by a palisade. Access to the bailey was through a fortified gatehouse. The donjon was reached by means of ladders or, more elaborately, a staircase and bridge, leading to another gatehouse. Sometimes the supports of the donjon began at ground level and the motte was piled up around them, sometimes leaving an open space within the supports which formed a cellar (i.e. the dungeon), as at South Mimms for example. These arrangements were later duplicated in stone.

Castles were constructed at strategically or tactically appropriate locations. Many of them, especially those built by order of King William, were built within existing fortifications. The first castle the Normans threw up in England was located within the remaining walls of the Roman fortress of Anderida and many 'campaign castles', not all of which had a motte, were similarly placed within existing fortified locations. One example of that was the Iron Age enclosure called Belsar's Hill near Ely. Elsewhere the castles were placed within the walls of English 'burhs', usually in a corner of the existing enclosure. A good example is Warwick where the motte was placed within the burh and adjacent to the cliff edge overlooking the river Avon. It is still there today in the grounds of Warwick Castle. It is known locally as 'Aethelfleda's mound' because Aethelfleda, sister of King Edward the Elder and known as the Lady of the Mercians, built the original burh there in 914. At Peterborough the Norman abbot, Turold, built a motte adjacent to the abbey church and within the precincts of the abbey, it is known as 'Mount Turold'.

But outside the towns other sites had to be found for castles. Many would naturally have been built in the open on part of the new lord's demesne but it also seems that Norman lords chose to erase all memory of their English predecessor's lordship by building their motte within the existing thegnly residence with its fortified enclosure, consisting usually of a palisaded bank and ditch and entered by way of a fortified gatehouse, the 'burhgate'. This is reckoned to have been done by Richard fitzGilbert when he built his castle at Clare. Others who could have done so in East Anglia include William de Warenne at Castle Acre and William and Robert Malet at Eye. If castles were built on the site of the existing thegn's dwellings, that would explain why there is little archaeological evidence of the nature of their residences.

They are somewhere under the motte and bailey castles or their later enlarged replacements, just as many English (i.e. 'Anglo-Saxon') Churches were demolished, either in their entirety or partially, and 'Norman' churches built to replace them.

That this was the case can be demonstrated from the location of a number of castles whose environment has been explored. Castles in the open countryside tended to be built on slopes, or where there was no slope, false crests. This was done to present them as dominating the surrounding landscape. A good example of this is Castle Acre. It can be viewed from the A1065 a few miles north of Swaffham, lying on the crest of the hill. At Castle Acre, William de Warenne was the successor of the East Anglian thegn called Toki. The Earl had a large manor there worth nine pounds (over 2,000 silver pennies) in 1086. Toki had built a manor house at Castle Acre in the centre of his lands and Warenne replaced it with a manor house built of chalk and flint and added a bank and palisade. He replaced the timber gatehouse with one of chalk clunch and added a church. The manor dominates the Nar valley. Then there was Richard fitzGilbert's castle at Clare (with its associated Priory). It came to Richard from Aelfric son of Wihtgar (and possibly a descendant of King Edgar's great thegn Wulfstan of Dalham). Aelfric had been Queen Emma's steward. His father had a pre-Conquest manor house at Clare, with a tower (i.e. a gatehouse or burhgate). Richard's motte and bailey was built just north of Wihtgar's thegnly residence. At Eye in Suffolk, the thegn Eadric of Laxfield had a manor house set in a park which was obscured by the post-Conquest layout of Eye. Eadric had been exiled in King Edward's time, possibly as an associate of Osgod Clapa. William Malet's castle, built early in 1071 replaced the manor house. It became the centre of the Malet honor. It really does seem that the castles built outside the towns were often sited on the manors held by dead or exiled thegns. That the thegns had such residences is demonstrated from the evidence not only of archaeology but of laws and charters. But the Norman castles became the location for the exercise of private jurisdiction, over the tenants of the lord's manors as well as being both military strong points and family residences.[13]

Appendix 3

The Battlefield of Hastings

The site of the Battle of Hastings occupies a natural amphitheatre lying between two hills, Caldbec to the north and Telham to the south. King Harold is said to have taken up a position, after emerging from the forest of Andredesweald, on a ridge overlooking the area where the battle was fought. That ridge is now occupied by the buildings of Battle Abbey. The High Altar of the Abbey Church, now long since demolished, was located by the Normans on the exact spot where King Harold's Standard had been placed and where his dead body was found.

The whole area in front of the position of the Church was lowered and flattened when the Church and the Abbey were built in order to provide a platform for the monastic buildings. Some of those buildings, both those erected in the eleventh century and those built later, had to be supported by substantial arches built out over the edge of the ridge and down the slope in front of it. These rose in stages up the hill, becoming smaller as the building moved further onto the ridge. There is also a nineteenth century terrace walk along the front of the ridge, which self-evidently was not there in 1066. This shows that the rise of the last part of the hill, up to the ridge, would have been both higher and steeper than it is today, presenting a real obstacle to men on horses attempting to attack the English position.

As a result, the knights on their horses would have been almost level with the English warriors of the shield wall formation, rather than above them and able to strike downwards. The sight of the spears and axes of the defenders glittering in the sun, together with the noise of battle and the hostile battle cries of the English would have 'spooked' the horses, causing at least some of them to shy away from the shield wall and preventing the knights from pressing home their attack. It would not have been possible to launch a solid cavalry charge capable of smashing into the shield wall up such a steep rise. In addition, the Norman horses were not armoured nor did they wear blinkers and were open to being stabbed by the English spearmen or cloven in two by the axemen.

The ground to the right and left flanks of the English position also falls away steeply, mostly over very rough ground, much of it, even in dry weather, is still wet and marshy, another obstacle to cavalry. In October 1066, after the rains of mid-September caused by the equinoctial gales (the Equinox in 1066 was on 16 September by the Julian Calendar, not six days later as under the Gregorian system) so the whole battlefield was most likely very wet and muddy, if not marshy. Even in 2008 the ponds at the bottom of the slope, created by the monks of Battle, lying roughly where Duke William's centre would have been, like other ponds and lakes around the battlefield created by local landowners, remain full of the water which drains down from the ridge.

The monks who built Battle originally started building well down the slope, to take advantage of the availability of water by tapping into the springs, but King William insisted on the Abbey being built on the ridge. He promised the monks a plentiful supply of wine for drinking as a reward for doing so. The ponds and lakes now drain the battlefield very effectively but they were mostly not there in 1066.

The slope of the hillside leading down from the English right is rough and, in places, very steep and there is a pond, deeper now (after enlargement) than it would have been in 1066, and adjacent to it a mound or hillock, about half way down the slope. Both were probably there at the time of the battle and the hillock is probably the one shown in the Bayeux Tapestry (plate 71). But both have been enlarged since 1066. That whole side of the battlefield was probably something of a morass which would have become harder to cross after men and horses had charged across it several times. The slope on the English left wing was also rough and probably steeper than it is now. The Norman knights certainly found it impossible to turn the flanks of the English position.

To run up the hill in full armour, as the Norman heavy infantry were expected to do (and they most likely formed the bulk of the Norman army), would have taxed the strength of the strongest and even the horsemen would have found it difficult. The slope, viewed from the probable Norman position, rises gently at first and then gets steeper and steeper, and reaches its sharpest angle in front of the English line. The overall angle subtended by the slope, from the Norman lines to the crest of the ridge looks today as between forty and forty-five degrees.

The English had the advantage of a strong defensive position and would have been assisted by gravity when hurling their spears and other missiles at the enemy. They could strike downwards at both charging foot soldiers and at horsemen and could easily have hacked at horses' backs with their dreaded two-handed battleaxes.

A line of shield men could thrust forward effectively to repel attackers, pushing them back down the hill before resuming their former defensive posture. The English line, the shield wall, was not so densely packed as to restrict their manoeuvres or prevent them from striking out at the enemy. Little is said by the Norman writers, who describe the battle, about the role of the infantry, partly out of sheer snobbishness, giving greater attention to the exploits of the knights, men of greater social and military status, and partly because the infantry made little impression on the shield wall. Even the archers (and the Normans had many more of those than King Harold) would have had problems with firing uphill at a line of men equipped with shields and, once they had expended the arrows in their quiver, would have been forced to retreat to obtain a fresh supply. Nor could they replenish their supply of arrows by using those fired at them by their opponents since the English had fewer archers.

The hillock on the right hand side of the slope was, it is thought, occupied by lightly armed English troops, possibly including some archers and perhaps slingers, who were able to deliver a dangerous cross fire of missiles to enfilade the Norman left, manned as it was by the Breton contingents. So the Bretons' approach up the slope would have been greatly impeded and they would have found it difficult to deal with men who could retreat rapidly into the woods if attacked and return after the knights had passed. Some of these English fighting men could have been equipped with javelins, which the English called 'ategar'.

Duke William and his leading barons must have been daunted at the prospect of attacking an army in such a well established position, though the Duke, by the careful placing of his men, made the best he could of his forces. Towards the closing stages of the battle, with the English line still unbroken, he is said to have ordered his archers to fire over the heads of the men in the frontline, so that the arrows would fall vertically down onto the men behind. But it should perhaps be considered that it was in fact an obvious tactic to adopt for archers faced with the task of firing up hill at an enemy looking down on them and that, in itself, might account for the use of this tactic. King William might just have been given the credit for it. The obvious response of the men in the rear would have been to cover themselves with their shields, performing the 'testudo' or tortoise manoeuvre. It is therefore likely that the tactic only became effective towards the end of the day as men grew weary and the numbers of the English were reduced.

A 'shield wall' formation of about one thousand men could have occupied the width of the ridge and, if the English army was ten or twelve ranks deep (and reinforced continuously from behind as more men advanced out of the woods and along the causeway leading to the ridge – it ran along the line of Battle High Street), then King Harold could easily have had an army of ten or twelve thousand men, or even more if there were more than twelve ranks. The Annals of St Maixent claim that the Duke had 14,000 men and that, allowing for some of them being baggage handlers, servants, cooks and so on, is not an impossible figure. The English army is not likely to have been any smaller (and the Normans thought it was larger), otherwise it could not have held out for nine hours until King Harold himself was first wounded and then killed. A Norman force of 14,000 represents, if the fleet is accepted to have been one of 700 ships, an average of only twenty men per vessel.

Only the events of the closing stages of the conflict, during perhaps the last half hour, and the death of King Harold himself, rendered defeat inevitable. The field of battle was certainly large enough to accommodate a struggle involving some twenty-four thousand men. The Normans had no reserves to call on, whereas the English, who were alleged to have begun the battle before all their men were in battle array, could well have received reinforcements throughout the day. In the end, the Norman archers played the part of artillery and the Knights provided the Duke with the necessary mass of manoeuvre.[14]

Appendix 4

Earl Harold in Normandy

A much disputed question is that concerning exactly what commitments, if any, Earl Harold entered into in Normandy. It is bedevilled by the readiness of historians to allow themselves to accept and be misled by the specious coherence of the case presented by the Norman writers, especially William of Jumièges and William of Poitiers despite the complete absence of any sort of independent verification for it.

That there is no contemporary record of the affair in English sources can be accounted for firstly by the failure of the monks who wrote the Anglo-Saxon Chronicles to maintain a comprehensive record of events during the last ten years of the reign of King Edward, and secondly by the effect on their freedom to write of the Conquest itself. As was said in the days of Henry I, 'The feet of those who bark shall be cut off'. King Henry did not permit much in the way of overt criticism or opposition and neither his brother, William Rufus, nor his father, King William, had done so either. Those who wrote the chronicles did so aware that they were, in a sense, public documents, open to inspection and being read by visiting Norman Bishops or Abbots and lay lords.

Three versions of the Anglo-Saxon Chronicle cover the period 1060 to 1087 but all three deal very inadequately with the years 1063 to 1065. Version C, the Abingdon Chronicle, ends abruptly in 1066, because the ending of the Chronicle has been lost. Its full coverage of events actually ends in 1055 and it only resumes its account at August 1065 and then describes events quite fully from then until the defeat of King Harald Hardrada. It also has an addition in a twelfth century hand which adds the story of the Norwegian who held the bridge at Stamford Bridge. Some scribe took up his pen to describe the course of the tragic events of 1065, the fall of Earl Tostig and the death of King Edward and extended his account to include the battle of Stamford Bridge. The silence of this version about Earl Harold's journey is simply due to the fact that the chronicle had not been kept for ten years, from 1055 to 1065.

Version D, the Worcester Chronicle, ends in 1079 (with a late addition to the entry for 1080 actually relating to 1130; the defeat of Angus, Earl of Moray). It omits the year 1064 entirely and for 1063 and 1065 records the activities of Earl Harold in Wales and the fall of Earl Tostig with an account of Earl Harold's part in it. It shares much of its information with Version C and might be that version's source (or they shared a common one.) The simplest explanation for the missing entry is that the scribe knew of nothing worth recording for 1064. It was not unusual for the scribes to make entries under the wrong date.

Version E, the Peterborough Chronicle, is a copy made to replace an original destroyed by fire in 1116. The monks borrowed a version, which has since perished, probably from St Augustine's, Canterbury, to which they added information of their own, especially as regards events at Peterborough after the Conquest. It ends in 1154. But the manuscript from which it was copied also omitted any record for 1064. The Peterborough text recounts the events of 1065 under the date of 1064 and then jumps to date the events of the following year correctly under 1066. So the presumed text from St Augustine's also found nothing worth recording under 1064. Some historians, convinced by the Norman accounts, think the scribes left out 1064 out of embarrassment, unwilling to record Harold's conduct in Normandy. Yet all three versions insist on saying that King Edward entrusted or granted the kingdom to Earl Harold, thus implicitly denying any previous grant to Duke William.[15]

The fourth relevant source, the Worcester Chronicle known as that of Florence of Worcester (but now acknowledged to have been most likely actually written by another Worcester monk called John), in addition to other sources, drew much of its information from yet another, no longer extant, version of the Anglo-Saxon Chronicle. This chronicle also has nothing to say about events in England or Normandy in 1064. It fills the gap with an excursus about events in Jerusalem instead, which it inserts between the betrayal of Gruffydd of Wales by his own people and the report of the building of a hunting lodge at Portskewett by 'the valiant Earl Harold' in July 1065. The events of 1065 then follow in their proper place. Surely the author of that Chronicle could not have been ignorant of the story of Harold's sojourn in Normandy, yet he omits it simply, apparently, because it was not in any of the sources he used.

Either the scribes knew nothing worth recording for 1064, the simplest explanation, or, unable safely to deny the Norman version of events, they preferred discreet silence. The latter explanation, as also that which accounts for the silence by alleging that it could not be denied, ignores the fact that other Anglo-Norman writers, William of Malmesbury, Eadmer of Canterbury, and Henry of Huntingdon, had no hesitation in doing so and do deny those parts of the story which could be safely denied. They do not directly deny King William's right to the throne, which in any case rested on conquest.

The Norman case rests on the writings of William of Jumièges and William of Poitiers, which make a number of quite incredible claims. The former alleges that King Edward owed his accession to the English throne to Norman intervention, though he has to admit that the English authorities did not permit Edward to come to England with more than a token escort. Much more reliable sources attribute Edward's recall to England and accession to the direct invitation of his half-brother, King Harthacnut, and the influence of the great Earls, both Godwine of Wessex and Leofric of Mercia. William of Poitiers alleges that Earl Harold swore a quite unbelievably complex oath.

Some historians readily accept the main thrust of the Norman claims, others regard them as a tissue of lies. One writer has commented that the two Williams were 'Doctor Goebbels with two heads'. Their writings are, as far as the claim to the throne is concerned, essentially only one source. They probably depended for their information on the contents of the case, possibly drawn up by Abbot Lanfranc, for presentation to Pope Alexander II. That case was presented at Rome, at the Lateran Palace, by a Norman embassy, led by Archdeacon Gilbert of Lisieux, and accepted by the Pope, under the influence of Archdeacon Hildebrand (the later Pope Gregory VII) with no opportunity being permitted to the English to contest it. Duke William actually had the Channel Ports watched to ensure that no English embassy could be sent to Rome.

There is, however, an independent version of Earl Harold's visit to Normandy, created under the auspices of Odo, Bishop of Bayeux. It is the work of English artists and needlewomen working under the direction of an unidentified designer chosen by the Bishop. This is the stunning pictorial version of these events, the famous Bayeux Tapestry.

The Tapestry, actually a piece of embroidery, presents a visually compelling story covering the events of what is probably 1064 to 1066, extending from Earl Harold's decision to set out on a voyage in the Channel to his death and the defeat of the English army at Hastings. What is most striking about it is, that while it presents a coherent story, the designer of the Tapestry carefully avoids committing himself to explicit testimony about the meaning of the scenes he presents. At crucial points in the account of Harold's journey to Normandy and his conduct while there, the Tapestry fails to spell out, perhaps even deliberately, the significance of the scenes it contains. In so doing it actually fails to substantiate the case presented by William of Poitiers, and, by implication, that of William of Jumièges.[16]

One possible reason for this lies in the fact that, though commissioned by a Norman lord, usually taken to be Odo, Bishop of Bayeux, the Conqueror's half-brother, the Tapestry is of English workmanship. Cyril Hart has shown, by detailed analysis, that about one third of all motifs and scenes in the Tapestry are derived from images in manuscripts from the pre-Conquest monastery archive at Canterbury, and that, it is suggested, is as close as one can get to proof. Had the whole archive survived many more prototypes could well have been found.[17]

The Tapestry makes no effort to spell out in the captions which accompany the scenes, exactly what is being said. The first scene (plate 1) shows an unidentified figure, presumably, from what follows, Earl Harold, talking to King Edward. The King, although old, seems in good health. As he subsequently is shown setting out on a sea voyage, the Earl was presumably obtaining the King's permission to do so. The King is shown admonishing him; he points a minatory finger at the Earl. The caption simply reads 'Edward Rex'. No attempt is made, as so easily might have been, to explain that Edward is 'sending' the Earl anywhere, least of all that he is being sent to Duke William. It does not say, 'Here King Edward sends Harold to William', yet it does trouble to tell the viewer that the next scene is 'Where Earl Harold and his horsemen ride to Bosham Church'. A statement which adds little to the story. The Earl then dines at Bosham and is then shown wading out to board a ship. It is said merely that he 'crosses the sea'. No attempt is made to add 'to Normandy'. He is then blown by a strong wind and reaches the territory of Count Guy, that is Ponthieu.

The voyage is a peaceful one with no military implications, those aboard are not armed nor wearing armour. Nor is it, as William of Malmesbury suggested, a fishing trip, the vessel is no fishing boat. There is no shipwreck either, but William of Poitiers calls it a 'forced landing', and the boat was blown to Ponthieu by a strong wind, possibly of gale force. Harold is arrested by Count Guy and taken to the castle of Beaurain, a long way from the Norman border on the opposite side of Ponthieu. He is granted the honours of his rank (just like the thegn Hereward, who landed in Guînes in 1063 and fell into the hands of Count Manasses the Old); he carries his falcon on his wrist but is still a captive. Guy grants Harold an audience, presumably to discuss the payment of a ransom. The men of Ponthieu were known for capturing voyagers who landed on their shores, robbing the lesser men and ransoming the nobility.

Some unknown watcher, possibly a Norman agent, observes the meeting. The implication is that this man sent word of Earl Harold's predicament to Duke William, as, in the next scenes the Duke's messengers come to Count Guy. There were probably several exchanges between the two courts, and, as a result, Count Guy took the Earl and handed him over to the Duke. Where this was is not stated but the building shown has been identified as probably the famous Tower of Rouen. William of Poitiers presents this as the rescue of Earl Harold from the clutches of Count Guy by Duke William, so saving him from maltreatment or even torture. In effect Earl Harold has fallen into a trap.

Count Guy of Ponthieu had, as a result of involvement in earlier conflicts, become the vassal of the Duke, owing him the service of one hundred knights, and so he had no option but to hand the Earl over to him. It has been described as one gangster having to give in to a bigger one. Yet, when Hereward revealed his identity to Manasses the Old, he was released and treated with honour. There is only the word of William of Poitiers to say that Harold was in danger, though he could have been. The other William tells a similar story.

Both Norman writers then allege that Earl Harold, of his own free will according to one, 'performed fealty to him (William) in respect of the kingdom with many oaths'. Neither writer says anything about Harold accompanying the Duke on a campaign in Brittany but both the Tapestry and Orderic Vitalis say that he did, though the Tapestry puts this as occurring before the oath and Orderic puts it afterwards. None of the sources agree about where this oath took place. William of Jumièges gives no location at all, William of Poitiers puts it at Bonneville-sur-Touques, Orderic says it was Rouen and the Tapestry shows it as Bayeux. None of the writers name the witnesses of this significant event and there is no evidence that the agreement was ever put in writing, as perhaps, if genuine, it ought to have been.

The Tapestry shows an interesting scene in which Harold is escorted to Duke William's 'palace', the Tower hall at Rouen, where discussions take place between the two men. The Tapestry presents the two men as of equal status; Earl Harold is Duke (Dux) of the English and William is Duke (Dux) of the Normans. Then, after King Edward's death it always refers to Earl Harold as King. Either the designer, or the composer of the captions, by doing this, is taking sides. But the Tapestry is silent about the content of these discussions and, curiously, that scene is followed by the most puzzling scene in the whole Tapestry. A woman fully robed with her head covered and standing within an odd structure is shown being touched or perhaps struck by a tonsured cleric. The caption reads 'Where a cleric and Aelfgiva...', the sentence has no verb. A wide variety of solutions, none of them satisfactory, has been proposed. One point is that if the gesture is in fact a blow to the face, it might be intended to ensure that the woman never forgot what she was witnessing, that is, the discussion between the Duke and the Earl. She holds her hands raised as a sign of submission. She has never been identified but there is a possible candidate.

Most of the other references to the Norman Conquest in Western European sources, other than those from Normandy and England, stress or comment that the cause of the invasion was connected to Earl Harold's failure to keep a promise to marry the Duke's daughter, to which is added in some accounts, an agreement that his sister, Aelfgiva, should marry some prominent Norman (see the references to this matter in Chapter 2). The name Aelfgiva, that is either Aelfgifu in Old English or Aelfgytha, is spelled just like that of Harold's sister, as given in an entry in Domesday Book. She is listed as holding a small estate before 1066.

That the figure in the Tapestry is this particular Aelfgiva cannot be verified but as every other scene is essential to the story and as the marriage arrangements were part of it, this identification best fits the known facts. All other suggested 'Aelfgivas' are ladies who play no part in the affairs of 1064. It is possible that Aelfgiva was a member of Earl Harold's party captured in Ponthieu and that she was present at Rouen. In that case, then the cleric is simply pointing out her presence in a dramatic manner and striking her lightly on the face to ensure that she does not forget the agreement which has been reached. Similarly her presence is emphasised by the structure with spiral columns around her, indicating the place where she was being kept. Such structures were used in English sculpture to frame human figures in this period and the designer has made use of that convention.

The Tapestry then moves on to devote considerable space to the campaign in Brittany, during which Earl Harold distinguished himself by rescuing two Norman knights from a patch of quicksand. The account ends with a scene in which Duke William is shown bestowing arms on Harold, possibly as a reward for his feat of strength. It is certainly a Norman military ritual and some assume that the Duke was 'knighting' Earl Harold, others assert that to say that is to go beyond the evidence. The gift of armour may merely be a reward for the rescue of the Duke's men. A Norman viewing this would see the Duke treating the Earl as his vassal, although there is no indication that Harold had done homage. That was alleged to happen later, though the Tapestry shows no such scene. Even if the gift of arms and armour was a 'dubbing' to knighthood, Harold, whose lord was King Edward, would have viewed this as applying only when he was in Normandy, and, as a known student of French customs, have accepted it as an indispensable part of being initiated as a knight.

The scene then moves to Bayeux but the Tapestry does not really insist that what followed took place there. Bayeux is simply where the Norman army disbanded after Brittany. Bonneville-sur-Touques is a castle just off the route from Bayeux to Rouen. Here, then, Harold is shown apparently taking the famous, or infamous, oath. The most striking thing about this scene is that the Tapestry signally fails to say what the oath was about. There is no attempt, as there easily could have been, to add a phrase such as 'concerning the throne' or 'concerning the crown'. It simply says that Harold took an oath 'to Duke William', which might very well have been an elaborate form of homage. An Earl such as Harold would surely not have willingly or unwillingly knelt and placed his hands between those of the Duke. English nobles are described only as 'bowing' to a lord when swearing a hold oath, the oath of commendation to a lord. Harold accepts French custom in so far as agreeing to swear on relics. The relics are not, as later stories alleged, concealed in any way. They had certainly been specially brought together in one place so that Harold could be made to swear on them. But the Tapestry is deliberately vague about what Harold actually swore.

The Tapestry borders are full of imagery which combines fashionable ornamentation with subtly complex meanings and references, especially when the images are of rows of paired animals. They are drawn to fill blank spaces and come from a bestiary. The borders below the scene in which the oath was taken are of particular interest. The scene itself shows the Duke enthroned (but not crowned, he is no king) and bearing a sword. He is dominating and threatening. The Earl is surely subject to duress. In the border subversive anecdotes, probably taken from the fables of Aesop, are illustrated. In plate 3, where Harold dines at Bosham, in the border a crow drops its food into a fox's mouth. Does this imply that Harold, like the crow, is to be the victim of flattery or deceit? Historians have identified a number of fables in the Tapestry borders; that of the Fox and the Crow, that of the Wolf and the Lamb and that of the Wolf and the Crane.[18]

The Fox in the story persuaded the crow to sing so that he would drop his piece of cheese. The moral is that one should never trust flatterers. The Crane pulled a bone from the Wolf's throat and the moral of that is never expect gratitude for a good deed. The Lamb should never have trusted the Wolf. So these images comment on the action above and point out the hidden danger for the unwary from the crafty and deceitful. A Norman might deduce that this is about Harold. He is of fine appearance but, to a Norman, that conceals an inner man who is false. Another way of looking at it is to suggest that Harold should have been aware of deceit and not have allowed himself to trust what the Duke has told him and that the viewer should beware of taking things at face value.

Most historians accept the minimal interpretation, that the whole affair is about the succession to the English throne, but there is absolutely no independent verification for that interpretation. Harold swore something that gained for him his freedom. He also clearly swore under duress, knowing perfectly well that he would not be released unless he did so. Whatever the Pope was told about the oath, it is plain that he was told, as William of Poitiers asserts, that Harold swore of his own free will. But Harold himself was never given the opportunity to testify whether he did so or not.

The version of the oath put about by William of Poitiers is frankly implausible. It is just too elaborate. Harold is said to have sworn to act as Duke William's 'vicarius', or representative, at the Court of King Edward (though there is no sign that he made any attempt to do so), and use all his influence and wealth to that end. He was to ensure the Duke's succession to the throne. He was to garrison the 'castle' at Dover with the Duke's knights (though none went to England with Harold) and maintain garrisons in other castles elsewhere in England. This seems to be based on the fact that, when William of Poitiers eventually came to England, he found a castle had been built at Dover and was probably told about the castles on the Welsh border and Robert fitzWymarc's castle in Essex.

The writer then admits what is far more probable, that the Earl had made ceremonial homage to the Duke who had then confirmed him in his possession of all his estates in England (which were not yet William's to give). He then spoils his case by alleging that King Edward was ill and not expected to live much longer which is obviously false. Edward did not become ill until late in November 1065 and in the autumn of that year had been fit enough to go hunting.

Earl Harold is shown returning to England and the story here ends as it began with an audience given to the Earl by King Edward. It is widely commented that the Earl is drawn in a posture of apology and humiliation. He appears almost to cringe before a minatory and stern King who might also be thought to be saying, 'I told you to be careful!' The accompanying axe men who escort the Earl and guard the King are shown pointing to both of them, thus stressing the significance of the interview. The caption to the scene says nothing, as usual, of what is being said. One later writer does suggest that the King did say to Harold that he had warned him to be careful because he knew Duke William well and that he would seize an advantage if he could, but this was written with hindsight after the event.

The account in the Tapestry then jumps forward to the death and burial of the King in his newly consecrated Church at Westminster. This is early January 1066 and nothing is shown to indicate what Earl Harold had been doing since 1064. This accords with the Norman attitude in their writings, which was to connect the swearing of the oath directly to the death of King Edward and Harold's coronation as though the one followed immediately after the other, and that King Edward had sent Earl Harold to Normandy because he was ill and expecting to die, and wished to confirm his promise of the succession. In fact the Earl was back in England by July 1065 (if not earlier), well before the King's death.

The whole story of the alleged promise and the oath extracted from Earl Harold only emerges after both the King and Earl were safely dead and neither could contradict the Norman version of events.

Appendix 5

Hereward

Enough is known about the Lincolnshire thegn known as Hereward to provide an outline sketch of his career and to present him as a by no means untypical example of an eleventh century Anglo-Danish thegn.

His date of birth is naturally unknown and no documents survive which say anything about his early youth. He was, however, allegedly exiled in 1063 when he was already a man. If he had been about eighteen years of age, then a date of birth in 1045 or thereabouts is possible. Since he was one of those driven into exile as a result of the Norman Conquest, his date of death is not known. But enough is known of him to show that he was born into a noble family of thegnly rank and that his father was a King's Thegn with wide and extensive estates.

According to the traditions of both Peterborough and Crowland Abbeys, Hereward was the nephew of Abbot Brand of Peterborough. The 'Annales Petro-Burgenses', a collection of traditions written down in the fourteenth century, say that Abbot Brand was the 'patruus', that is, paternal uncle of Hereward; therefore one of the Abbot's four brothers, Asketil, Siward, Siric and Godric, was his father. The five brothers were the sons of a thegn called Toki. Since Asketil owned property in Lincoln from which three burgesses rendered to him the sum of five shillings (in rent), it suggests that the rich landowner of Lincoln, Toki Autison was Asketil's father. Toki of Lincoln was a well-respected man with the rights of 'sake and soke, toll and team' in Lincolnshire, owning some sixty 'messuages' (houses with attached land) in Lincoln, with his own Hall and Church, and many other estates in six shires. His lands were confiscated after the conquest and fell into the hands of a baron called Geoffrey Alselin. Toki's father, Auti, was the moneyer of Lincoln and it was probably he who had established the family's fortunes.

Of the four brothers of Abbot Brand, Asketil (who is usually referred to by the shortened form of his name, Askill or the Norse version, Eskill) is the best candidate for Hereward's father. Askill was dead before Brand became abbot at Peterborough, and had probably died in the fighting, either at Stamford Bridge or Hastings. He held most of the family's land and he was a King's Thegn, one of those with 'seat and special duty in the King's hall'. Godric, the youngest, survived to become Abbot at Peterborough himself in 1098, only to be deposed for simony by Archbishop Anselm in 1101, because he and the monks had been compelled to pay money to King William Rufus for the confirmation of Godric's election. His English name suggests that Toki's wife, whose name is not known, was an Englishwoman. His father's name was Danish and so were the names of his brothers, but an English mother could well have wanted her youngest son to have an English name. The other two brothers, Siward and Siric were still holding small estates in 1086 as tenants of Geoffrey Alselin. A 'Siward filius Toki' was still alive in the reign of William Rufus. These three were too young for any one of them to have been Hereward's father since Hereward himself had probably been born in about 1045.

Asketil held land not only in Lincolnshire but in at least five other shires and, as the likelihood of there having been two equally rich King's Thegns called Asketil, with large estates in the East Midlands, is remote, he may safely be further identified as the thegn Askill of Ware. The estate at Ware was probably his main residence. It was worth £50 a year and included a park for wild beasts. In 1086 it had a listed population of about forty, including a priest and a reeve, suggesting an overall population of up to 200 persons. In total Asketil's lands were worth £245 a year (58,800 silver pennies) and included 110 carucates and 124 hides. Hereward certainly was, therefore, as his father's heir, as Geoffrey Gaimar claimed, a nobleman and 'one of the first in the land'.

This identification of Hereward as the son of Asketil eliminates all legendary accretions to his story alleging that he was son of a thegn or lord called Leofric of Bourne, even of Leofric Earl of Mercia, and related to King Edward. The confusion arose because the lord of Bourne in Lincolnshire was Earl Morcar, Leofric's grandson, and that estate, along with several estates belonging to Hereward, were all passed after the Conquest to the Breton called Ogier.

Furthermore, Hereward was never known in his own lifetime, nor for a couple of centuries at least, as 'the Wake'. The cognomen was not recorded until the fourteenth century. It arose because several of Hereward's estates, together with the manor of Bourne and other lands, were formed by Henry I into the Barony of Bourne and given to the brothers William and Richard de Rullos (from Roulours in Calvados). William had no heir and Richard became lord of Bourne. He married a Breton heiress, Emma, daughter of Enisan de Musard, a vassal of Count Alan of Richmond. Their daughter,

Adelina, was married off by Henry I to Baldwin fitzGilbert, who bought the barony from the king along with permission to marry Adelina. Baldwin was the son of Gilbert of Clare and descended through Richard fitzGilbert from Gilbert Count of Brionne. The daughter of Baldwin and Adelina, Emma, then married Hugh Wake, a knight from Guernsey, who became lord of Bourne, and their son was Baldwin Wake, ancestor of the Wake barons of Bourne. At some unknown stage the Wakes, to give an air of antiquity and legitimacy to their ownership of the barony, claimed to be descended from Hereward, and in due course he became known as 'le Wake'.

Hereward's career began, probably in 1063, when, having quarrelled with the Abbot of Crowland, Ulfcytel, because he failed to pay the rent he owed for an estate at Rippingale near Bourne, and having upset his father by other unruly behaviour, causing riots and disturbances, he was exiled by King Edward at his father's request. He was therefore not in England when the Normans invaded. By ignoring the more fabulous accretions to his legend, historians have established that much of his career in exile can be corroborated.

Setting out by sea after his decree of exile was issued, Hereward, like Earl Harold in 1064, landed unexpectedly in France and was arrested by the men of Count Manasses I of Guînes. Released on establishing his identity he travelled to St Omer and began a career as a mercenary soldier. He took service with the Bishop of Cambrai, Lietbert, which is established because he witnessed a charter issued by the Bishop. He is almost certainly the 'Miles Herivvardi' who signs with other witnesses. ('Hereward' in Latin is written in English sources as Hereuuardus and the use of 'v' for 'u' is quite common). The legendary account of his career mentions other lords with whom he took service or whom he encountered, they are real people; Baldwin, Count of Hainault, Arnulf the Vicomte of Picquigny, and even Henry II of Brabant. Hereward also took part in 'military spectacles' at Bruges and Poitiers, and this is thought to be one of the earliest references to the tournament.

His most spectacular career move, according to the Gesta Herewardi, was to accompany the Count of Flanders' son (that is Robert the Frisian) on a campaign in an area called 'Scaldemariland' in order to compel the inhabitants to pay their traditional dues to the Count. Hereward is described as playing a leading role in the campaign and to have been the commander's 'Magister Militum', that is the knight commanding the mercenary troops. Remarkably, that story can be verified. The story comes from the monastery of Echternach, and is embedded in the Vita Sancti Willibrordi written by Abbot Thiofrid of Echternach. He says that the monastery held lands in the Island of Walcheren in the Scheldt Estuary and relates how a son of Count

Baldwin endeavoured to extract unpaid taxes from the inhabitants of the islands of the estuary.

He is said to have led an army of French and German mercenaries by land and sea across the 'Scaldemermur', that is, the Scheldt Estuary, which is known to have been called 'Scaldemermur' and 'Scaldemariensis' and lay in the province of Zeeland.

The islanders are said to have successfully repelled the attack and to have captured two banners which were then sent to Echternach in thanks to St Willibrord for his protection. The islanders could not decide whether to make peace or continue the war, so Abbot Thiofrid agreed to mediate between them and the Flemish army. (The Count's son was certain to have been his second son, Robert the Frisian). Terms were agreed, the Gesta Herewardi claims the islanders had to pay twice as much tax as they had done previously. The area had been given to the Counts of Flanders in 1012 by Henry II of Germany. Robert the Frisian celebrated his birthday with his parents at Whitsun 1067 and Count Baldwin died on 1 September. That puts the war nicely as being fought between 1066 and 1067, and allows for the return of Hereward to England in the year 1067, after his uncle had become Abbot of Peterborough.

The rest of Hereward's career was to take place in England from 1067 to 1071. He was, in due course, driven out of Ely and, according to the Gesta spent some time as an outlaw in the 'Bruneswald' or Forest of Bromswold. Most of his exploits there are mere legend and can be discounted. Equally improbable is the suggestion that he was reconciled to King William. That is most likely a confusion with another thegn called Hereward who was still alive and holding lands in the West Midlands in 1086. It is thus unlikely that the Lincolnshire Hereward merely lived out the rest of his life under Norman rule. Equally unlikely is Geoffrey Gaimar's story that he went on campaign to Maine and was ambushed by a party of jealous Normans while on his way back and, in a ferocious struggle, after killing at least seven of them, he was slain and beheaded. It resembles the accounts of the death of Earl Edwin of Mercia, even down to the beheading, which may be the source of Gaimar's story.

It is more probable that Hereward simply did what so many others did and fled into exile. A curious story from Norfolk suggests a solution. It is said that a certain lady called Wilburga of 'Taunton' (perhaps Terrington) gave one carucate of land to the Church of King's Lynn so that prayers could be said for her ancestors. She had made a will after she married a man called Hereward, in the reign of Henry II. She wanted prayers said for her husband and 'for Hereward his father and Hereward the Exile his grandfather'. The tale cannot be verified but the chronology just about fits. Similarly, there was a gift to the Abbey of Bury St Edmunds, between 1121 and 1148, by a woman called Goda (that is Gytha) 'daughter of Hereward'. She gives 'all the land of Hereward... to be held peacefully and quietly and honourably' under the Abbot, 'just as the grandfather and the father of Hereward and he himself held it in the vill of Great Barton'. It is just conceivable that 'Hereward the Exile' did return to England eventually, perhaps in the reign of William II rather than William I, acquired lands in Norfolk and Suffolk and died in old age. He might then have been buried, as tradition claims, at Crowland.[19]

Appendix 6

The Bayeux Tapestry

The 'Tapestry' is in fact a long, narrow linen hanging on which is embroidered, in woollen thread, an account of the Conquest of England from Earl Harold's embassy which ended up in Normandy to his death on the Field of Hastings. It is now just under sixty-five metres long but was once somewhat longer having lost some material at both ends. It first came to light in 1476 in the Treasury of Bayeux Cathedral (hence its name) but it is widely accepted that it had been kept there ever since it was first made during the eleventh century. Some restoration work has been done to some parts which has affected the interpretation of some scenes.

It is a remarkably ambiguous work and can be 'read' in at least two contrasting ways. To a Norman observer it conveys the official account of the Conquest, endorsing in particular the alleged perjury of Earl Harold, but to other observers, and notably to eleventh century English eyes, it conveys a note of dissent. At crucial points it fails to spell out clearly the meaning of the scene presented, leaving it to the observer to supply a meaning. Rather subversively, it refers to Harold consistently, after the death of King Edward, as 'King Harold', although from about 1070 onwards Anglo-Norman sources continue to call him 'Earl' and deny him the title of King.

Although efforts have been made to assign various origins to the tapestry, the consensus remains at present that it was made in England by English needlewomen, probably in the Canterbury area (using images from illustrations found in Canterbury archives) at the behest of Bishop Odo of Bayeux when he was also Earl of Kent, probably around 1077.

Captions

Plate I. This shows King Edward, enthroned, in converse with two men, one of whom is Earl Harold. The King is named, anachronistically, as 'Edward Rex' and is the work of restorers. Elsewhere he is called 'Eadwardus'.

Plate II continues 'Ubi Haroldo Dux Anglorum et milites equitant ad Bosham.'

That is, 'Where Harold, Duke of the English and (his) fighting men ride to Bosham'. More subversion, the scribe who devised the captions puts the Earl on the same level as William, who is 'Dux Normannorum' or Duke of the Normans.

Plate III. Harold is shown entering Bosham Church, presumably in order to pray for a safe and successful journey. Several features of the Church are intact today, notably the great Chancel Arch shown in this scene.

Plate IV. Earl Harold and his companions dine in an 'upper room' at his house or lodge at Bosham. It is perhaps meant to imply a 'last supper'.

Plate V. 'Here Harold goes to sea'. He has a hawk on his wrist, no one carries a weapon; it is a peaceful journey. The border below shows the fables of the Fox and the Crow (Beware of Flatterers) and the Wolf and the Lamb (Beware of the deceitful).

Plates VI and VII. In these scenes a strong wind (vento plenis) brings the ship to the country of Count Guy (Wido), of Ponthieu. There is no indication of the original destination. In the border the fable of the wolf and the crane.

Plates VIII and IX. Earl Harold is apprehended (arrested or seized) by Count Guy and taken to his Castle of Beaurain by armed men. He looks apprehensive. There he was held captive.

Plate X. The two nobles confer. Guy is seated on a throne. A lurking figure in a skullcap watches from behind a pillar. No such figure is shown accompanying Earl Harold. He may be a Norman cleric.

Plates XI and XII. A defiant Count Guy is addressed by Norman messengers from Duke William. Two figures, a tall man with a spear and a bearded dwarf holding the reins of a horse are present. One of these is called Turold but which one remains uncertain. Several 'Turolds' are associated with Bishop Odo which might account for this person being singled out in this manner.

Plate XIII. This is a flashback; it shows messengers hastening to Count Guy and another messenger is talking to Duke William. It explains what has happened earlier. The messenger could be an Englishman sent by Earl Harold to seek the Duke's aid.

Plates XIV and XV. Count Guy surrenders Earl Harold to Duke William. Harold is labelled 'Dux' and William is 'Normannorum Ducis'. They are given equal rank.

Plates XVI to XVIII. The Duke conducts the Earl to the Palace at Rouen, the great 'Tower Hall' of that city. Harold is accompanied by an armed guard of four men.

Plate XVIII also contains the most mysterious scene in the whole Tapestry. A veiled woman is shown standing between two ornamental pillars, which emphasise her presence. She is being struck by a cleric. The caption reads, 'Where Aelfgiva and a cleric...' There is no verb. Aelfgiva is the Latin for the English name 'Aelfgifu'. The only relevant Aelfgifu is Earl Harold's sister of that name. All scenes in the Tapestry relate to the story being told, therefore so must this one. Several sources maintain that Duke William offered Harold a marriage alliance; he was to marry a daughter of the Duke and his sister to marry a Norman noble. Possibly she is a witness to the agreement and is being formally struck to impress memory of it upon her.

Plates XIX and XX. A new chapter begins; Duke William leads his army to Mont-Saint-Michel in Brittany. The border shows the fable of the fox and the crow again.

Plate XXI. They arrive at the River Couesnon and Harold (again the Duke) rescues two Normans who have been trapped in the quicksands. The designer of the Tapestry is stressing his great strength and heroism.

Plates XXII to XXIV. Count Conan of Brittany flees from the city of Dol, which surrenders without a fight. Norman knights fight the Bretons and capture the castles of both Rennes and Dinan. The garrison of Dinan led by Count Conan surrenders the keys.

Plate XXV. Earl Harold, who has distinguished himself during the campaign, is given arms and armour by the Duke. He is thus regarded by many historians as accepting the Norman status of knighthood from Duke William and therefore becoming a vassal of the Duke. But there is no certainty that this is the ceremony of 'dubbing' to knighthood and the Tapestry certainly does not say it was. Harold was an English Earl and had no reason to accept a lower status.

Plates XXVI and XXVII. The most crucial scene of all. Apparently at Bayeux Earl Harold swears an oath before the Duke on two reliquaries containing the remains of Norman saints. Remarkably the Tapestry says nothing about the content of that oath, though it could easily have done so. Other sources say the oath was taken either at Rouen (Orderic) or at Bonneville-sur-Touques (Poitiers). William of Jumièges gives no location. Although the oath apparently causes Duke William to invade England, the Tapestry avoids saying what precise justification he had for doing so. Also William of Poitiers says the oath was taken before the expedition to Brittany. The matter remains confused and confusing. This vagueness could be deliberate.

Plates XXVIII and XXIX. Earl Harold returns to England and reports to King Edward. The Duke was to claim that Harold had promised to support his bid for the throne, yet the King is angry and Harold almost cringes before him. Edward is alleged to have wanted the Duke to be his heir, in which case he should be pleased! The fable of the wolf and the crane re-appears in the border. The fables warn against trusting the deceitful.

Plates XXX to XXXII. Westminster Abbey is shown to have been consecrated (December 1065). The King's body is being carried there to be buried. So the Tapestry has moved on to show King Edward's death. By showing first his funeral and then, one above the other, his deathbed and his death, the Tapestry shows how rapidly everything happened. Present at his deathbed are his wife, Queen Edith, Earl Harold and Archbishop Stigand. A fourth person supports him on a pillow. This scene is exactly as described in the Vita Edwardi which implies that the fourth man was the Staller, Robert fitzWymarc. The King, says the caption, addresses his vassals. He stretches out his hand to touch that of Earl Harold.

Plate XXXII – XXXIII. Two men, possibly Palace officials, point back to the dead King and offer the crown to Earl Harold. 'They gave the royal crown to Harold', says the caption. Immediately after this Harold is shown enthroned and crowned and a Sword of State is borne before him. Archbishop Stigand stands at his right hand. He is not shown actually crowning the new King. The Tapestry avoids the issue.

Plates XXXIV and XXXV. It is now spring, 1066, men stare in wonder at Halley's Comet and Harold, now holding a spear, hears the news. An English ship arrives in Normandy. As the next scene shows the Duke, who has been given a message from England, ordering the construction of a fleet of ships, perhaps this ship brought news of King Harold's rejection of the Duke's claims.

Plates XXXVI to XXXIX. Duke William orders ships to be built and their construction is displayed.

Plates XL and XLI show the ships being loaded with supplies and arms.

Plates XLI to XLIII show the Duke crossing the sea in a great vessel accompanied by other vessels of varying sizes, carrying men and horses.

Plates XLIV to XLVI show the disembarkation at Pevensey.

Plates XLVI to XLVIII show horsemen riding armed to Hastings . They are foraging for food.

Plates XLIX to LI show the food being prepared and served. Bishop Odo blesses the food and dines with Duke William and his brother Robert of Mortain. The Duke consults them about the next move, seated in a lodge of some king which has been commandeered. Wadard, who was one of Bishop Odo's vassals, is given inexplicable prominence; perhaps he had charge of the commissariat.

Plate LII The Duke orders a castle to be built at Hastings within the 'ceastra', that is, the Roman ramparts above the port.

Plate LIII-LIV. News is brought to William concerning King Harold. Perhaps this is Robert fitzWymarc who is said to have warned the Duke of King Harold's approach accompanied by a large army. He told William of Harold's destruction of the Norwegian army and advised him to sit tight within his defences and not to attempt to give battle. Nearby an English house is set on fire and a woman and child escape from it.

Plates LIV to LVII. The Norman army goes out from Hastings and advances to give battle to the English. The Duke hands his battle standard to one of those knights.

Plates LVIII to LIX. The Duke asks a knight called Vital (possibly the one who became a tenant in Kent under Bishop Odo) whether he has seen Earl Harold's army and he points towards scouts on a hill behind him which might be Telham Hill.

Plate LX A mounted warrior informs King Harold of the approach of the Norman army.

Plate LXI to LXIV The Duke exhorts his men to prepare for battle manfully and wisely... The knights, mostly ready to use their spears as javelins, advance preceded by archers.

Plates LXV and LXVI Battle begins and the knights advance against the English shield wall. Both sides hurl javelins at each other as the knights approach the shield wall from all directions. Dead men fill the lower border of the Tapestry. Some have been beheaded or have lost limbs. No attempt is made, nor could be, to show different waves of attack.

Plates LVII to LXXI show the deaths of Earls Gyrth and Leofwine. There is no support in the Tapestry for the idea that the Duke himself killed Earl Gyrth. Many men, both Norman and English, are slain. The Tapestry calls all of the Duke's men 'Frenchmen', just as the Anglo-Saxon Chronicle usually does. The final scene in this section shows a group of Englishmen repelling enemy attacks from a small hillock. The Englishmen wear no armour and so are not regular troops.

Plates LXXII to LXXIII. Bishop Odo encourages the young knights (pueros). The Bishop holds a staff or baton, possibly a mace used also to indicate authority. Duke William raises his helmet to show his face to his men, possibly to show he is not dead. Eustace of Boulogne draws attention to this.

Plates LXXIII to LXXV William's men launch a renewed attack against the English and the Tapestry remarks that 'Those who were with Harold fell'. Suggesting that it was now his Housecarls who were under attack. The Normans are attacking from both left and right.

Plates LXXVI and LXXVII. The final crucial scene of the Tapestry; the death of King Harold. The interpretation of this scene is still highly controversial. Norman knights assault four men, one of whom is killed immediately. The fourth is apparently struck in the eye by an arrow. This figure is labelled 'Harold' and must be the King. Then another figure is shown struck down by a knight wielding a sword and above that the caption reads 'Rex interfectus est', the King is killed. The whole caption thus reads 'Here Harold the King was killed'. The problem is that this area of the Tapestry has been heavily restored. The drawings of the Tapestry made by Antoine Benoît for Bernard de Montfaucon were published in 1733 by Antoine Lancelot. The figure of Harold in the engraving holds a much longer object which has no flights and does not touch his face, it could be a spear. All arrows shown are short and have flights. The word 'interfectus' is a restorer's conjecture as much of the word had been lost. It might have said something like 'in terra iactus est', that is 'is struck to the ground'. No definite conclusions can be drawn because of the damaged state of the Tapestry.

Plates LXXVIII and LXXIX The English, their King slain, turn and flee pursued by knights and archers. The actual end of the Tapestry is missing and some believe it once showed King William enthroned as King but there is no evidence whatsoever to prove it. It is unlikely that there was much more than a yard or so of cloth lost.

Notes

Chapter 1: The Norman D-Day

1. Bayeux Tapestry Plate 44.
2. William of Poitiers' Gesta Guillelmi in E.H.R. II. pp. 221-2. See Livy Book 29. 25.
3. Tetlow. *Enigma*. pp. 146-8. Lindsay p. 48. Howarth. p. 146. Rayne Patterson. p. 137.
4. Chronicle of St Maixent. Cited in A.N.S. 9. 1986.
5. Bayeux Tapestry Plates 37-41 and 46-50. Van Houts A.N.S. 12.
6. William of Malmesbury Gesta Regum 238; 10.
7. Roman de Rou 11697. Poitiers op.cit. p. 139.
8. William of Poitiers op.cit. p. 218 & pp. 223-4.
9. op.cit. p. 222.
10. op.cit. p. 224.
11. Bayeux Tapestry Plate 58.

Chapter 2: A Disputed Coronation

1. Barlow. *Vita Edwardi* p. 80 Bayeux Tapestry Plates 31 & 33.
2. William of Poitiers op.cit. p. 223. Bayeux Tapestry Plate 32. Barlow op.cit. p. 79.
3. Bayeux Tapestry Plates 32 & 33. Anglo-Saxon Chron. C & D 1066.
4. Lindsay p. 86. Need for Witan's consent to the succession; Malmesbury G.R. 238. Eadmer p. 5. Hamlet I. i. 180.
5. *English Romanesque Art. 1066-1200*. Arts Council. pp. 324-5. Florence of Worcester. Stevenson. 1066.
6. R.A.D.N. No. 229. William of Jumièges in E.H.D. II. p. 215. Lindsay p. 98. For Quevilly Freeman. Vol. I p. 248. Maybe the Duke at first hoped to have a grandson with a claim to England.

7. Douglas. *William the Conqueror*. pp. 173-4. Lindsay p. 91. Poitiers op.cit. pp. 84-6.

8. William of Poitiers op.cit. p. 223. As Garnett has pointed out, the claim that King Edward had designated William as his heir is derived from ducal ceremonies in Normandy during which the dukes named their heir to avoid unrest when they died.

9. *King Harald's Saga* para. 76. E.H.D.II Douglas and Greenaway identifies the daughter as Agatha. Marriage mentioned in non-Norman sources see Freeman Vol. 3 p. 689. Chron. St Andreas, Cambrai ii. Cap. 32.

10. William the Conqueror p. 102. William of Poitiers op.cit. p. 220.

11. Julius Caesar II. ii. 30. William of Malmesbury G.R. 225. 6. Van Houts E.H.R. 110 1995. Orderic II 142.

12. Letters of Gregory VII to William I, April 1080. E.H.D. II p. 644. William of Poitiers op.cit. p. 219. C. Morton in Latomus xxxiv 1975; *Pope Alexander and the Norman Conquest.* A minority view suggests that there was no Papal blessing in 1066 and that it was granted retrospectively through legates in 1070. There is little to corroborate such a view.

13. Lillebonne; see Freeman Vol. I p. 294.

14. *Ship List of William the Conqueror.* Liber qui modernum regum Francorum continent actus c. 1114. Text gives 'centum quinquagenta milia', and 'milia quingenta' means thousands upon thousands. Wace Roman de Rou in Oman, England before the Norman Conquest. p. 64.

15. Bayeux Tapestry Plates 39-41.

Chapter 3: Feints & Diversions

1. Domesday Book Berkshire fol. 56v.

2. A.S. Chron. C, D & E 1066

3. Harald's Saga Paras 78 & 79.

4. op.cit. as above Para 80.

5. William of Poitiers op.cit. pp. 219-21.

6. Miracles of St Edmund 172. by Herman the Archdeacon.

7. Poitiers op.cit. as above p. 220.

8. Howarth op.cit. p. 127.

9. The Bayeux Tapestry shows what some think was the masthead light Plate 44, but as it has no 'cressets' supporting torches, see Plate 24, this

is doubtful. Lindsay p. 144.

10. Domesday Hampshire fol. 52.
11. Bayeux Tapestry Plates 42-46.
12. William of Poitiers op.cit. p. 221.

Chapter 4: The Thunderbolt From the North

1. *Harald Hardrada*. Marsden. pp. 207-16.
2. *Fulford 1066* Jones. pp. 165-70.
3. *Fulford* op.cit. Chapter 6. Marsden op.cit. pp. 215-6. Harald's Saga Para. 85.
4. Chambers. p. 307.
5. Harald's Saga Paras 86-93.
6. op.cit. above Para. 91.
7. Vita Edwardi p. 58.
8. Chron. D. 1066.
9. Waltham Chronicle 1066.
10. Chron. D 1066.

Chapter 5: The War Between Duke William &
Harold, King of the English

1. This account is based on the text of William of Poitiers (in E.H.D. Vol. 2) and that of the Carmen de Haestinge Proelio integrated with that of the Anglo-Saxon Chronicles. Quotations are from these sources unless labelled otherwise.
2. Howarth op.cit. p. 169.
3. Wace; Roman de Rou.
4. Gerald of Wales pp. 226-7.
5. Chronicle of St Maixent Book ii 211. F. Baring in E.H.R. 20, 1909 argued that Harold had twelve to fifteen thousand men. Bacharach B.S. A.N.S. 8. The MilitaryAdministration of the Norman Conquest.
6. See discussion in Lawson; *The Battle of Hastings*.
7. See Lawson op.cit. p. 141 footnote.
8. Wace; Roman de Rou.
9. Bayeux Tapestry Plates 65 to 79.
10. Andrew Roberts; Article in *Sunday Telegraph* 30 January 2005.

'Oops! Who said charge?

11. Geoffrey Gaimar op.cit. (Stevenson) p. 794 and Wace op.cit.
12. Bayeux Tapestry Plates as above.
13. Bayeux Tapestry Plates 3, 10, 14 & 17, 25 & 26, 76 & 77.
14. Enguerrand had married a sister of Duke William. Historians disagree about the identities of the four knights. This account uses the most probable quartet. Lindsay op.cit. p. 89.

Chapter 6: From Victory to Kingship

1. This chapter is based mainly on the Anglo-Saxon Chronicles and Florence of Worcester, plus William of Poitiers op.cit.
2. Gillingham in A.N.S. 22 2002. quoting Poitiers. William of Newburgh 1. 13.
3. Battle Abbey and Battlefield Guide.
4. William of Poitiers op.cit. p. 229. Carmen De Haestinge Proelio 587-92.
   A.N.S. 6. William of Malmesbury op.cit. 247:1. Waltham Chronicle.
5. Anglo-Saxon Chron. E 1066. Chron. St Riquier iv c. 23. Anglo-Saxon Chron. D 1066. William of Poitiers op.cit. p. 229.
6. op.cit. as above p. 229. Domesday Kent fol. 1. William of Poitiers op.cit. p. 230.
7. Op. cit. above p. 229. Carmen. 660ff.
8. Carmen 611ff.
9. Davis op.cit. p. 11.
10. Carmen 660ff.
11. Jumièges op.cit. p. 214.
12. Peterborough Chron. E 1087.
13. Poitiers op.cit. p. 231.
14. Orderic Vitalis op.cit. 1067.

Chapter 7: King William Has His Triumph & England Rebels

1. Regesta No. 8.
2. Domesday Berkshire fol. 56V.
3. Domesday Surrey. Fol. 36.
4. This chapter's narrative is derived from William of Poitiers, the Anglo-Saxon Chronicles and Orderic Vitalis. Kapelle; *Norman Conquest of the North* is very useful.
5. Vita Herluini p. 10.

6. Harmer. Writs pp. 29 & 60. Regesta I. No.9. Select Charters. pp. 83-3. Domesday II. Fol. 59
7. Domesday Buckinghamshire fol.153.
8. Orderic 523-4. Eadmer p. 7.
9. Dialogue. Book I. x.
10. Anglo-Saxon Chron. D. 1066.
11. Jumièges. pp. 218 & 236. Orderic Latin text. 507D.
12. Abingdon Chronicle Book One.
13. Kapelle. pp. 106-8. Simeon H.R. 72. Orderic 508B; Jumièges vii 39; Poitiers p. 157.
14. Simeon op.cit. 92.
15. Adam of Bremen III 53.
16. Anglo-Saxon Chron. D. 1067.

Chapter 8: The First Stirrings of Revolt

1. This account uses the Anglo-Saxon Chronicles together with Orderic, the works published as Simeon of Durham, and the Church Historians of York (such as Hugh the Chanter).
2. Barlow. *Norman Conquest and Beyond*; Orderic Book. II. pp. 208-19. Garnett. *Conquered England*. And Domesday Devon. Fol. 100.
3. Garnett. *Conquered England*.
4. Orderic Vitalis Book II pp. 180 & 220-37.
5. Anglo-Saxon Chron. D. 1067.Vita Lanfranci P.L. Vol. CL Col. 53.
6. Chronicle D 1067 for 1068. Regesta No. 22.
7. Geoffrey Gaimar anno 1067. Domesday Lincs. Clamores fol. 376V.
8. Jumièges vii 40.
9. Orderic op.cit. 511C.
10. Orderic op.cit 512-512B.
11. Chron. D 1067 for 1068. Regesta No. 23.
12. Simeon op.cit. H.R. 84-94.
13. Orderic op.cit. 511C.
14. Regesta I. No. 178. Oxford English Dictionary; 'woodmen or wild men, or green men covered with green boughs'.
15. Norfolk Churches pages V and 22. Carola Hicks *Cambridgeshire Churches* pp. 238-9. Petite Larousse Illustré.
16. Domesday Lincs. fol. 341 & Kent fol. 10.

Chapter 9: The North in Flames

1. Kapelle W.E. *The Norman Conquest of the North*. p. 108.
2. Principal sources for this chapter as for chapter 8.
3. Chronicle E for 1068-9. Simeon H.R. 84-91. Orderic ii. 222 & 228 plus 226-28. Kapelle pp. 111-12. Symeon of Durham H.R. 186-97. H.D.E. 98-9.
4. Orderic. II. 220-37.
5. Kapelle p. 114. H.D.E. 99-100. Chron. D 1068 for 1069. Orderic op.cit. II. 226-7. Domesday Book II fol. 59. Florence 1069.
6. Kapelle p. 112. and 116-7.
7. Orderic II 222-3. Malmesbury. Gesta Regum 253. Symeon H.R. II 87-8. Chron. D 1068 for 1069.
8. Acta Pont. Ebor. X in Scriptores 1703.
9. Malmesbury G.R. 249.
10. Malmesbury Gesta Pontificum Ch. 115.

Chapter 10: The Harrying of the North

1. Symeon of Durham H.R. 1070. ii. 181 & 188 H.D.E. Chapters 50-51. Florence 1070. Orderic II. 196. De Obsessione Dunelm. i. 220.
2. Orderic 515c as quoted in Freeman op.cit. Book IV.
3. Symeon H.D.E. Ch.50. Orderic II. 234-5.
4. Evesham Chronicle pp. 90-91. Florence op.cit. 1070.
5. Kemble C.D. IV No. 263.
6. Domesday Book Essex Fol. 42. Surrey Fol. 31v.
7. Chronicle entries; D 1070, E 1069 for 1070, E 1006, C 1041. Florence 1070.
8. Malmesbury G.R. 249. D.B. Shropshire Fol. 252. Yorkshire Fol. 298.
9. D.B.Lincs. Fol. 336.
10. Liber Eliensis Book II 132. D.B. Hampshire Fol. 48.
11. D.B. Hampshire fol. 118.
12. Dialogue of the Exchequer Book I. x.

Chapter 11: Hereward Defies the Conqueror But Ely is Betrayed

1. Chron. E. 1070. Thierry *Norman Conquest* p. 244 quoting Abingdon Chronicle.

2. Chron. E 1069. Malmesbury G.R. 264.

3. Domesday Book; Lincs. Fols 346, 364, 376v, 377 & 377v. Chron. E 1070. Hugh Candidus also. Hart; *Danelaw*.

4. Chron. E. 1070. Chron. D 1071 for 1070. Hugh Candidus and Annales Burgo-Spaldenses.

5. Liber Eliensis II. 102.

6. See Gesta Herewardi.

7. Liber Eliensis II 102. Gesta Herewardi thoughout. Hart op.cit. The Danelaw; Hereward and his Companions.

8. Lib. El. II. 103. The account in this work is confused chronologically and has to be re-ordered by reference to the chronology in other chronicles. As related in the Gesta Herewardi. and Lib. El. II 102.

9. Chron. D 1072 for 1071. Florence 1071.

10. Lib. El. II 102. For Earl Edwin see Orderic's account. Orderic had visited Ely and other Fenland abbeys early in the Twelfth Century. Geoffrey Gaimar seems to have known a version of Orderic's story about Earl Edwin which did not name the Earl and so took it to refer to Hereward.

11. See Lib. El. II and Gesta Herewardi plus Hugh Candidus.

12. Chron. E 1071. Regesta I. No. 155.

13. Deduced from accounts in Gesta and Lib. Eliensis plus topographical works about the river Great Ouse.

14. Lib. El. II 106.

15. Fire in the fens; see Astbury; *The Black Fens*. Victoria *County History of Cambridgeshire Vol. I*.

16. Gaimar Stevenson trans. p. 798. and Chron. E. 1086.

17. Gaimar op.cit pp. 798-9. for circa 1072. See Rex; *Hereward the last Englishman* Ch. 11.

18. Much of this chapter is based on original sources as cited and on Rex; *Hereward,* and *English Resistance*.

Chapter 12: The Normanization of England Begins

1. Florence 1070. Chron. A 1070. Malmesbury G.R. II 228. 1 & 249. 1.

2. Davis. *Wales* op.cit. p. 101.

3. Florence sub anno 1070.

4. As above.

5. Vita Wulfstani ed. Darlington. Barlow Vita Edwardi p. 118. Gervase of

Canterbury. Chron. ii. 285.

6. Bates *William the Conqueror* pp. 215-6.
7. Discussed by R.A. Brown in *Origins of English Feudalism* & same author in *The Norman Conquest*.
8. *Battle Abbey and Battlefield* ed. J. Coad English Heritage 2007. p. 33.
9. Douglas op.cit. p. 321ff.
10. *Ten Articles* of William I. in Robertson; Laws. Cl. 7. From Textus Roffensis and Quadripartitus.
11. Dialogue of the Exchequer Book I viii.
12. Douglas op.cit. 323.

Chapter 13: King William Deals With Scotland

1. Douglas William I. p. 219 footnote. Lib. El. II. 134.
2. Origins of English Feudalism pp. 137-8. Abingdon Chron. ii. 3. Castle guard at Windsor ii 3-7. Lib. El. II 134.
3. Chron. D 1073 for 1072. E 1072. Florence 1072.
4. Simeon H.R. 1080.
5. Kapelle op.cit. pp. 135-6. De Obsess. Dunelm. In H.R. 1074.
6. Chron. E 1073. D 1074 for 1073.
7. H.R. Simeon. Accused of being 'on the side of the enemy when the Normans were slain at York.' Domesday Book Bucks. 146v.
8. Chron. D 1075 for 1074. Irish Annals for 1073-74. Ep. Lanfranc Nos 54 & 57.
9. Gaimar op.cit. pp. 798-9.
10. Douglas op.cit. pp. 228-30.

Chapter 14: The Revolt of the Earls

1. Domesday Book Hunts. Fol. 203v. Godwine; Little Domesday Fols. 131 & 262.
2. Chron. E 1075, D 1076 for 1075, Florence 1074-5. Malmesbury G.R. III 255.
3. Florence 1074-5, Chron. E 1075. Jumièges G.N.D. vii 25.& viii 15. Orderic op.cit. 534 A-D.Latin text.
4. Douglas op.cit. pp. 231-3. Malmesbury G.R. 313-4. Death of Waltheof under English law Orderic 535a.
5. Florence 1075.

6. Letters of Lanfranc Nos 28, 38, 46, 47.
7. Domesday Book Cambs. Whaddon Fol. 196v Lib. El. II. 107.
8. Chron. D 1076 for 1075, E 1075.
9. Chron. E 1075, D 1076 for 1075. Malmesbury G.R. ii 313.
10. Impact of Rebellion on Little Domesday. A.N.S. 25 2002.
11. Laws, Robertson. V Aethelred 30 & VI Aethelred 37 and Writings of Wulfstan II, Archbishop of York c. 1016.
12. Harald's Saga 97.
13. Pseudo-Ingulf. Historia Croylandensis, Stevenson. pp. 675, 668-70. Orderic II. 320-21. based on information received from his visit to Crowland in 1119.

Appendices

1. Vita Edwardi pp. 48-9. Chron. D 1048 for 1049.
2. Chron. D. 1046 for 1045, C 1049, D 1050 FOR 1049.
3. Chron. E 1048 for 1051, C 1051, D 1052 for 1051.
4. As above especially D 1052 for 1051. See John E. *Reassessing Anglo-Saxon England.*
5. Chron. D 1052 for 1051.
6. William of Jumièges op.cit. in E.H.D. II. p. 215.
   William of Poitiers op.cit. in E.H.D. II. p. 223.
7. Chron. C 1054, D 1053.
8. Vita Edwardi p. 23.
9. Chron. D 1057, E 1057.
10. Vita Edwardi p. 33.
11. William of Poitiers op.cit pp. 217-8. Bayeux Tapestry Plates 1 to 30.
12. English Castles Chs. 2 & 3.
13. Wareham. *Lords and Communities.*
14. Battle Abbey and Battlefield.
15. Garmonsaway ed. Anglo-Saxon Chronicle Introduction xxxvi to xli.
16. Bayeux Tapestry ed. Wilson. E.H.D. Vol. II. Musset op.cit.
17. Hart cited in Review; A. Burghart. *Times Literary Supplement* 20 July 2007.
18. Articles in Anglo-Norman England nos. 9, 21 & 23. Garnett op.cit. in T.R.H.S.
19. See *Hereward the last Englishman*; Mellows Hugh Candidus. Hart, *Danelaw & English Charters.* Keats-Rowan *Domesday People and*

Domesday Descendants. Round. Studies. Van Houts A.S.E. 28
Hereward in Flanders.

Bibliography

Recommended Reading

A Brief History of the Normans. F. Neveux. Trans. Howard Curtis. Constable & Robinson 2008. A readable survey of the Normans and their World.

Anglo-Norman England. M. Chibnall. Oxford 1986. One of the best surveys of Norman rule in England.

The Battle of Hastings. M.K. Lawson. Tempus 2002. Provides a thorough grounding in the nature of the sources and the problems they pose.

Harald Hardrada; the Warrior's Way. J. Marsden. Stroud 2007. Provides a unique account of career of the 'thunderbolt of the North'.

1066 The Year of the Three Battles. F. McGlynn. Pimlico. 1999. Overturns many of the myths surrounding the events of 1066.

Hereward; the Last Englishman. P. Rex, Tempus 2007. The most up-to-date account of his origins and career.

La Tapisserie de Bayeux. Lucien Musset. Trans. R.A.W. Rex. Boydell 2005. A full colour reproduction of the Tapestry with detailed commentary.

The Norman Conquest of the North; the Region and its Transformation. W.E. Kapelle London 1979. Provides information not readily obtainable elsewhere.

The English and the Norman Conquest. Ann Williams, Woodbridge 1995. Analyses the fate of those Englishmen and women who survived the coming of the Normans.

The Norman Conquest. R. Allen Brown. Edward Arnold 1989. A compendium of sources on Anglo-Norman Feudalism, providing insight into the Conquest from a variety of perspectives.

The Late Anglo-Saxon Army. I.P. Stevenson. Tempus 2007. A useful analysis of battle tactics and equipment.

The Normans and their Histories; Propaganda, Myth and Subversion. E. Albu, Woodbridge 2001. A remarkably critical survey of Norman spin.

Bibliography

The Abbey of Abingdon, its Chronicle and the Norman Conquest.
J. Hudson. Anglo-Norman Studies 19, 1996. (Cited as A.N.S.).

A Brief History of the Normans. François Neveux. Constable & Robinson 2008.

Alexander II and the Norman Conquest. C. Morton. A.N.S. 13. 1991.

Amatus of Montecassino; Storia de Normanni. Ed. V. de Bartholomeis. Rome 1935.

Anglo-Norman England 1066-1166. M. Chibnall. Oxford 1986 – a scholarly and readable overview.

Anglo-Norman Feudalism and the problem of continuity. J.O. Prestwich. Past and Present 26, 1963.

The Anglo-Saxon Age c. 400-1042. D.V.J. Fisher. Longman 1973.

Anglo-Saxon Chronicles. Ed. and Trans. J. Stevenson. London 1853.

Anglo-Saxon Chronicles. Ed. and Trans. M. Swanton. London 2000.

Anglo-Saxon Chronicles. Ed. and Trans. G.N. Garmonsway. Everyman, London 1955.

Anglo-Saxon England. Sir Frank Merry Stenton. Oxford 1988.

Anglo-Saxon Military Institutions on the Eve of the Norman Conquest.
C.W. Hollister. Oxford 1962.

Annales Burgo-Spaldenses. In Historiae Anglicanae Scriptores. J. Sparke. London 1723.

Arms, Armour and Warfare in the Eleventh Century. I. Peirce. A.N.S. 9 1986.

The Art of War in the Middle Ages. Vol.1 378-1278. Sir Charles Oman. London 1924.

Authority and Interpretation of the Bayeux Tapestry. N.P. Brookes and H.E. Walker. A.N.S. 1. 1978.

The Battlefield of Hastings. F. Baring. E.H.R. 20. 1005.

The Battle of Hastings. J. Bradbury. Stroud 1998.

The Battle of Hastings 1066. M.K.Lawson. Tempus 2002 – an invaluable resumé of the sources.

Battle of Hastings. Weekend Telegraph. Gen. H. Essame. 7 Jan. 1966.

Battle of Hastings. Sunday Times Magazine. Gen. Sir Bernard Montgomery. 24 April 1966 - great General says William hit Harold for six!

The Battle of Hastings. H. H. Wood. Atlantic Books 2008.

The Bayeux Tapestry and Schools of Illumination. C.R. Hart. A.N.S. 21 1998.

The Bayeux Tapestry: Invisible Seams and Visible Boundaries. G.R. Owen-Crocker. Anglo Saxon England 31. 2002.

The Bayeux Tapestry; Why Eustace, Odo and William? A.N.S. 12 1989.

The Black Fens. A.K. Astbury. Cambridge 1958.

The Blinding of Harold and the Meaning of the Bayeux Tapestry. D. Bernstein. A.N.S. 5 1982.

Blood Feud; Murder and Revenge in Anglo-Saxon England. R. Fletcher. Penguin 2002.

The Buildings of Battle Abbey. I.N. Hare. A.N.S. 2 1979.

Cambridgeshire Churches. Carola Hicks. 2007.

Campaigns of the Norman Conquest. M. Bennett. Osprey 2001 – a useful summary from a military historian.

Chronicle of Florence of Worcester. Ed. and Trans. J. Stevenson. London 1853.

Conquered England. G. Garnett.. Oxford 2007.

The Constitutional History of Medieval England. J.E.A. Jolliffe. London 1967 Edition.

Coronation and Propaganda. Some Implications of the Norman Claim to the Throne of England 1066. G.Garnett. T.R.H.S. 5th. Ser. xxxvi 1986 – a fascinating critique of the Norman case.

The Danelaw. C.R. Hart. Hambledon Press 1992.

The Deeds of the Bishops of England; William of Malmesbury. Ed. and Trans. D. Preest. Boydell 2002.

Domesday Book. Ed. and Trans. A. Williams and G.H. Martin. Penguin 1992.

Domesday Book and Beyond. F.W. Maitland. Cambridge 1887. 1964 Ed.

Domesday Descendants K.S.B. Keats-Rowan Woodbridge 2003.

Domesday People. K.S.B. Keats-Rowan Woodbridge 1999.

The Dukes of Normandy and their Origin Rt. Hon. The Earl of Onslow. London 1945.

The Ecclesiastical History of England and Normandy. Orderic Vitalis. Ed. and Trans. M. Chibnall. Oxford 1969-80.

Edward the Confessor. F. Barlow. London 1979.

Edward the Confessor and the Norman Succession. E. John. E.H.R. 94. 1979.

Edward the Confessor, Duke William of Normandy and the English Succession. D.C. Douglas E.H.R. 68 1953.

Edward the Confessor's Promise of the Throne to Duke William of Normandy. T.J. Oleson. E.H.R. 72 1957.

Edward the Confessor's Return to England in 1041 J.R. Maddicott. E.H.R. 118. 2004.

England Before the Norman Conquest. R.W. Chambers. London 1928

– contains sources not readily available elsewhere.

England Before the Norman Conquest. Sir Charles Oman. London 1921 – rather old-fashioned but readable.

England Under the Normans and Angevins. H.W.C. Davis London 1949.

The English and the Norman Conquest. A. Williams. Woodbridge 1995 – a fascinating account of the survival of the English under Norman rule.

English Castles. R. Allen Brown. London 1954.

English Charters of Eastern England. C.R. Hart. Leicester 1966.

English Historical Documents Vol. II. Ed. D.C. Douglas and G.W. Greenaway. London 1953 – an absolutely essential aid to the study of this period.

English Resistance; the Underground War Against the Normans. P. Rex. Tempus. 2004.

The Enigma of Hastings. E. Tetlow. New York 1974 – idiosyncratic but invaluable on the Bastard's cross channel journey.

Feudal Documents from the Abbey of Bury St Edmunds. D.C. Douglas. Oxford 1932.

The Feudal Kingdom of England. F. Barlow. Longmans 1966.

The Forgotten Battle of 1066; Fulford. C. Jones. Tempus 2007 – an invaluable local study.

From Thegnage to Barony; Sake and Soke, Title and Tenants-in-Chief. D.Roffe. A.N.S. 12 1989.

Geoffrey Gaimar *L'Estorie des Engles.* Ed. and Trans. J. Stevenson. London 1854.

Gerald of Wales; *Journey through Wales and Description of Wales.* Trans. L. Thorpe. London 1978.

Gesta Herewardi. Original text in Robert of Swaffham; Register. Peterborough M/S. 1 Camb. Univ. Library.

Gesta Herewardi. Trans. Hardy & Martin, in Rolls Series 1888.

Gesta Normannorum Ducum; a History Without an End. E. Van Houts. A.N.S. 2 1979.

Gesta Normannorum Ducum. William of Jumièges. Ed. and Trans. E. van Houts. 2 vols. Oxford 1995.

Gesta Regum Anglorum. William of Malmesbury. Ed. and Trans. R.A.B. Mynors et. Al. Oxford 1998.

Guillaume le Conquerant. Michel de Boüard. Librairie Arthème Fayard 1984.

Harald Hardrada; The Warrior's Way. J. Marsden. Stroud. 2007 – a very useful history of Hardrada's career.

Harold and William; the Battle for England 1064-1066. B.R. Patterson.

Tempus 2004.

Harold, the Last Anglo-Saxon King. Ian W. Walker. Stroud 1997.

Harold, the Last English King. P. Rex. The History Press 2008.

The Hastings Hundreds. D. Ingram. The History Press 2008.

Hereward and Flanders. E. van Houts. Anglo-Saxon England 28 1999.
    – a vital contribution to our knowledge of Hereward's career.

Hereward the Last Englishman. P. Rex. Tempus. 2005.

Hereward the Saxon Patriot. Lt. Gen. T.L. Harward. Wisbech 1896 – a quite
    barmy book.

Hereward the Wake and the Barony of Bourne. D. Roffe. Lincs. Hist and
    Arch. Vol. 29 1994.

History of the Norman Conquest. 6 Vols. E.A. Freeman. Oxford 1862
    – Freeman's work still covers ground no one else has touched.

Holding to the Rules of War. J. Gillingham. A.N.S. 25 2002.

Hugh Candidus Chronicle; ed. W.T. Mellows Oxford 1941.

Kings and Lords in Conquest England. R. Fleming. Cambridge 1991.

The Kingdom of Northumbria A.D. 350-1100. N.J. Higham. Stroud 1993
    – a most useful survey of Northumbrian history.

King Harald's Saga. M. Magnusson and H. Pálsson. Penguin 1966.

The Impact of Rebellion on Little Domesday. L. Marten. A.N.S. 25 2002.

The Language of the Bayeux Tapestry. I. Short. A.N.S. 23 2000 – very
    intriguing.

La Tapisserie de Bayeux. Lucien Musset. Trans. Richard Rex. Boydell.
    2005.

The Late Anglo-Saxon Army. I.P. Stevenson. Tempus 2007.

*Le Mémorial des Siècles: XI Siècle, les Évènements. La Conquête de
    L'Angleterre par les Normands.* Ed André Maurois. Paris 1968 – a very
    useful collection of sources.

Liber Eliensis. Ed. and Trans. J. Fairweather. Boydell 2005.

The Location of Early Norman Castles. A.G. Lowerre. A.N.S. 25 2002.

Lords and Communities in Medieval East Anglia. A. Wareham. Boydell.
    2005 – an invaluable and scholarly survey.

Millenium. Tom Holland. Little, Brown 2008.

The Military Administration of the Norman Conquest. B.S. Bacharach.
    A.N.S. 8. 1985.

Naval Logistics of the Cross Channel Operation 1066. C.M. Gillmor. A.N.S.
    7 1984.

Norfolk's Churches. R. Tilbrook and C.V. Roberts. Norwich 1997.

The Norman Conquest. D.J.A. Matthew. London 1966.

The Norman Conquest 2. Vols. Augustin Thierry. London 1861 – another very strange work.

The Norman Conquest. H.M. Thomas. Rowman and Littlefield. 2008.

The Norman Conquest and Beyond. F. Barlow. London 1983.

The Norman Conquest of Leicestershire and Rutland. Ed. C Phythian-Adams. Leicester 1986 – a regional introduction to Domesday Book.

The Norman Conquest of the North; the Region and its Transformation 1000-1135. W.E. Kapelle. London 1979 – a vital contribution to the history of this region.

The Norman Conquest Through European Eyes. E. van Houts H.R. 110 1995.

The Norman Heritage 1066-1200. T. Rowley. London 1983.

The Normans and their Histories: Propaganda, Myth and Subversion. E. Albu Woodbridge 2001 – an absolutely fascinating argument.

The Normans and their World. J. Lindsay. Granada Publishing 1974.

The Normans and the Norman Conquest. R. Allen Brown. Woodbridge 1969 – strongly pro-Norman.

The Origins of English Feudalism. R. Allen Brown. London 1973.

The Participation of Aquitanians in the Conquest of England 1066-1100. A.N.S. 9 1986.

Peaceable Power in English Castles. C. Coulson. A.N.S. 23 2000.

Problems Connected with the English Royal Succession 800-1066. A. Williams. A.N.S. 2 1979.

Reassessing Anglo-Saxon England. E. John. Manchester 1996.

Regesta Anglo-Normannorum. Vol. 1 Ed. H.W.C. Davis. Oxford 1913.

The Road to Hastings. P. Hill. Tempus 2005.

Saxons, Normans and their Buildings. E. Fernie. A.N.S. 19 1996.

Scotland. A New History. M. Lynch Pimlico 1992.

Secrets of the Bayeux Tapestry. Brenda and Brian Williams, Pitkin Guide 2008.

Select Charters. Ed. W. Stubbs. Oxford 1900.

The Ship List of William the Conqueror. E. van Houts A.N.S. 12 1989.

Some Notes and Considerations on Problems Connected with the English Royal Succession 860-1066. A. Williams. A.N.S.1 1978.

Studies in Peerage and Family History. J.H. Round. 1901.

Time and the Hour. Collected papers of D.C. Douglas. London 1977.

Towards an Interpretation of the Bayeux Tapestry. H.E.J. Cowley. A.N.S. 9 1986.

Unification and Conquest. P. Stafford. London 1989.

Vita Edwardi Regis the Life of King Edward Who Lies at Westminster. Ed. and Trans. F. Barlow. Oxford 1992.

The Warenne view of the past. E. van Houts. A.N.S. 25 2002.

Where Did All the Charters Go? Anglo-Saxon Charters and the New Politics of the Eleventh Century. C. Insley. A.N.S. 24 2001.

William the Conqueror. D. Bates. Tempus 2004.

William the Conqueror. D.C. Douglas. London 1964.

The Year of Three Battles. F. McLynn. Pimlico 1998.

1066 The Year of the Conquest. D. Howarth. Collins. 1977.

List of Illustrations

14. King Harold, enthroned in state. With special permission from the city of Bayeux.

15. An awestruck crowd points up at the 'hairy star', that is, Halley's Comet. With special permission from the city of Bayeux.

16. A nobleman (possibly Count Eustace of Boulogne). With special permission from the city of Bayeux.

17. The Norman Knights are shown riding 'manfully and wisely' into battle. With special permission from the city of Bayeux.

18. The advance of the knights continues. With special permission from the city of Bayeux.

19. The Norman knights attack the English shield wall. With special permission from the city of Bayeux.

20. A dramatic visualisation of the intensity of the fighting as English thegns repel a Norman charge. With special permission from the city of Bayeux.

21. Bishop Odo of Bayeux is the central figure here. With special permission from the city of Bayeux.

22. King Harold. With special permission from the city of Bayeux.

23. The Tower of Earl's Barton Church. Author's Collection.

24. The battlefield of Hastings. Author's Collection.

25. Ely monastery. Author's Collection.

26. King William's Seal. Author's Collection.

27. Rougemont castle. Author's Collection.

28. Abbayé aux Hommes, Caen. Author's Collection.

29. Bayeux cathedral. Author's Collection.

30. The Norman gateway at Dover. © Christina Rex.

31. Burial Place of William of Normandy, Caen. Author's Collection.

32. Bosham harbour. © John Taylor.

33. Bosham Church. © John Taylor.

34. Exterior of side aisles; All Saints, Brixworth. © Christina Rex.

35. Norman Doorway. © Christina Rex.

36. Round Tower of Church of Burnham Deepdale. © Christina Rex.

37. 'Saxon' arch leading to Cloisters; Ely Cathedral. © Christina Rex.

38. Tower and turret of Ely Cathedral. © Christina Rex.

39. Fortifications of the Warenne Castle at Castle Acre. © Christina Rex.

40. Probable crossing point of the Norman Army on the 'Old West River'. © Christina Rex.

41 & 42 Wicken Fen, Cambridgeshire. © Christina Rex.

43. Edward the Confessor. © John Brooks and Jonathan Reeve JR1117slide 10001100.

Genealogical Tables:

Index

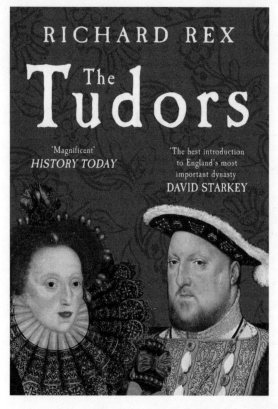

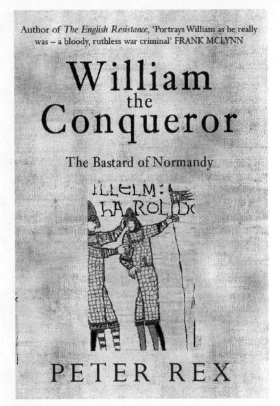